# OUTCASTS:

## The Lands That FIFA Forgot

### by Steve Menary

http://outcastsbook.blogspot.com/

First published in the United Kingdom
by Know The Score Books Limited, 2007
www.knowthescorebooks.com

# Know The Score Books Publications

| CULT HEROES | Author | ISBN |
|---|---|---|
| CHELSEA | Leo Moynihan | 1905449003 |
| MANCHESTER CITY | David Clayton | 9781905449057 |
| NEWCASTLE | Dylan Younger | 1905449038 |
| SOUTHAMPTON | Jeremy Wilson | 1905449011 |
| WEST BROM | Simon Wright | 190544902X |

| MATCH OF MY LIFE | Editor | ISBN |
|---|---|---|
| ENGLAND WORLD CUP | Massarella & Moynihan | 1905449526 |
| EUROPEAN CUP FINALS | Ben Lyttleton | 1905449577 |
| FA CUP FINALS 1953-69 | David Saffer | 9781905449538 |
| FULHAM | Michael Heatley | 1905449518 |
| LEEDS | David Saffer | 1905449542 |
| LIVERPOOL | Leo Moynihan | 190544950X |
| MANCHESTER UNITED | Ivan Ponting | 9781905449590 |
| SHEFFIELD UNITED | Nick Johnson | 1905449623 |
| STOKE CITY | Simon Lowe | 9781905449552 |
| SUNDERLAND | Rob Mason | 1905449607 |
| SPURS | Allen & Massarella | 9781905449583 |
| WOLVES | Simon Lowe | 1905449569 |

| GENERAL FOOTBALL | Author | ISBN |
|---|---|---|
| 2007/8 CHAMPIONS LEAGUE YEARBOOK | | 9781905449934 |

| BURKSEY | Peter Morfoot | 1905449496 |
|---|---|---|

The Autobiography of a Football God

| HOLD THE BACK PAGE | Harry Harris | 1905449917 |
|---|---|---|

| MY PREMIERSHIP DIARY | Marcus Hahnemann | 9781905449330 |
|---|---|---|

Reading's First Season in the Premiership

| OUTCASTS | Steve Menary | 9781905449316 |
|---|---|---|

The Lands That FIFA Forgot

| PARISH TO PLANET | Dr Eric Midwinter | 9781905449309 |
|---|---|---|

How Football Came To Rule The World

| 2006 WORLD CUP DIARY | Harry Harris | 1905449909 |
|---|---|---|

| AUTOBIOGRAPHY | Author | ISBN |
|---|---|---|
| TACKLES LIKE A FERRET | Paul Parker | 190544947X |
| (England Cover) | | |
| TACKLES LIKE A FERRET | Paul Parker | 1905449461 |
| (Manchester United Cover) | | |

| CRICKET | Author | ISBN |
|---|---|---|
| GROVEL! | David Tossell | 9781905449439 |
| The Story & Legacy of the Summer of 1976 | | |
| | | |
| MOML: THE ASHES | Pilger & Wightman | 1905449631 |
| | | |
| MY TURN TO SPIN | Shaun Udal | 9781905449422 |
| | | |
| WASTED? | Paul Smith | 9781905449453 |
| | | |
| LEAGUE CRICKET YEARBOOK | | |
| Midlands edition | Andy Searle | 9781905449729 |
| North West edition | Andy Searle | 9781905449705 |

| RUGBY LEAGUE | Author | ISBN |
|---|---|---|
| MOML Wigan Warriors | David Kuzio | 9781905449668 |

# Forthcoming Publications

| CULT HEROES | Author | ISBN |
|---|---|---|
| CARLISLE UNITED | Paul Harrison | 9781905449095 |
| CELTIC | David Potter | 9781905449088 |
| NOTTINGHAM FOREST | David McVay | 9781905449064 |
| RANGERS | Paul Smith | 9781905449071 |

| MATCH OF MY LIFE | Editor | ISBN |
|---|---|---|
| ASTON VILLA | Neil Moxley | 9781905449651 |
| BOLTON WANDERERS | David Saffer | 9781905449644 |
| DERBY COUNTY | Johnson & Matthews | 9781905449682 |

| GENERAL FOOTBALL | Author | ISBN |
|---|---|---|
| UNITED THROUGH TRIUMPH AND TRAGEDY | | |
| | BIll Foulkes | 9781905449781 |
| MARTIN JOL: THE INSIDE STORY | | |
| | Harry Harris | 9781905449774 |

**Know The Score Books Limited**
118 Alcester Road, Studley, Warwickshire, B80 7NT
Tel: 01527 454482 Fax: 01527 452183
info@knowthescorebooks.com
www.knowthescorebooks.com

A CIP catalogue record is available for this book from the British Library

**ISBN: 978-1-905449-31-6**

Jacket Design by Chris Burke
Book Designed and Edited by Andy Searle

Printed and bound in Great Britain by
William Clowes Ltd, Beccles, Suffolk

*To Lesley, Lucie & Scott*

# ACKNOWLEDGEMENTS

This book would not have been possible without help from a number of people, who I would like to thank - in particular Gavin Hamilton at World Soccer for commissioning work that enabled me to research large sections.

Thanks also to Brian Oliver at The Observer and Andy Lyons at When Saturday Comes, who commissioned work that helped write this book as did Jens Sejer Anderson, who also asked me to speak on the same subject at the 2005 Play the Game conference in Copenhagen.

A big thank-you to Allison Heller at Housebuilder, Emma Crates at Construction News and Tracey McVeigh at The Observer, who all commissioned journalism un-related to this book but which helped pay for some of the trips to find the teams covered here.

Thanks to Mark Cruickshank for kindly supplying the results section included here, to Soren Andersen, Jennifer Tennant and Rafael Maranhao for their translations, and Arnon, Slavic and Massimo for their great company at the ELF Cup. Also thanks to Jean Luc Kit and Christian Michelis at the NF Board, Andreas Herren at FIFA, Andrin Cooper at the FA; Thomas Helseth at the Norwegian Embassy in London, Brian Partington at the Island Games Association and Steffen Frahm and Bastian Kaufhold at the Wild Cup.

In individual places, I am very grateful for their help from: Jens Brinch, Jens Tang Olesen and Irene Jeppson at Sermitsiaq (Greenland); Peter Coleman and Vince Stravino (North Mariana); Patrick Watts (Falklands); Michael Nybrandt (Tibet); Joseph Nunez (Gibraltar); Pèire Costa (Occitània); Cengiz Uzun (Northern Cyprus); and Ante Jovna Gaup, Leif Isak Nilut, Hakan Kuorak (Sápmi).

Thanks also to Claire Faragher, to Andy Stevens for his proof-reading skills, Tom Green for his help with the website and Adrian Chiles and David Conn for giving this book some credibility

Finally, a big thank-you for the cover and many of the photos and much else to Chris Burke and the biggest thank-you of all to Simon Lowe for being willing to publish this book.


Steve Menary, August 2007

# CONTENTS

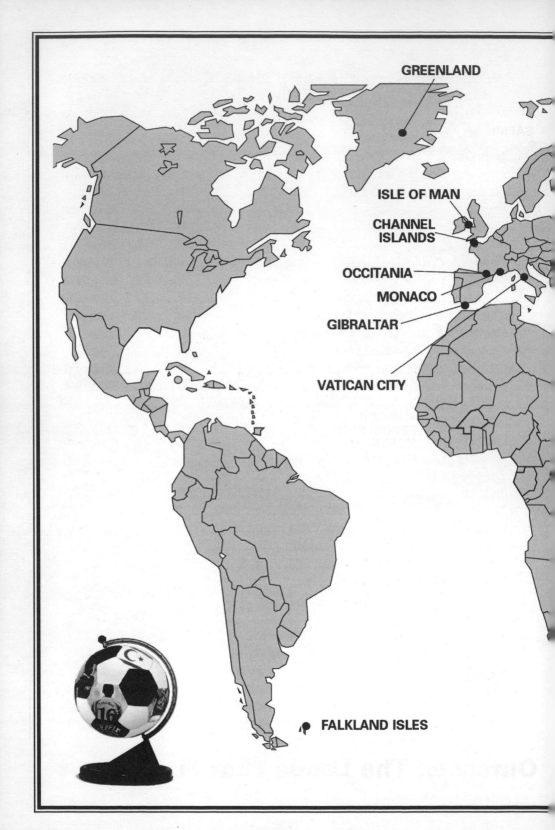

GREENLAND

ISLE OF MAN

CHANNEL
ISLANDS

OCCITANIA

MONACO

GIBRALTAR

VATICAN CITY

FALKLAND ISLES

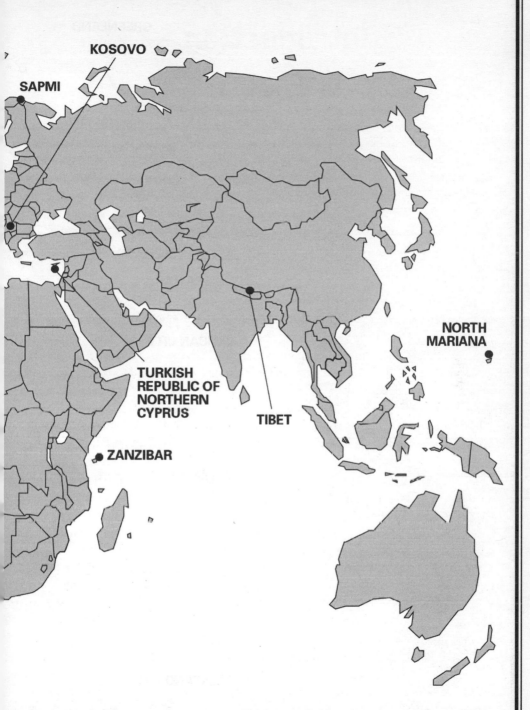

KOSOVO

SAPMI

TURKISH
REPUBLIC OF
NORTHERN
CYPRUS

TIBET

NORTH
MARIANA

ZANZIBAR

# Outcasts: The Lands That Fifa Forgot

# Introduction

## by David Conn

There are so many fascinating stories in this book that, as a football commentator might say, it is difficult to pick out the highlights. Perhaps the most significant phrase of all is one written almost in passing in Chapter 5, the fascinating account of football's place in the life and history of those blasted islands, the Falklands. Describing the moment it dawns on the manager, Patrick Watts, that his ecstatic match commentary is useless because he has lost his connection to Port Stanley where there has been a power cut, Steve Menary writes that "as the only journalist there," he thought it would be only decent to lend Watts his tape recorder.

That phrase is clearly written not to boast of the extreme lengths travelled to produce this engaging, warm and human story of football in the outer reaches of the world. It was just a fact. Steve Menary has gone to the places other journalists have never reached, and returned to write his far-reaching book. No other journalists felt that the Island Games tournament in the Shetlands was one which need trouble their diaries, but in this book the most important stories are the ones flung far from the great clubs and nations which fill the back pages.

Like the best sports or football books, this one places the game, and its universal, great appeal, in the widest context - charting, unexpectedly at times, great social and historical events, swirling around what might be simple tales of 22 men and a ball. It says a great deal about the connectedness of the modern world, and football's central place in it, that a book about the most obscure corners of human habitation can discover so much that feels centrally relevant. A great deal is revealed by these small communities' relationships with the great countries around them, and anybody who has ever played or supported football will recognise the same passions and tensions in the game being played out on the Shetland Isles as at Wembley, Hampden Park or anywhere.

Steve Menary is a journalist with a great capacity for research and chasing down the relevant facts, and here he has applied that appetite to the most ambitious of targets: world football, at its edges. For readers who want to know their writers have given them 100%, there will be no doubts here. Beyond the sheer lengths gone to witness and understand what football means in the lands that FIFA forgot, he has also delivered an absorbing, engaging and thought-provoking account of the miracle which is football itself, a common language in a close, divided world at the beginning of the 21st century.

# Foreword

## by Adrian Chiles

I write this in a close season. It could be any close season in British football. The weather's rubbish and there is nothing but transfer news and speculation in the newspapers. The facile annual merry-go-round of footballers' endlessly changing loyalties is well under way. Oh yes, and a famous footballer who recently became a father has been caught with his pants down in a hotel somewhere with some woman he met in a casino, or something.

The big clubs are firmly stamping their carbon footprints down on money-spinning tours on other continents. Some of the smaller clubs are paying big bucks to some famous foreign teams to come over and field uninterested second strings in pre-season friendlies.

We idly wonder who'll do well in the coming season but any accountant could tell us who's going to finish where. All they have to do is write down a list of clubs in order of how big their wage bills are. At the end of the season the league table, in any division, will more or less exactly match the accountant's list.

So where is the soul of football? I think it's in this book. For sure, there's something magnificent in the big players, big teams, the big championships and the monstrously beautiful stadiums. But nothing ever moves me so much on planet football as the sight, from the air, of a pitch scratched out on some unsuitable earth. I saw one in Bosnia once, in the middle of the war. And in South Africa too, twenty years ago. Even, often, on some crappy scrap of ground in a rougher part of Glasgow, Hull, Clapham Common or wherever

The stories in this book of these countries' attempts to make their way in the lower reaches of FIFA's consciousness are movingly analogous to all those pitches carved so determinedly into the ground.

# INTERNATIONAL

Adj 1. existing or occurring between two nations
2. agreed on or used by all of many nations
Noun 1. *Brit* a game or contest between teams from
different countries
2. *Brit* a player who has taken part in a contest between
teams from different countries
3. (International) any of four nations founded between
(1864-1936) to promote socialism or communism

**Oxford English Dictionary 2006**

# Preface

## by Steve Menary

This is a story of jealousy, excuses, death, collusion, nepotism, political intrigue, bitterness, war and shenanigans and mal-administration; all in the name of football. It is full of ludicrous desires, dedication beyond belief, egos, one-upmanship and attempts to achieve the impossible.

But it is also a story of the triumph of humanity over despotism, spirit over administrative constriction and the expression of nationality in the purest sense over politically-drawn boundaries. Football is a sport which has been consumed by politicking, consumerism and money for much of our times. The process of writing this book brought me, over two years, into contact with hundreds of people who play the game for the very best of reasons - for the love of the game itself. That they do so in order to express some kind of national identity, barred by the powers-that-be, made the task all the more joyful.

Some of the people I met were incredible characters with amazing personal stories who rejoice in playing football or running their 'national' team simply because they can. I found their stories inspirational, astounding, often maddening, but always interesting. I hope you do too.

Wading through the minefield of FIFA statutes and UEFA avoidance tactics led me to the conclusion that, just maybe, the success of the 'nations' described in this book is because they are outside FIFA's auspices and not inside. No matter what their aspirations, the sheer determination to play and represent their country shows how important football is as a force in the modern world, irrespective of who controls the game.

# OUTCASTS - THE CAST

Mark Blair - Isle of Man goalkeeper
Jens Brinch - Greenlandic sports administrator
Eric Clague - Isle of Man football historian
Martyn Clarke - Falklands Islands' footballer
Peter Coleman - US attorney & North Mariana Islands FA secretary
Pèire Costa - Occitan football activist
Kalsang Dhondup - Tibetan football coach
Matt Fallaize - former Guernsey FA secretary
Steffen Frahm - former St Pauli football administrator
Ann Garrett - Isle of Man FA secretary
Andreas Herren - FIFA head of media
Rick Holden - former Manchester City player and Isle of Man coach
Jean Luc Kit - football statistician & NF Board general secretary
Niklas Kreutzmann - Greenland captain
Håkan Kuorak - Sami FA vice-president
Kevin Manning - Isle of Man manager
Christian Michelis - NF Board president
Gill Morgan - former Jersey FA secretary
Leif Isak Nilut - Sami FA president & theatre producer
Christoph North - Monaco FA secretary
Joe Nunez - Gibraltar FA president
Michael Nybrandt - Tibetan activist
Jens Tang Olesen - Greenland manager
Stephan Ottenbruch - German film producer
Brian Partington - Island Games Association chairman
Colin Ramirez - Gibraltar captain
Edmund Rugova - Kosovo coach
Alisan Saltik - German film director
Nigel Shimmin - Isle of Man captain
Ferdi Sabit Soyer - North Cyprus prime minister
Vince Stravino - North Mariana Islanders footballer
Coskun Ulusoy - North Cyprus footballer
Cengiz Uzun - North Cyprus football organiser
Patrick Watts - General Manager, Falkland Islands FA
Georges Wuethrich - Chagos supporter & NF Board activist

# CHAPTER ONE

# The World According To FIFA

*"Any association which is responsible for organising and supervising football in its country may become a member of FIFA. In this context, the expression 'country' shall refer to an independent state recognised by the international community."*
**FIFA statute, Article 10**

## 8 March 2005, Zurich

UNNOTICED BY most of the international sporting community, a notice slips out of FIFA's headquarters in Switzerland rejecting an application from Zanzibar to join the international order of the world's most popular game. As the African island of Zanzibar is not a country but part of Tanzania, the rejection should come as no surprise, but ten months previously FIFA had welcomed the French territory of New Caledonia - population 211,000 - as its 205th member, stating with a tinge of regret that there were hardly any territories left to accept.

The international footballing aspirations of Zanzibar's 981,000 people, whose football association has been around since 1926 - predating Tanzania's formation by nearly 40 years - were ignored by FIFA, but the African island's situation bears many similarities with New Caledonia. Neither territory is in the United Nations (UN), but both are members of one of the six regional confederations that provide FIFA with its membership, so what was the difference?

Andreas Herren, FIFA's head of media, tries to explain: "In the case of New Caledonia, there is an ongoing process of autonimisation (sic) with a referendum for independence planned for 2012. Also, while the New Caledonia FA is part of the French FA, the distance to France is such that no club in New Caledonia can compete in the competitions being played on the French mainland.

"As for Zanzibar, there is no independence process even though there is some local autonomy. Also, as the distance between Zanzibar and Tanzania is very short - 40 minutes by boat, flight connections on a daily basis - this criterion is not valid. What is more, previously clubs from Zanzibar played in the Tanzanian competitions."

# OUTCASTS: The Lands That FIFA Forgot

They did, but not any more. Zanzibar has its own President following the 1964 Glorious Revolution, which led to it joining with the state of Tanganyika to form Tanzania. It is no small satellite island in the manner of the Isles of Man, Wight or Sheppey; it is a partner in the modern country of Tanzania and was never swallowed up by a larger entity. As a nation state it has played internationals as part of the Council of East and Central Africa Football for 75 years. But, after being rejected by FIFA, Zanzibar was then also thrown out of the African regional confederation, the Confédération Africaine de Football (CAF), and forced to restore ties with the Tanzania Football Federation (TFF) which had been severed in 2002 due to island Zanzibar allegedly moaning about being ignored by the mainland Tanzanians.

After being shunned by FIFA, Farouk Karim, then vice president of the Zanzibar Football Association, grumpily stated: "We have no way out but to co-operate with the TFF."

Zanzibar's rejection was well-timed by FIFA, which six months later, in September 2005, held its 55th ordinary congress for the first time in Africa. The lingering bad smell of problems would not have helped the atmosphere.

Following Zanzibar's rejection and New Caledonia's acceptance, two more countries were then accepted into the fold with East Timor and Comoros taking FIFA's membership roster up to 207 national teams, proving that there are still more members to be found out there past the footballing frontiers set by FIFA.

Both independent states and members of the UN, the admission of East Timor and the Comoros was at least consistent. For FIFA, there were clearly to be no more colonies or territories, only independent countries. So then, how does FIFA square the circle that still leaves a big discrepancy between its 207 members and the 192 places on planet earth recognised as countries by the UN? And how do they attempt to curb the playing of football as an expression of 'national' identity amongst these places which have not found haven within their walls?

\*\*\*\*\*\*\*\*\*\*\*

Until the early years of the 21st century, lax rules, regional power politics and confederations desperate to use an apparently bulging membership to justify more lucrative places at the World Cup finals meant the definition of "international football" had been tested to the limit for decades. And nowhere was the concept of international football stretched further than the Caribbean. The best example is probably found in the British colony of the Cayman Islands. Accepted into FIFA in 1992, the Cayman Islands Football Association (CIFA) took a novel approach to raising a team to attempt to qualify for the

2

2006 World Cup finals in Germany to justify its continuing status. Instead of using players from the 41,000 people living on the Caribbean islands for a two-leg home and away tie with Cuba, the Caymans' Brazilian coach Marcos Aurelio Tinoco supplemented his squad with people who had simply worked there. The aim was to provide a competitive team and the Caymans did score a first World Cup goal through defender and captain Thomas Elliot after 72 minutes. Despite this, the islanders still lost the home leg 1-2 and were thumped 0-3 in the return in Havana to dash unlikely dreams of qualifying for Germany.

At least this time the players had actually been to the Caymans, which was more than could be said for the team representing the Islanders in the qualifiers for the 2002 World Cup in Japan and South Korea. Then, preparing for another two-legged tie against Cuba, CIFA took an approach more akin to raising a Sunday morning pub team. Recruiting an overseas agent to drum up a squad, Barry McIntosh's brief was not to track down islanders that had quit the Caymans to work overseas, but to provide an entire squad with just about any players that he could find. Of the 24 players asked to play by McIntosh, only two reportedly said 'no', with Manchester United defender David May one of the pair to spurn an opportunity to play World Cup football. Players that were more enthusiastic included Motherwell's Ged Brannan, Martin O'Connor of Birmingham City and Wayne Allison, who had played in that year's Worthington Cup final for Tranmere Rovers.

McIntosh defended the CIFA's policy, telling The Guardian: "These players have agreed to join up with us not for the money, but simply because they wish to play international football. We are doing nothing wrong and perhaps more importantly we are doing nothing new. The United States has taken players from Puerto Rico under the same system, as has Jamaica from England. The Cayman Islands is a British dependency. We use the same passports; we have the Queen's face on our currency. When you have something new in life it does take time for people to appreciate what the benefits can be."

The Caymans' policy came under fire from all directions and only seven UK-based players travelled to the Caribbean for the home game with Cuba. FIFA then intervened before the kick-off and barred the UK-based players and the Caymans went down to a 0-4 defeat to Cuba, ending the World Cup adventure of this quixotic international side.

One player reportedly interested in playing for the Caymans, London-born Barry Hayles of Fulham, then transferred his international ambitions to Jamaica; a country which had qualified for the finals in France 1998. FIFA has since tightened up regulations allowing players to switch nationalities with such frivolity. From 2005 players that have been capped at junior level but entitled to dual nationality can change allegiance, but only provided they have not played full international football and are under 21 years-old. Amazingly, though, players such as England Under-21 star Carlton Cole, who was born in Surrey but is eligible for Nigeria, are still giving interviews to the press about how they want to switch nationality; even though, at 23, he is no longer eligible. This rule change has forced the Caymans to take a different tack, but the Islands' FA remains a member of FIFA, which takes its 207 members from six regional confederations.

According to FIFA's membership rules, which were tightened up in 2003, all full members must also be full members of a confederation before joining the world body. FIFA itself was established back in 1904, but most of these six confederations were set up much later. UEFA and the Confederación Sudamericana de Fútbol (CONMEBOL) are the game's heartland in terms of playing strength and no country from outside these two regions has won or even contested a World Cup final. CONMEBOL's origins date from 1916, while UEFA's are as recent as 1954.

The CAF (Africa) was set up in 1957 and is expected to provide a future World Cup winner, maybe in 2010, when South Africa will become the continent's first country to stage the World Cup finals, although no nation from Africa has, yet, even reached a semi-final - a feat achieved by 2002 joint host South Korea.

South Korea is a member of the Asian Football Confederation (AFC), which was set up in 1954 and whose membership was swelled in 2005 by Australia's decision to abandon its own Oceania Football Federation (OFF) - set up in 1966 - and join the AFC.

Australia's move was partly to provide more competitive games than tiny Pacific rivals such as the United States administered territory of American Samoa, which let in a world record 31 goals without reply in a 2001 qualifier against the Socceroos for the finals in Japan and South Korea.

Australia's successful qualification for the 2006 finals was through Oceania, whose members include New Caledonia, but has only previously provided two World Cup finalists - Australia in 1970 and New Zealand in 1974. That lack of success is due to the winner of the Oceania region inevitably facing a play-off against a South American or Asian team with Australia, invariably Oceania's top team, usually falling at the last hurdle up until 2005, when Uruguay were overcome and a finals place claimed again after a 36 year wait.

Leaving Oceania means Australia can aim for one of the four World Cup places on offer to the Asian region for the 2010 tournament in South Africa. The move also, crucially, provides Australia and the Asians with far more saleable matches for TV than the Oceania champion's league could offer.

4

# The World According To FIFA

The sixth and final confederation is the Confederation of North, Central American and Caribbean Association Football (CONCACAF). Set up in 1961, CONCACAF is traditionally dominated on the field by two-times World Cup hosts Mexico and, more recently, by the United States. The US may not have taken football to its heart, but, apart from South Korea in 2002, this region has provided the only other World Cup semi-finalists outside of Europe and South America with the US making the last four at the first tournament back in 1930.

The reason these six confederations provide FIFA with more members than there are countries recognised by the UN is that some confederations have a far looser idea of what constitutes a 'nation' than others, allowing places such as the Caymans to join.

During the 1990s, UEFA's membership surged as a host of new members emerged from the break-up of Yugoslavia and the Soviet Union. A number of smaller nations, such as Andorra and San Marino, also began playing regularly due to generous grants available through full membership of both UEFA and FIFA. When the Danish territory of the Faroes started playing in 1994, this prompted more contentious territories to look into playing internationals, such as Gibraltar, and led to FIFA instituting a membership survey. In the pre-amble to the survey results, FIFA congratulates former president Dr Joao Havelange for ushering China and South Africa - one-time pariahs in the international community - into the fold of world football. No mention is made of why colonies were ever admitted, but this first happened in 1932, when the Netherland Antilles joined FIFA. A hiatus followed before Puerto Rico (officially an 'unincorporated organised territory' of the USA) joined in 1960, then another lull before the 1990s boom in membership.

"We can only point out that the affiliations were made in accordance with the FIFA statutes and in line with FIFA's goal to make the game truly universal," adds Andreas Herren in defence.

That is the crux. FIFA wants football to stay the world's most popular sport and demonstrated amazing double standards to ensure this. Non-contentious colonies like the Cayman Islands are let in, but the likes of Zanzibar are excluded. Why? Well, when Gibraltar tried to join UEFA in the late 1990s, politics intruded and Spain threatened to quit all European and international competitions rather than suffer the indignity of playing the Rock's national side in a qualifier.

Of course, no Champions League could be complete without Real Madrid or Barcelona or the finals of an international tournament without the Spanish national side, even if the national team never win anything. So, to ensure Gibraltar could be barred entry, UEFA altered its clause on membership to provide clear criteria of what a country really is: Article 5 of UEFA's statutes on membership says:

> "Membership of UEFA is open to national football associations situated in the continent of Europe, based in a country which is recognised by the United Nations as an independent state, and which are responsible for the organisation and implementation of football-related matters in the territory of their country.
>
> In exceptional circumstances, a national football association that is situated in another continent may be admitted to membership, provided that it is not a member of the confederation of that continent or any other confederation and that FIFA approves its membership of UEFA. A national football association that wishes to become a member of UEFA shall submit a written application for admission. The congress shall have the power in its discretion to accept or refuse an application for membership.
>
> The executive committee may admit a national football association into membership on a provisional basis. A decision on full admission must be taken at the next congress."

UEFA declines to explain why these amendments were made, but a letter to another European international aspirant, the Channel island of Jersey, from the English FA chairman Geoff Thompson explains what UEFA was belatedly trying to achieve. The letter made clear that associations from inside another UEFA member were clearly not to be encouraged to join, saying the amendments are designed as:

> "1. Protection of existing associations, to prevent the emergence of several associations in their country, i.e. territory
> 2. UEFA membership in future should depend on unequivocal criteria (a country which is recognised by the United Nations as an independent state."

This change to the entry criteria blocked new entrants to UEFA such as Greenland. The irony is that UEFA's new rule was not retrospective, so it protected the four teams from the United Kingdom. Also, the Faroe Islands, which enjoys the same system of self-rule as the Greenlanders as part of the Danish commonwealth, was allowed to remain both a UEFA and FIFA member. Those organisations also permitted Kazakhstan to transfer from the AFC to UEFA in 2004. This was apparently due to Kazakhstan's close proximity to other Caspian nations already playing as part of Europe, such as

Azerbaijan, rather than the oil that is slowly making the country very rich. FIFA may have tightened its entry criteria, but theirs is still far woollier than UEFA's in making clear what the definition of a country really is, and the UN is not, whatever their spokesmen may say, the yard stick. Article 10 of FIFA's statutes on admission says:

"Any association which is responsible for organising and supervising football in its country may become a member of FIFA. In this context, the expression 'country' shall refer to an independent state recognised by the international community. Subject to paragraph 5 and six below, only one association shall be recognised in each country.

1. Membership is only permitted if an association has already been a provisional member of confederation for at least two years.

2. Any association wishing to become a member of FIFA shall apply in writing to the FIFA general secretariat.

3. The association's legally valid statutes shall be enclosed with the application for membership and shall contain the mandatory following provisions

(a) always to comply with the statutes, regulations and decisions of FIFA and its confederations

(b) to comply with the laws of the game in force

(c) to recognise the court of arbitration for sport as specified in these statutes

4. Each of the four British associations is recognised as a separate member of FIFA

5. An association in a region which has not yet gained independence may, with the authorisation of the association in the country on which it is dependent, also apply for admission to FIFA.

6. The regulations governing the application of the statutes shall regulate the details of the procedure for admission.

7. This article shall not affect the status of existing members."

FIFA using the UN to define a country would be hypocritical as its own statutes also protect the rights secured by England, Scotland, Wales and Northern Ireland, enshrined many decades ago as independent teams, even though all four are represented at the UN by the United Kingdom. Instead FIFA uses the vague term 'international community' to exclude places such as Zanzibar that are no more of a country than England, Scotland, Wales and Northern Ireland, while allowing those 'native' Cayman Islanders a sight of World Cup qualification. Few people in the UK would question the right of any of those four British teams to play internationals as they have all been doing so for more than a century, but elsewhere this situation is seen as an anomaly that needs addressing - and one which the proposed British team to compete in the London 2012 Olympics can only complicate.

What makes FIFA's role intriguing is that not all members of the UN play international football as part of FIFA. Tiny countries like Kiribati, Nauru, Palau, Tuvalu and the Federated States of Micronesia struggle to find the resources to play international football and are not getting any help, as members of the 'international community', from FIFA either - despite fitting their entry criteria perfectly. Monaco and the tiny Vatican State are not members of FIFA, but do enjoy membership of the UN, which insists there is no co-operation with any of the football bodies over membership and recognition of what is a country.

Brendan Varma from the Office for the Spokesman for the UN Secretary General says: "Membership… is open to all other peace-loving states which accept the obligations contained in the present charter and, in the judgement of the organization, are able and willing to carry out these obligations. The admission of any such state to membership … will be effected by a decision of the general assembly upon the recommendation of the security council."

The four teams of the UK, which as a single entity sits on the UN security council, plus the likes of the Caymans, New Caledonia and the Faroes, are only a handful of the inconsistencies on FIFA's membership roster. When asked how many FIFA members were independent states, John Schumacher of FIFA's media department helpfully said: "We invite you to do the comparison count by yourself."

Trawling through FIFA's 207-strong membership roll, a large number of members are clearly not independent nations, yet all receive US$1 million every four years as part of the world body's financial assistance programme. That money is also a huge political tool and enables regional power brokers such as Trinidad & Tobago boss and CONCACAF strongman Jack Warner to move up through the regional hierarchy into FIFA.

Known locally as 'Teflon Jack', Warner was deemed in February 2006 to have a "conflict of interests and that the code of ethics had been violated as a result" of ticket allocations for that year's World Cup finals made to the Trinidad & Tobago FA that were being distributed by a travel agency owned by his family. Warner was never punished by FIFA, but he is certainly guilty of using his position in CONCACAF to test the idea of international football and provide a block of voters, who, awash with FIFA grants, are willing voters to support Warner and his protector, FIFA boss Sepp Blatter, come election time.

CONCACAF is brimming with non-countries that have gone on to join FIFA. Gallingly for Gibraltar, this list includes a large number of other UK colonies, including Bermuda, whose players include 1970s West Ham striker

Clyde Best and Sean 'The Goat' Goater, who played in the Premier League for Manchester City. Other UK colonies in CONCACAF include teams turning out in the colours of the tiny Turks & Caicos Islands; the 21,000 people of the British Virgin Islands and the mere 13,000 people of Anguilla.

Most bizarre of all, FIFA and CONCACAF's membership roll includes Montserrat, which in June 2002 took on Bhutan in a game termed as 'the alternative World Cup' - the pair were then FIFA's lowest ranked members - with the British island colony slumping to a 0-4 defeat.

The island had a historically tiny population of around 9,000 residents, but Montserrat was decimated by the eruption in 1997 of the La Soufrière volcano that caused many locals to flee their wrecked island. According to a report from the BBC World Service, that disaster left the island without a single football pitch. Montserrat has since used funding through its FIFA membership to rebuild its sporting facilities and would surely be a willing supporter of Warner and Blatter come election time.

Other CONCACAF colonies also in FIFA include the Dutch possessions of Aruba - population 70,000 - and a team representing the 216,000 people of the Netherlands Antilles, which are being split up and could soon multiply into a number of other potential FIFA members and Warner supporters.

A number of US-controlled territories also play international football under the guise of CONCACAF and FIFA, including Puerto Rico - population 3.9 million - and the 125,000 people of the US Virgin Islands.

Like CONCACAF, Oceania bulked up its wafer thin membership roster in a bid for a guaranteed World Cup finals place - a bid that never paid off and is unlikely to now that Australia have decamped for Asia. New Caledonia was not even the first French territory from Oceania to join FIFA, as Tahiti - population 262,000 - achieved that a decade and a half earlier. Other Oceania non-countries include the 70,000 people of American Samoa (another 'unincorporated' territory), who are probably glad that Australia have quit for the Asian zone after their World Cup thrashing.

Meanwhile non-countries playing internationally elsewhere include, in Asia, the 164,000 people of Guam, a US territory, and China's two special administrative regions, Hong Kong and the former Portuguese colony of Macau - populations of 7.4 million and 470,000 respectively. All three are AFC and FIFA members.

Curiously, when England last played Hong Kong in May 1996 in a game watched by 26,000 people in the Hong Kong stadium, the match was not deemed a full international, despite the former colony regularly playing internationals including the 2006 World Cup qualifiers. Instead, politics ensured that England's 1-0 win goes down in history as an unofficial match against a 'Hong Kong XI'.

Taiwan also plays regular international football, though unrecognised as a state by the United Nations. As recently as 2005, China - a member of the UN Security Council - passed an anti-secession law declaring that if Taiwan tried to gain full statehood, then the Chinese would invade the island that their then-ousted leaders fled to more than half a century ago. At one stage a few decades ago, the Taiwanese had to play in the Oceania qualifiers along with Israel, which was also not welcome in its own confederation. Times have moved on. China has been welcomed to the FIFA fold and Taiwan took part in the 2006 World Cup qualifiers, easing Macao out 6-1 on aggregate over two legs as a member of the AFC. In the next group stage, the amateur Taiwanese lost all six matches, but did score four times - an improvement on their six defeats and no goals scored in the 2002 campaign.

One of those defeats was to Palestine, another place not generally regarded as independent - certainly not in Israel. Having been accepted by FIFA as a member back in 1994, the Palestine association do not dare play home matches on the Gaza strip. Instead, the Qatari capital of Doha has made the Palestinians welcome, while training camps are held in the Egyptian town of Ismailia, 120-km north of Cairo.

In total, 23 of the world body's 207 members are not fully independent countries at all but some form of 'non-country' in UN terms (see Fig.1 in appendices). That is nearly 10 per cent of all FIFA's members and that is without considering the 53 countries in the British Commonwealth, whose head of state - however nominal - is actually the Queen of England.

Then there are also 'territories' that are members of regional confederations but have not yet joined FIFA, which requires provisional membership of a regional confederation for a minimum of two years. The French-run island of Reunion in the Indian Ocean is an associate member of CAF, but not yet part of FIFA. Like Greenland and the Faroes, the French colonies are run as departments that send representatives to the French parliament in Paris and can also, unlike the two Danish territories, enter teams into the French version of the FA Cup.

Neither FIFA nor UEFA accepts associate members. CONCACAF, however, which has accepted another two French territories, Guadeloupe and Martinique, as members on this basis. Also in this confederation is French Guyana, which rarely enters representative sides, although a side from the French colony was put out to play Jamaica over two legs in CONCACAF's Gold Cup in 2005, losing 0-5 away from home before churning out a 0-0 draw in the South American heat. The colony, probably best known as a jail for French criminal-turned-celebrity author Papillon, has not escaped FIFA's attentions. In February 2004, the world body and the French Football Federation agreed plans to channel funding for football into the colony under

FIFA's Goal programme. Two more French overseas territories, Martinique and Guadeloupe, are also CONCACAF members and beneficiaries of the Goal programme without being members of FIFA.

The Goal initiative produces many benefits, such as spending more than £400,000 on re-establishing football in Montserrat, when there was a far more pressing need for state rebuilding funds, but there have also been more dubious uses of Goal cash. In Antigua & Barbuda, more than £200,000 went missing on a new FA headquarters that was never built. The Antigua & Barbuda FA secretary general, Paul 'Chet' Greene, a friend of 'Teflon Jack' Warner's, went unpunished.

Perhaps equally disturbing is how Goal cash can go to football associations, such as French Guyana, that are not even FIFA members. This funding appears to be made through the colonial authorities, such as the French Federation in French Guyana, but FIFA will not confirm this. Instead of providing someone to discuss the aims of the Goal programme, FIFA just lifted the following bland statement from its website and emailed it over as a reply to my enquiry:

"The Goal Programme inspired by FIFA President Joseph S Blatter was launched for the 1999 to 2002 period with funds of 100 million Swiss Francs. The programme then graduated to the Goal II stage, again with funds of 100 million Swiss francs (£41 million) available for the 2003 to 2006 period. The aim of the programme is to further financially underprivileged associations, providing headquarters, natural and artificial turf pitches, training and education centres and other facilities essential to a basic infrastructure. It is intended that each member association will have its own House of Football by the year 2006. So far, 78 of the 207 projects in the pipeline have officially been launched, with a further 20 already completed. Such is the success of the programme that 35 member associations are already working on a second project. One condition for approval of a second scheme is that the first Goal project has been finished and is fully operational."

Another French overseas territory, Saint Martin, also benefits from Goal cash, as does Sint Maarten, the Dutch colony on the other side of the same Caribbean island. Both are associate members of CONCACAF, but not members of FIFA.

Like CONCACAF, the Oceania federation also needs to bump up its membership roster as Australia's defection proved a body blow to the region's chances of ever commanding an automatic World Cup qualifying slot. With this surely in mind, in November 2006 at the Oceania annual congress celebrating the federation's 40th anniversary, the OFC found four more members adrift in the Pacific. The new associate members included Palau, Tuvalu (the island which found fame as the .tv internet extension so fondly purchased by western television companies) and the Federated States of Micronesia. As members of the United Nations, if this trio can graduate to full Oceania membership - according to FIFA's membership rules - they can then join the cash cow that is the world body.

That might be more difficult for the fourth new member, Niue Island. One of the world's largest submerged coral atolls with a population of just 1,500, Niue is self governing, but has all its external affairs and defence issues administered by the government of New Zealand, which also provides the official currency.

Including Niue, there are 30 places that are not countries as recognised by the United Nations that play international football under the aegis of FIFA and its six regional confederations, yet FIFA's decision to bar Zanzibar suggests that the door has now been firmly closed on non-countries. Of those 30, 23 are members of FIFA. They look set to remain anomalies, while other territories seeking to join them on the international stage are left kicking their heels on the touchline, only able to look in on the global brotherhood of football.

Or are they? What happens to the territories that missed FIFA's cash-laden boat? To the places from Zanzibar to the Channel Islands and Gibraltar to Greenland that want to express their national identities on a football pitch, but no longer fit into FIFA's world view? Where are these outcasts from FIFA, the national teams that cannot exist?

# CHAPTER TWO

# The Channel Island Divide

*"To play for your country is every sportsperson's ambition and although the Channel islands obviously have a far smaller population than the senior world soccer powers such as Brazil, Italy or England, the thrill and pride with selection is just as meaningful."*
**Foreword to 'A History of Channel Island Football'**

## 2 May 2005, Guernsey

"WE'VE GOT TO GET off the island or we won't ever get any better. It's the only way to improve," says a friendly female security guard at the exit of Guernsey's neat, new and unsettlingly silent airport. A former table tennis player for Guernsey in her youth, she runs off a list of some of the island's sporting successes, like Andy Priaulx, the racing driver who won the inaugural 2005 FIA world touring car championship, and Martine Le Moignan, a former women's squash world champion, although there is no mention of team sports - or Matthew Le Tissier.

The Le Tissier name features regularly in the history of the Jersey versus Guernsey annual derby, the Muratti Vase, although the Southampton legend never played in a single game; unlike his brother Mark Le Tissier, who won the Ossie Eloury trophy for Man of the Match in the 1985 contest.

Another Le Tissier, Kevin, is still considered a better player on the island than his brother Matt by many who saw him play, but was said to lack the same ambition - a criticism also levelled at the one-club Southampton player. One of 25 players inducted into the Muratti Hall of Fame for the centennial match in 2005, Kevin Le Tissier scored 22 goals in 20 Muratti appearances between 1982 and 1998, including the event's very own 'Hand of God' incident at Jersey's Springfield ground in 1992.

Only one player has played in the inter-island derby then gone on to win a full England cap and that was another man who turned out for Saints, but, unlike Le Tissier, could not prevent the south coast club from eventual relegation in 2005. Graeme Le Saux played for Jersey in the 1987 Muratti at the Track in Guernsey, where he was Man of the Match and helped set up the winning goal in extra time for a 4-3 win for the visitors.

13

"What a future this lad has," wrote local football pundit Rex Bennet in the Guernsey Evening Press as he awarded Le Saux top marks for his performance.

After leaving Jersey side St Paul's for Chelsea, Le Saux made his debut against Portsmouth at the end of the 1988/89 season, and was transferred in March 1993 to Blackburn Rovers for £700,000. In 1994, Le Saux made his England debut and went on to win the Premier League title the following season and 36 England caps before failing to impress Sven-Göran Eriksson. Le Saux returned to Chelsea in August 1997 before signing for Saints in August 2003 - too late to play with Le Tissier - as part of a £7 million deal that took Wayne Bridge to Stamford Bridge. Due to Le Tissier's refusal to leave Saints, Le Saux's transfer fees make him the Channel Islands' most expensive football export.

Having two players in the England squad was an aberration for Channel Island football and the Muratti is a world away from the England v Italy match in 1997 that was Le Tissier's only real opportunity for England. Established in 1905, the series also includes another Channel Island in Alderney, which appeared in the final in rotation with the other two larger Channel Islands until 1937 and beat Guernsey 1-0 in Jersey in 1920 for their only Muratti win. After winning that game, Alderney had a street party, but their two star players, Allen and Rudoi - their forenames remain unknown to this day - were not there as they were on a steam ship immigrating to America and have never been heard of since.

That game is just one colourful chapter in the Muratti's history, which was suspended in World War Two after the islands were occupied by invading German forces. Unofficial games were still played, however, including one in a German concentration camp between interned Islanders that saw Guernsey thrash Jersey 6-1.

"Some of the locals think that the Muratti is much more important than a mere international," says Frank Cusack, a Glaswegian civil engineer who moved to Guernsey in 1980 and spent three years working on a history of the fixture published in time for the 2005 match.

Despite being ejected from a guaranteed final slot, the Ridunians - as Alderney are known locally - still make an effort for the annual semi-final defeat with shops decked out in the side's colours of blue and white. Alderney suffered a series of thrashings after 1937, but the play-off has been closer in recent years and Guernsey only won 2-1 to secure a place in the centennial Muratti - the Ridunians' best result for 51 years. That performance did not go down well with Guernsey coach Steve Ogier, but the Guernsey Football Association expects a big crowd for the centennial event. The home side are hoping to avenge a 0-3 thrashing in Jersey in 2004 and the GFA are anticipating a near capacity crowd.

# The Channel Island Divide

"I'm sure you won't have too much trouble finding the ground," says Matt Fallaize, the GFA secretary. "Everyone should know where you need to go - after all, 5,000-plus souls will be making their way there."

Along with the rest of the Channel Islands, Guernsey is a remnant of the medieval dukedom of Normandy. More recent influences are also apparent in house names on the walk into St Peter Port. Strathmore, Ventnor, Valetta and Finlandia might be the result of permanent incursions or long-gone holidays; people doing the reverse of Alderney's mysterious 1920 match winner and immigrating to the Channel Islands, a feat now impossible for all but a handful of the super rich.

That restrictive entry policy - one almost unique to western Europe - is a result of laws passed by the governments in the two main islands to create the tax haven that exists today. Neither part of the UK or the European Union, the two Channel Islands have their own parliament and a level of autonomy that must have been viewed with envy by nationalists in Wales and Scotland prior to the election of the New Labour government in 1997, even with reforms since pushed through.

The legal system on the Channel Islands dates back to the 13th century and until the end of the 15th century, the islands were ruled together by a governor on behalf of the British royal family - although that lineage is still only recognized as the Duke of Normandy and not the Queen of England. In 1470, two Bailiwicks were created with separate governors. Jersey existed alone, while another Bailiwick encompassed Guernsey, Alderney and the smaller isles of Sark, Jethou, Brecqhou, Lithou and Herm. At just 1,300-odd acres and with a population of only 500, Sark is ruled as a medieval fiefdom within that Bailiwick, but did field a team at the 2003 Island Games - a sort of biennial Olympiad for small islands - that was held in Guernsey, only to succumb to a series of double figure defeats.

The past 100 years of Channel Island football is dominated by Guernsey and Jersey and, although some locals suggest some of the better players have come from outside the islands, many surnames resonate with the islands' links with France, including GFA secretary Matt Fallaize.

In Guernsey, there are two Col Fallaize's - a big one that is an island football legend with 16 goals in 19 Muratti appearances and a small one. Matt Fallaize is the son of the smaller, but despite his lack of football achievements, the surname certainly has pedigree. According to research by the Landmark Trust, which buys, restores and rents out historic buildings as holiday accommodation, a Norman baron, William de Falaise, arrived in England after the Norman Conquest. This Falaise was granted the Manor of Stoke in Somerset and subsequently founded the Priory of Stoke between 1100 and 1107 in the reign of Henry I and his legacy remains in the renovated Stogursey Castle near Bridgwater in Somerset.

# OUTCASTS: The Lands That FIFA Forgot

In his excellent history of the tournament, Cusack selected best-ever post-war teams with players such as Colin Gervaise-Brazier, Colin Renouf and Kevin Le Tissier making the Guernsey side; Bram Le Rich, Grahame Le Maistre and Dempsey Poindestre in the Jersey team and Mark Treais in Alderney's best XI.

In a foreword to Cusack's book, publisher Tony Williams writes: "To play for your country is every sportsperson's ambition and although the Channel Islands obviously have a far smaller population than the senior world soccer powers such as Brazil, Italy or England, the thrill and pride with selection is just as meaningful."

FIFA supremo Sepp Blatter was even persuaded to write a pre-amble to the book, although he carefully contradicted Williams by refusing to identify any of the three islands as countries. Blatter wrote: "For the last 100 years, the football communities of Alderney, Guernsey and Jersey have held a remarkable competition, the Muratti Vase, which has, through the powerful bond that only football can create, brought together the people of the Channel Islands year after year in the spirit of fair play and competition."

Of course, none of the Channel Islands are countries, but then neither are those 23 FIFA members identified earlier and Matt Fallaize is expecting significantly more than the sub 1,000 fans found at competitive matches for some smaller members among even the UEFA elite, such as Andorra.

***********

In St Peter Port, the capital is quiet for a bank holiday and the second day of summer and amazingly the shops appear shut. Has everyone really quit St Peter Port for the Muratti as Matt Fallaize said? Has capitalism been put on hold for football? The sight of Boots' gaping front door suggests otherwise, but there are precious few shoppers inside. A few drag racers exhibit cars on the sea front and pubs, some advertising the typical stodgy fare of Premier League matches, are open; but the place is almost deserted.

The first signs of the Muratti are in the queue for the bus, which - an hour before kick off - is full, though the only evidence of football are two fans, one male, one female and both wearing a red Jersey top over a full range of tattoos with rings and piercings. As the Jersey fans board, the driver, in a broad Glaswegian accent, jokes about only accepting their Jersey one pound notes for the fare today as it's a bank holiday. The Jersey fans return the driver's joke and sit down as the bus pulls away, the aisles rammed with people, but still no other signs of the football apart from a police van chugging up the hill ahead of the bus.

# The Channel Island Divide

As the bus crests the hill and drops into Grange Road, the first fans appear in dribs and drabs and the passengers at the front erupt at the sight of the supporters in Guernsey green and white shirts. The bus terminates by the grammar school on Footes Lane, where football fans are everywhere, milling about, collecting tickets, hooting horns and from their midst comes Matt Fallaize.

As members of the English FA, Guernsey and Jersey are on the same level as county teams in the UK mainland, but Fallaize is the complete opposite of the ageing former players often seeking solace for loss of playing status in junior football officialdom. Youthful and engaging, Fallaize worked on the island's daily newspaper, The Guernsey Press, before joining the GFA as full-time secretary in spring 2004. He is almost swamped by his green FA blazer, but he is not overawed by his big day and has big plans - bigger even than the Muratti.

The GFA receives assistance from financial giant Credit Suisse, which has offices on the island and sponsors Guernsey's under-21 and under-18 representative teams. Credit Suisse is based in the same Swiss city of Zurich as FIFA and Fallaize is asking for their help in joining the international game.

"We're currently exploring whether Guernsey could potentially be recognised as a nation in its own right and the early indications are positive, but the matter requires considerable further investigation," he says.

"There's no single impetus as such. It was down to a culmination of factors. One of our executive officers is heavily involved in Guernsey cricket and recently played a leading role in securing associate member status of the ICC [International Cricket Council, the game's global governing body] for Guernsey. He is keen to pursue the UEFA/FIFA line."

Fallaize looks up proudly at the £1.2 million Garenne Stand at Footes Lane that is the main stand for the Muratti match and mostly full an hour before kick off. Built for the 2003 Island Games, the ground includes a running track and today boasts three temporary stands erected for the Muratti.

"Those other three stands cost about £140,000. It holds five thousand people, but we're hoping to get about 4,700 today," says Fallaize, scanning hopefully around the rest of the ground.

Then his phone goes and he departs, but not before promising to find Stanton Monks prior to kick-off and a few minutes later the former Jersey FA secretary makes his way out of the ground.

"We started looking into the possibility of joining UEFA when I was secretary, but they moved the goalposts," Monks says, smiling at his own football cliché. "Gibraltar was one reason, but there was a number of reasons really including the number of other applications that they were expecting. We took some advice and were told that unless we handled our own international relations, we couldn't join."

With the ground filling up, Monks promises to find former Jersey FA president Brian Ahier, who visited FIFA with a lawyer in 1999, for more details, then disappears into the Garenne Stand. The rest of the stadium may only be temporary and uncovered, but the ground is up to lower Football League standards, with decent floodlights, although the crowd look like they are at a village fete.

Many fans are wearing the 1,000 Guernsey green T-shirts distributed by sponsors Cable & Wireless, while others have made the effort to wear green clothes. The pitched battles of Marseilles in France 98, anti-Pope and Irish chants found at any England match or inter-club feuds that scarred matches such as Southampton FC's first match hosting England are worlds away; although the Muratti did suffer some crowd problems in the 1980s as the plague of hooliganism sweeping across Europe reached the Channel Islands.

These days, alcohol is not sold at the ground, which partly explains the good behaviour. But lack of pre-match alcohol is not the only reason; some fans had been at The Doghouse pub on the way to Footes' Lane prior to the game. Something else is missing and that is the sort of intolerance often seen among pockets of football fans; the Muratti is more akin to a fete.

Before the game, the Guernsey rugby team, who won the inter-island Muratti against Jersey for the first time in 10 years, 28-24, are paraded before the crowd. Kitted out in blazers, they then take their seat in the temporary Cherry Godfrey South Stand - ending a 10-year wait for a win was obviously not enough to earn a seat in the main Garenne stand.

In the South Stand, a boisterous band of young male fans, who had probably been in The Doghouse before the game, test out anti-Jersey songs before God Save the Queen is played over the PA and the crowd falls eerily silent. Pockets of fans briefly sing along, but are quickly shamed into silence. Everyone looks uncomfortable, seemingly keen for the anthem to pass. When it does, the Cherry Godfrey South Stand boys resume their chants. Like most of the ground, the stand is named after a match sponsor, who, as the programme goes to great pains to point out, have, along with a number of others, helped provide the money for the temporary stands and giant screen.

Matt Fallaize's target of 4,700 fans appears optimistic as Guernsey only has a population of 65,000, but with tickets starting at £8 he thinks getting five per cent of the population to the game is a reasonable target. That attendance would generate £49,164, but the GFA would still be out of pocket and that is one reason why the dream of international football may not be realised. Frank Cusack adds: "The GFA are looking into the possibility of entering major competitions, but although there is the will I believe that the main stumbling block may be the cost - but one never knows."

# The Channel Island Divide

As members of the English FA, Guernsey receive sizeable annual grants for a range of activities from development to ground improvements and therein lies a fundamental problem; the English FA could not conceivably fund a rival FA they may meet in competitive internationals. If the GFA did achieve full member status of UEFA they would receive a minimum annual grant of 500,000 Swiss francs and possibly up to 1.1 million Swiss francs depending on commitments to areas like club licensing and women's football. Guernsey could also net another U$1 million every four years as members of FIFA if they join the world body.

That would surely compensate for loss of FA cash, but even with this generous funding other existing members of UEFA are unable to field sides at junior levels. Northern Ireland, for example, has not entered sides in UEFA's U-21 championship due to lack of cash. The crowd and receipts target at the 2005 Muratti has not met Matt Fallaize's goal, but attendances are on the up again after a lean period. They are unlikely to match the 12,000 people who crammed into the old Guernsey stadium, the Track, to see the home team win 3-1 after extra time in 1951, however.

As the game kicks off, the Cherry Godfrey South Stand get stuck into more chants: "Have you ever seen a local, ever seen a local, ever seen a local in your team? Have you fuck!"

A few smiles ripple out from the crowd, but some fans seem unsure if that refers to the visiting Jersey squad or the hosts. Only later when the south stand pour out "Where's the local in your team?" and "Your Irish, Scots and Scousers" along with "Illegal immigrants" is it clear that the earlier chant was solely aimed at Jersey. Despite this jibe, getting permanent residency on the island is not easy and if Guernsey were to play internationals, with Matt Le Tissier now working as a TV pundit, they would have to rely on mainly home-grown players.

Guernsey and Jersey have striven for some time to play a better standard of football and joined the English South West Counties league a decade ago. As part of this competition, both play regular matches against county sides such as Devon, Dorset, Cornwall and the Army and Navy's representative sides.

"That has given us a leg-up," admits Tristram Morgan, Guernsey's number 10 at the Muratti. "Our league only has seven teams in it. Below that it's reserve football or the Sunday league. The trouble is that there's no motivation and we are playing the same sides all the time. That's where the South West Counties has been really good."

A tidy midfielder, Morgan plays for island side Vale Recreation and is one of the home side's better players at the Muratti.

"We play in the Island Games and won the gold medal at the last one in 2003 [when Guernsey were hosts], but they'd certainly have to have some more regular training sessions [to play internationals]," he concedes with a smile. "But it would be great if they could bring World Cup qualifiers here. Why not?"

Why not? Guernsey's seven-team league may not seem like much of a testing ground, but at least they have a national league. UEFA had to help San Marino develop a league and Liechtenstein still does not have a national league for its handful of clubs, though top side FC Vaduz does play in the Swiss Second Division. No bar to entry there then.

GFA Referees Secretary, Graham Skuse, hails from Llanelli in Wales and puts the standard at the Muratti on a par with the Welsh Premier League sides that play in UEFA club competitions every year. Both teams try to play football on the floor, but defence dominates and there are few clear cut chances. Fifteen minutes pass before the Guernsey keeper makes the first save.

The first half drags with little to separate the two sides and the only goals by half-time are those shown on the giant screen of the home side's 5-1 win in the women's Muratti the previous day. Rain starts to pour and most supporters flee for any cover they can find with security guards doing little to stop them. In true Channel Island fashion, everyone is effortlessly polite and no-one drops litter.

On the pitch, a blazered and determined Guernsey official tries to sell raffle tickets to help raise cash to send a team to the 2005 Island Games, while the announcer tells the crowd they can expect this sort of weather every day at this year's tournament in the Shetland Isles.

The sun comes out for the second half and the crowd returns, a teenage girl looking for a bag hurriedly abandoned quarter of an hour earlier. The bag sits unmolested by either fans or the security team, who obviously are not expecting any bombs to be smuggled into Foote's Lane.

The second half starts in a similar fashion with neither side looking capable of making a breakthrough. Despite solid performances in midfield from Morgan and the opposing Jersey number 10, the match misses a touch of quality.

What it needs is a bit of class, some Brazilian flair. Jersey have Brett Pitman playing in the Football League with Bournemouth, but Guernsey boast a Zico: Ryan Zico Black. Named after the Brazilian World Cup winner, he turned out on a semi-professional basis for Northwich Victoria and Morecambe, but like Le Tissier, having bigger fish to fry, neither has ever played a Muratti.

Morecambe FC's official website says of Zico Black: "It was rare to see Zico play the full 90 minutes, but he produced some excellent performances in a Morecambe shirt, but he also produced some pretty dire ones.

Inconsistency was probably his biggest problem, but the talent was definitely there. Zico had bags of potential, but ultimately he failed to achieve it at Morecambe."

After being released by the Lancashire side, Zico Black was then picked up by Northern Irish side Glenavon before returning to Britain with Lancaster City. Despite being born on the island in 1981, Zico Black secured representative honours for Northern Ireland at Under 18, Under 19 and Under 21 level.

Northern Ireland is a popular choice for Guernsey players with David Waterman, another islander playing semi-pro on the mainland, making 13 appearances for the province's Under 21 team. After leaving club side Northerners, Waterman, who was born in 1977, was picked up by Portsmouth and made his debut for the south coast side at 18 as a substitute against Grimsby. At 25, he moved on to Oxford United before going part-time with Weymouth under then boss Steve Claridge in 2004/05.

As the second half draws to a close, Morgan mars an otherwise good performance with a wayward late shot and the match limps into extra-time with neither side capable of a breakthrough. Extra-time also fails to produce anything close to a breakthrough, although home captain John Nobes does have to make a superbly timed goalmouth challenge in the last minute to send the match to a replay for only the sixth time. The result is the same as the first Muratti at Foote's Lane in 2003, but lacking the excitement of that 3-3 draw.

After the game, Fallaize admits: "The match was like a typical Italian match with the defences on top and few chances. Perhaps it wasn't the best football played in a Muratti, but the event and the occasion was enjoyed by everyone."

The standard was not brilliant, but did have a first class regular in referee Philip Joslin, who took charge of the 1998 FA Cup final between Arsenal and Newcastle and also refereed at Euro 96. With only four players dismissed in a century, he had little to worry about at the Muratti. The English FA has provided the man in black since 1905, when a Guernsey man, H Le Mesurier, refereed a stormy Muratti in Jersey that Guernsey won by a single goal and the referee needed police protection after leaving the match.

After the 2005 game, the post-match behaviour could not have been more different to an England match with the crowds waiting for cars to pass instead of running between them or hammering their bonnets with drunken fists. Perhaps good behaviour is simply a feature of the Muratti as even spectators leaving the match all stuck to the pavement. When the narrow winding footpaths away from Foote's Lane got clogged up by the crowds, no-one strayed onto the road to overtake, everyone just waited patiently.

The match attracted interest from the commercial sector with a bidding war for the radio coverage rights with Island FM and Channel 103FM wrestling the rights off the BBC. But does the lack of venom between the supporters and players make the game less important, or was it because many from both groups know each other outside of football?

Guernsey centre-forward Paul Nobes, an electrician by trade and brother of Guernsey's best player on the day, John Nobes, says: "We all play inter-club competitions, so we get to know them through that and we also get to know them socially as well."

***********

Thirteen days after the original match, the two sides went head-to-head again on Jersey in front of more than 3,000 people in a match Fallaize enthusiastically described as a "classic". One up after just nine minutes through Darragh Duffy of Belgrave Wanderers, Jersey responded with two quick goals before Dominic Heaume, also of Belgrave, equalised before half-time. The match again went into extra-time, though not with the lethargy of the original. With four minutes of added time left, Jersey took the lead again only for Jon Veron of Northerners to equalise with the last kick of the game to take the Muratti into penalties on which Guernsey finally triumphed 3-2 with a kick to spare after keeper Pattimore saved three Jersey kicks.

The result returned the Muratti Vase to Guernsey for the first time since 2001, giving the team confidence ahead of the defence of their Island Games trophy that summer and boosting Matt Fallaize's dream of playing international football.

Paul Nobes thinks this is a realistic ambition too, adding: "You only have to look at some of the smaller teams that joined UEFA a few years ago. Originally, they were getting beaten by big scores, but the standard has improved as they got to play and practise more often and more of their players got to play elsewhere. Ryan Zico Black couldn't even break into the island set up, but he was confident that he could improve by going to the mainland and he can now play semi-professional football to a good standard. I don't think that the Muratti is always a good standard, but when we play in tournaments like the Island Games it's much, much better. And that's because we practise ten hours a week beforehand. We do two lots of training sessions, then a ball work session and a voluntary session, which is usually gym-work."

With Jersey's players and fans keen to catch ferries back after the stalemate at the original Muratti on Guernsey, former Jersey FA President Brian Ahier does not appear to meet me, but later by email he recollects his visit to Switzerland and offers a different story to Stanton Monks. He says: "It's some five years since I resigned as President of JFA and memories of my visit to FIFA with lawyer Steve Meiklejohn are at best patchy. As I recall we were well received and certainly not told that it would be impossible for us to enter international competition and the question of whether we could handle our defence affairs was not discussed.

"Possible problems highlighted were a need to prove independence from the FA and eligibility of players - we require 12 months residence in the Island in order to qualify to play representative football and this was thought by FIFA to be too short. The JFA was left to look further into the matter and, if thought appropriate, to make a formal application. The reason the matter has not been advanced is because the JFA have probably decided that they do not wish to pursue it further."

The JFA are certainly approachable, but they are not great at remembering what happened in the past and current President Charlie Tostevin is not optimistic about making the sort of progress that Guernsey is hoping for. He says: "If the opportunity came we would certainly be interested, but unless we become an independent state I don't think it will happen."

With no sponsor and cash in short supply, the JFA is not even sending a football side to the 2005 Island Games, where Guernsey are defending their title as they continue to look to broaden their horizons.

\*\*\*\*\*\*\*\*\*\*\*

On 1 September 2005, Guernsey's international dream appears to be gone as Matt Fallaize quits and Graham Skuse, his acting replacement, is not keen on the idea of internationals. Competing in the South West Counties league costs Guernsey around £50,000 a season - an expense covered mainly by Credit Suisse - but this arrangement is not like most leagues. Skuse explains: "When we enter the SWC we have to pay for 22 people to come over here. It's cheaper for us to play away in Devon or Cornwall. People talk about us playing Cyprus, say, but that's not a weekend trip, you need the Monday and the Friday off work as well."

The tide has turned against Guernsey's international ambitions for the time being and is moving towards their neighbours after a wide-ranging report in 2006 into the state of Jersey football. Compiled by a working party led by Meiklejohn and ex-Sunderland chairman Bob Murray, a resident on the island, the report advocates rejecting competitions like the South West Counties in favour of greater international exposure.

A similar report in 2000 came to nothing and, after this latest review, there were sweeping changes at the JFA with Tostevin replaced by Ricky Weir and the friendly secretary Gill Morgan also standing down to be replaced by Nicky Martini.

# OUTCASTS: The Lands That FIFA Forgot

Meiklejohn made another visit to UEFA on 23 May 2006, but this time took a member of the English FA with him, the JFA's aim being to play internationals with its parent body's permission - and financial support. The Portuguese island of Madeira was touted as potential opponents, along with the likes of smaller UEFA members such as Andorra or Luxembourg. Madeira was mentioned mainly because Jersey is packed full of migrant islanders from the Portuguese island, where the most famous footballer is Manchester United star Cristiano Ronaldo. Jersey v Madeira at the Springfield Stadium in St Helier with Ronaldo in the visiting side might appear unlikely, but Miguel de Sousa, a Madeira politician and football administrator, has expansion ideas too using the UK as a model.

De Sousa even visited the Welsh FA to see how it works. He says: "It seemed to me an acceptable model for Madeira and Portugal. It depends exclusively on the general assembly of the Federacao Portuguesa de Futebol. It does not depend on any government or politician will (sic). If the FPF's general assembly authorizes Madeira to create its own FA, UEFA will accept that. Once Madeira would not be part of the FPF anymore, it would make sense that Madeira would become part of UEFA."

The idea of 'nations' seceding in order to field football teams seems against all UEFA's latest principles, but Portugal's Iberian neighbour runs its own affairs just like that, with the country's autonomous regions like the Basque Country and Catalonia fielding 'international' teams regularly.

The Basque and Catalan-born professionals get together around the end of each year, areas such as Galicia less so, to play friendlies against UEFA members. These gatherings were banned under Spain's repressive ruler General Franco, but since his death in 1975 have increased and these are very competitive sides. For example, a Basque XI put four goals without reply in December 2006 past a Serbian side that had qualified for that year's World Cup finals.

In 'Morbo', his definitive history of Spanish football, Phil Ball explains: "As far as the Basques and Catalans are concerned, this is the constitution of the café con leche para todos (white coffee for everyone), deliberately drawn up by the Espanolistas whose intention was to subsume real regional culture and separatism under a political system that pretended to be devolving equal shares of democracy to everyone. There have been times when either of these teams [the Basque or Catalan XI] could have destroyed the Spanish national outfit given the opportunity."

***********

# The Channel Island Divide

So, could Jersey or Guernsey - both with probably more independence than the Basques or Catalans - play in such a format in 'a sweetened white tea for everyone' arrangement with the English FA's blessing? After the 2005 Muratti, the FA denied that any regional FA had ever considered seceding, although FA Chairman Geoff Thompson's warning letter to the Jersey FA in 2002 was in a response to a Jersey enquiry on that same subject.

In 2007, the English FA still have no real enthusiasm for Jersey's ambitions. On being asked if the FA knows anything about Jersey's international desires, FA Head of Media Adrian Cooper would only say: "The Jersey FA is one of The FA's affiliated associations and has been for several decades, but I don't know anything about meetings with UEFA about them playing matches."

On being asked if he could provide a little more detail, Cooper simply says: "I don't think there is anything we can add. I've seen that letter, which is from Geoff Thompson, which outlines the likelihood that UEFA and FIFA would oppose the Jersey FA playing representative football. I am not aware of any subsequent letters."

With this sort of support, the Channel Islands look set to remain an international football backwater.

Or do they? Before the estimable Gill Morgan departed, she travelled to London for a meeting of an organisation cheekily called the Non FIFA (NF) Board aimed at providing opportunities for the places that FIFA does not want to know.

# CHAPTER THREE

# The International Waiting Room Of The NF Board

*"Maybe we can all go round the world playing football.*
*Or maybe we will just play in Gatwick."*
**Alain Besage, Chagos footballer**

## 11 June 2005, The Royal National Hotel, London

OUTSIDE THE DRAB Royal National Hotel, tiny Roman soldiers sit in cases watching a giant model panzer patrol up and down. The military replicas are part of a toy show being staged outside the Bloomsbury hotel. Inside the hotel, the NF Board is about to start with plans for another replica - a world cup. Theirs is much like FIFA's, only for countries that mostly do not exist.

Formed in December 2003 at La Mort Subite bar in Brussels, the NF Board wants to be, in its own words, an 'international waiting room' for aspiring international football sides. On its website, the NF Board grandly states its aims:

> "The Association's object of business is to federate Football Associations which are not affiliated to FIFA, until their permanent affiliation to the said Fédération Internationale de Football Association, with the aim of organising football matches on an international scale regardless of political or religious factors.
>
> NF Board shall be apolitical and non denominational, and shall not be a rival organisation to FIFA; on the contrary, it wishes to complement it with the constant aim of connecting these two institutions.
>
> NF Board therefore wishes to prepare its member federations for international competitions and for arranging administrative organisations and matches, in accordance with the rules set by the IFAB (International Football Association Board), particularly in order to meet the conditions set out in the specifications for affiliation to FIFA."

# The International Waiting Room Of The NF Board

That sounds ambitious, but by 2005 the NF Board, a motley collection of footballing outsiders, remained largely unheard of. Those few people that knew about the organisation tended to dismiss it as a bunch of eccentrics: a spectre rising out of the internet that has failed to materialise into anything concrete. Part of the problem is that the French, Belgian and Swiss members appear rather secretive about where they come from.

Chairman Christian Michelis has been at the heart of the development of the Monaco national team but, himself prefers to be thought of as French rather than Monégasque. Is he the same person that attended the 1997 Island Games in Jersey as a media representative for Paris-based organisation Live Sports, which no longer seems to exist? Did that tournament provide a spur for the formation of the NF Board? And how did he link up with vice chairman Jean-Luc Kit, a tiny Frenchman dressed all in black with metal-rimmed sunglasses and a large quiff?

In 2000, Kit helped publish an encyclopaedic book on international football that put him in contact with the Rec Sport Soccer Statistics Foundation (RSSSF). The RSSSF was originally founded as the Northern European Rec (sic) Sport Soccer Statistics Foundation in January 1994 by three contributors to an online football news group, Lars Aarhus, who ran a vast archive on Norwegian football, Kent Hedlundh and Karel Stokkermans. At the end of that year, German Bernd Timmermann joined and began contributing German football results.

Since then, RSSSF (www.rsssf.com) has developed a massive archive of international football results with members contributing from all around the world to a free-to-access website. A fore-runner of online encyclopedia Wikipedia, RSSSF includes the most obscure games and results imaginable, including members of the putative NF Board.

Stokkermans is an official observer on the board of the NF Board but says: "We were approached by Jean-Luc Kit some three or four years ago and had a few discussions, though I have to admit that my and RSSSF's role in the NF board is a fairly passive one.

"I haven't yet managed to attend any of the official meetings; I only had some informal discussions with Jean-Luc. Christian and I haven't met in person. The first meeting with Jean-Luc also was more about the [football statistics group] OMF, which is to deal with unifying statistics on various types of football, including rugby league and union as well as many others, and not so much about the NF Board.

"I can't tell what exactly drove him to the idea of the NF Board and the corresponding world cup. My personal status is that of an observer, which means I get some round mails and made some suggestions on people to contact in a couple of territories for which RSSSF had or has correspondents."

# OUTCASTS: The Lands That FIFA Forgot

Other observers include Englishman Neil Morrison and Mark Cruickshank, who, like Stokkermans, was recruited via the internet. Cruickshank runs the vast resource of the Roon Ba website (www.roonba.co.nr) that, like the RSSSF, collates data on international football fixtures and results and also includes a vast hoard of info on non-FIFA football. Where the Roon Ba differs from RSSSF is that Cruickshank, a Scotsman living in Essex, also uses these results to rank more than 80 places or countries ignored by FIFA. Places as diverse as autonomous Spanish regions such as Catalonia to countries like Palau in the Pacific that have only managed a couple of representative games, or oddities such as Easter Island, a Chilean possession stranded thousands of miles from anywhere in the Pacific. That makes the lower end of the Roon Ba rankings as meaningful as FIFA's, but it is a brave attempt to work out who's best among all the also-rans and provides the NF Board with its own rankings.

Cruickshank says: "This was originally how I got involved, as I had always paid attention on my website to non-FIFA territories and had collected a number of results so as to produce the ranking. I was then invited to become a member, with this specific function. My interest in non-FIFA football stemmed from an interest in maps at an early age, where I always seemed to be trying to find the most obscure little islands possible. Also, being from a technically non-independent country myself, I was moved to find some way of making sure these teams got as much attention at last as the FIFA members."

Like Stokkermans, Cruickshank's role is passive, but even this affiliation is likely to be tested over the next four years as he undertakes a Masters degree in Phonology, the study of the way sounds function within a given language or across languages, at Essex University.

The NF Board appears more a meeting of internet minds, of the inhabitants of football-mad chatrooms on the Net, where sites detail the existence of SC Grytviken or results from a league on Ascension Island - the former highly unlikely as Grytviken, the capital of South Georgia, is largely uninhabited, apart from the odd visiting scientist. Could they get eleven players up for a team? If so, who would they play? Certainly not anyone from Argentina as the last Argentineans to visit South Georgia provoked the Falklands War.

That first meeting in Brussels did little to dispel the notion that the NF Board was a dream cooked up by internet obsessives. Gravitas was added by the involvement of Luc Misson, a lawyer with the FIFpro international players' union who worked on the Bosman case that unravelled many of the contractual agreements that bound professional players to clubs over the past few years.

# The International Waiting Room Of The NF Board

Michael Nybrandt, a young Dane who organised a friendly between Tibet and Greenland in 2001 that spurred the foundation of the NF Board, was also in La Mort Subite, but the teams there seemed fantastical to say the least.

Apart from Michelis and the Monaco team, also present were football representatives from Sápmi, the indigenous people of what most term as Lapland, a football association supposedly from Western Sahara, a disputed territory annexed by Morocco in 1979, and Northern Cyprus, a breakaway state only recognised by Turkey after it invaded the top half of the Mediterranean island in 1974.

The other team in Brussels was one of the most bizarre members of the NF Board - and there are quite a few candidates. The 2,000 indigenous people of the Chagos Islands were controversially removed by the British government in the early 1970s to make way for a US Air Force base that has since been used to bomb Libya and Iraq, the idea of a national team seems bizarre to say the least. Where would they play for a start? Would the USAF allow the Chagos players to return for home matches? Almost certainly not given the strategic importance of the islands to George Bush's ongoing War OnTerror. Perhaps a more important is the answer to the question, where would the Chagos islanders actually raise a team from given that the majority of the islanders were forcibly dumped by the British government into the slums of Mauritius and the Seychelles?

The NF Board's football dreams might have looked like a fantasy to outsiders but the meeting at the Royal National Hotel shows that the dreams of Kit and Michelis are grounded in reality.

\*\*\*\*\*\*\*\*\*\*\*

In the foyer of the Royal National Hotel, the NF Board's Swiss organiser David Aranda stands talking to three players from the Chagos team. Alain Besage and Patrick Boyer are in their mid-twenties and their parents, like most of the archipelago's inhabitants, were exiled to Mauritius, where around 6,000 people now claiming Chagos lineage still live. Both currently share a house near Gatwick Airport with Jean-Claude Luc, who lived on Diego Garcia, the biggest island on the Chagos archipelago, for three months before being taken along with his parents to the Seychelles, which houses another 2,000 people from the islands that are now known as the British Indian Island Territory. All three left wives and small children behind in Mauritius and the Seychelles to come and live at Gatwick Airport in Autumn 2004, when the British government finally gave in and offered the exiled Chagos islanders full UK passports.

# OUTCASTS: The Lands That FIFA Forgot

"I was a personal security guard to the president of the Seychelles," says Luc, who at 37 appears to be the unselected head of the Chagos Football Association. "I left because of the cost of living. In the military, we had good pay, but it was not enough. For people coming from the UK for a holiday it is OK, but not for us."

Not surprisingly, he misses his children. Along with his house-mates Luc works for Unilever and United Parcels and wants to save enough money to go home. That will be at least seven years away, so plenty of time to get a national team up and running and Luc is organising a Chagos team in exile to publicise the cause of his countrymen, with an orange strip already chosen.

"Maybe we can all go round the world playing football," says Alain Besage smiling before, his smile hardly budging, adding: "Or maybe we will just play in Gatwick."

The appearance of the Chagos team is partly explained by Besage's Aunt being married to NF Board member George Wuethrich, a portly IT consultant from Geneva.

"I spoke to FIFA, but they are not interested in having countries like the Chagos," says Wuethrich. "They rely on safe things and the Chagos are not safe."

\*\*\*\*\*\*\*\*\*\*\*

The idea of a Chagos national team might seem a remote possibility, but the islanders are in London and their dreams seem no less unlikely than many of the other people sitting in the meeting room at the Royal National. The idea of South Lower Saxonia from the Lower Saxony region of Germany playing international football seems crazy but two giant, friendly German skinheads with impeccable English are in London to represent the SNFB, the South Lower Saxonian Football Federation.

At least both those places could raise a team, which is more than Hugh Geoffrey Withers from Sealand could probably manage. Sealand is a World War II sea fort that was taken over by a tiny handful of people who set up the Kingdom of Sealand and seceded from the UK to avoid income tax. With Withers are two of Sealand's teenage 'royal princes', Liam and James, who both look racked with teenage ennui and are soon glancing at their watches and looking for an escape

Also there, sitting by Cruickshank, is Pèire Costa, the chairman of Occitània, a federation representing people that speak the ancient Gallic language of Oc, which began being swallowed up by the French as far back as the thirteenth century as the French kings gradually conquered their homeland. Costa is trying to keep alive the idea of Occitània through football. The London meeting is held in English, but Costa asks for everything translated into French, although it later emerges that he also speaks and writes pretty good English.

Franky Junior Reinhardt, the head of the Romany football association is supposed to be there according to a name card, but his seat is empty and so is one reserved for Western Sahara. But Taner Yolcu, the bald-headed overweight secretary of the Northern Cypriot Football Federation, made the Brussels meeting and is in London. So is Adam Amerkhanov, a friendly London-based player for the Chechen team. He is standing in for the Chechen federation's president, Andi Guitchkaev, who has, apparently and mysteriously, been unavoidably detained.

Three well-dressed men represent the football association of Somaliland, the British-controlled area of Somalia in the eastern horn of Africa that was part of modern-day Somalia before breaking away in May 1991 to become independent. Despite 3.5 million people living in Somaliland, the place is not on the international sporting and political map, although football is played by around 80,000 people there, mostly boys aged up to 18, the age many give up to work for their families. One member of the Somaliland association, speaking almost faultless English, explained that the Somaliland association's headquarters is based in the unlikely location of Birmingham.

Also in attendance are two representatives of the football federation of the Kurdistan region of northern Iraq, who sit by Nybrandt, who has returned from a three-month trip to Cuba to represent Tibet. Like Tibet, Gibraltar have played representative matches and the UK colony is represented by Gibraltar Football Association president Joe Nunez. Sitting down the table from Nunez is the Jersey Football Association's friendly secretary Gill Morgan. Alongside a handful of fantasy teams, the NF Board has drawn in teams that very much exist to try and realise their idea.

\*\*\*\*\*\*\*\*\*\*\*

The NF Board kick off by electing representatives to cover other parts of the globe and with apologies from interested places unable to attend, including the south Pacific republic of Kiribati and Greenland. Eight provisional members are then elected: Monaco; the Sápmi; Northern Cyprus; Tibet; the Chagos; Somaliland along with two absentees, Zanzibar and Western Sahara.

As the meeting progresses, a camerawoman from Norway's NRK station roams the room, but the presence of television cameras perhaps overstates interest in the meeting.

The BBC World Service failed to show and the only other journalist is a quiet young man from French sports paper L'Equipe, who scribbles away intermittently. The meeting is painfully slow, everything translated into French or English depending on the speaker until the subject of money is raised.

The NF Board can hardly be accused of greed as members will only be charged an annual fee of 150 euros, which was agreed at a previous meeting. That is unlikely to generate much cash and Michelis suggests 50 per cent of the gate receipts from home games go to the home team, 30 per cent to the visitors and the remaining 20 per cent to the NF Board to generate some more cash to pay for organisation. Hardly unreasonable, but Gill Morgan makes the point that the costs are all with the travelling team and suggests that the visitors receive 75 per cent.

"You're talking about a percentage of profits and that's not going to happen," bursts out Joe Nunez, who has been sitting through the previous conversation shaking his head. "Ten per cent of nothing is still nothing. Most of these games are going to lose money. Accept that and get over it, then in five to 10 years time start talking about sharing gate receipts."

Gill Morgan only half-jokingly suggests discussing how to share out the losses before the South Lower Saxony Skins make the point these are supposed to be friendly games and you put your friends up if they come to stay.

"We don't want to make a profit, but we also don't say give us your bowl and we will pay everything," says the larger of the two Skins, with a smile. "We want to be able to support the travel and hotel bills as no-one will be travelling to Tibet for 10 or 20 years, I think."

Eventually, everyone present agrees unanimously that a nominal fee of around 25 euros will go direct to the NF board and teams playing each other must agree how to share any profits or losses as they go along.

George Wuethrich mentions discussions with a Cree tribe from northern Canada that wants to organise an indigenous people's Olympics including a football tournament, before a break is taken for tea. On her way outside to assemble for a group photo Gill Morgan confides: "What worries me about all this is the cost of getting to these matches."

After having her photo taken with the rest of the representatives of the NF Board's provisional potential members, Morgan troops back inside as discussion moves onto their ambitious plans for a 16-team tournament to be held in November 2006.

On the way back inside, Taner Yolcu, as he lumbers his bulky frame up the hotel stairs, sweating heavily and looking none too healthy, confides that the event will be staged in Northern Cyprus. That is perhaps no surprise as

Northern Cyprus is the only real candidate, boasting 93 pitches and a number of professional standard stadia, the largest holding 28,000 people.

The Viva World Cup will, the NF Board soon confirm, be staged over a week in Yolcu's breakaway state with four groups of four. Apart from those present at the meeting, the NF Board executive claim that a number of other isolated federations also expressed an interest in playing in the Viva World Cup, including Catalonia in northern Spain, the Falklands, the south Pacific republics of Tuvalu and Kiribati, Greenland and the Isle of Man.

The NF Board has drawn up a long list of 101 potential members with contact details aimed at helping them organise matches against each other. Seemingly compiled by a World Soccer reader pining for the days when the bible of international football supposedly devoted tracts to obscure club matches in places like Albania, the list ranges from the realistic through the bizarre to the outright laughable.

Like Monaco, the Comoros Islands is also a member of the United Nations but not of FIFA and at the time appeared a reasonable candidate - until being swallowed up soon after by FIFA. Another forgotten UN member in the Pacific, the Federated States of Micronesia, also seems like a reasonable suggestion for an NF Board member (although Micronesia would be invited to join FIFA confederation Oceania 18 months later), but then up pops Cornwall.

Their inclusion seems ludicrous as Cornwall's recent 'international' representation goes no further than matches in the South West Counties league against Guernsey and Jersey, but the Roon Ba does detail three friendlies played by Cornwall in 1953 against Trinidad & Tobago. Half a century later, Cornwall's opponents would take on England in the 2006 World Cup; credentials indeed. Perhaps the re-emergence of a Cornish language prompted the inclusion in the NF Board's manual, but the Cornish FA are probably unaware of their own aspirations as the manual lacks any contact details.

The manual includes another batch of breakaway states such as Transnistria, which is trying to secede from Moldova, and Abkhazia which is seeking to split away from Georgia. For some reason South Ossetia, which has already split from Georgia, is missing from this ambitious list.

Nauru, with a population of 5,000 people but better known for vast guano deposits that brought the island a huge income until they ran out leaving a giant crater in the centre of the South Pacific island, is also included. So is St Helena, an island from the South Atlantic famous for being Napoleon Bonaparte's prison and place of death, with a similar size population to Nauru, but still owned by the British. St Helena has no airport, but sends athletes to the Island Games so perhaps their entry into the realms of NF Board international football is not so bizarre: Certainly not as bizarre as the inclusion of the Pitcairn Islands.

# OUTCASTS: The Lands That FIFA Forgot

Settled by mutineers from the Bounty led by Fletcher Christian and with a population of less than 50 people, there are no transport links to Pitcairn apart from a regular boat that stops for half a day once a year. Those are certainly major obstacles to Pitcairn playing international football, but not as problematic as most of their male population being locked up on the island for a series of sexual offences based on the naturally close blood relations to their womenfolk, rendering the idea of a Pitcairn Islands national team completely ludicrous.

Some potential teams are more in keeping with the NF Board's ethos of stateless nations, such as the Basque Country and Catalonia in Europe and the French-Canadians of Quebec. Other entries appear even more bizarre than Pitcairn - like the Antarctic and the Vatican City. The idea of a Vatican team seems ridiculous until Christian Michelis explains that Monaco has managed a game - a goalless draw - against the Vatican City, appropriately enough when the Papacy was held by former Polish amateur goalkeeper Pope John Paul II. But the Antarctic?

***********

Another debate starts about whether the Viva World Cup should be amateur or include semi-professionals or even full-time players? Gill Morgan wants to know if Graeme Le Saux, freshly retired from Southampton after the club's recent relegation from the Premier League, would be eligible to play? That conversation gradually leads into the most animated debate of the afternoon, one that finally gets to the heart of the values of the NF Board.

"How do you decide on nationality?" asks Joseph Nunez. "In Gibraltar, you have to be a registered Gibraltarian to play."

One of the South Lower Saxony Skins then adds: "We all want to win games, but we do hope that there is no cheating and the NF Board does not want to interfere with how we choose our team."

No-one certainly wants to argue with either of the amiable Skins. Occitània's Pèire Costa explains that his team has nothing to make them Occitanian other than a feeling of allegiance for their language and culture. Christian Michelis makes the point that Monaco supplements its Olympic team with people that have lived within a 20-km radius of the principality for a set period.

Like the debate over money, this seems impossible to resolve until Leif Isak Nilut, the President of the Sápmi Football Federation, does just that with an intervention unlikely to be seen at any UEFA or FIFA gathering.

A broad, friendly man dressed in a bright blue decorated traditional Sami jacket, he has been trying to catch the attention of the NF Board's executive for some time as the debate dragged on. Unlike the rest of the delegates, he moved seats at the break to sit by an attractive female representative for the Kurdistan Football Association.

Eventually, his polite finger-waving gains the attention of Christian Michelis, but Nilut does not speak, he stands up - and sings.

Nilut breaks into a heartfelt rendition of a traditional Sami song known as a yoik. The words come booming out of Nilut's chest and despite no-one else in the room apart from the two NRK journalists having the remotest idea what any of the words mean, everyone stays respectfully silent.

For a moment, no-one speaks. The sheer emotion of Nilut's song has conveyed not just what it means to be a Sami but to be a person from a state-less country. With that level of commitment to maintaining their identity at every member, the NF Board should be a massive success.

Nilut then launches into what the Sami think the NF Board is all about; this time in English. He says: "We play for the Sápmi team because that is who we are. We are not a state, we live in four different countries, but it's about where you belong. I hope that we can all agree on this because it's what the purpose of the NF Board is all about. We will have the best team possible in Cyprus."

As Nilut sits down the delegates applaud his performance, which in impenetrable song, then clearer words, has made everyone present realise what the NF Board should aspire to be about.

Sealand's Hugh Geoffrey Withers then makes a rare interjection, saying: "We would find it untenable were we placed in a position of being told how we should select our national team."

Being an offshore rig with a supposed population of just 21 (although five is more likely) and not enough space for a football pitch, Sealand has adopted a club side from Aalborg in Denmark. At this point, someone sitting with the NF Board executive, who was earlier praised for his work on 'statistics', starts talking about the majority of the Sealand population being immigrants. He agrees that strict rules on who plays for them could be a problem.

The seriousness of his comment makes a mockery of Nilut's impassioned statement. The big Sami is too polite to say anything but the urge to leap across the sparsely populated media desk and give him a good shake is hard to suppress. Later, the Sealand team are exposed as an elaborate joke. The side, featuring a 54 year-old bank manager as a left back and a 41 year-old headmaster on the wing, is run by a 47 year-old Danish hotel manager, Christian Olsen, who even plays an adopted national anthem before their friendly matches against Danish club sides.

Luckily, the rest of the room take little notice of Withers as Christian Michelis returns to Nilut's speech, saying: "We want to be different from FIFA, we want to be the football of the peoples. You must know why you want to play in the Viva World Cup and why you are using those players. If you want to play with people just from Occitània or with people who only have a Gibraltar passport, why not?

"People must choose why they want to play from the outset. We want the peoples (sic) to play football and not be so strict. We want to make a different game. There will be rules for the competition, of course, but we want to be together and play together."

For the second time that afternoon, the delegates break into spontaneous applause at this laudable objective. There is no vote, but the rules for the first Viva World Cup seem to have been decided: two halves of 45 minutes each way and bring whoever you want. To end the day, the Viva World Cup itself is unveiled; a pretty ugly sculpture by French sculptor Gérard Pigault, the trophy is titled the Nelson Mandela Trophy, which is a very political name for a supposedly non-political project.

***********

After the meeting, the idea that the NF Board is some kind of giant hoax remains hard to shake off, but within weeks of that meeting, the NF Board's initial provisional membership swells to 17 football federations, but Greenland is still not one of them. Nor are any of the Channel Islands, the Isle of Man or Gibraltar, despite Gill Morgan and Joseph Nunez's attendance in London.

Morgan says later: "There are certain issues regarding the NF Board. Firstly, Jersey and Guernsey and the Isle of Man are all affiliated to the Football Association. We get a lot of funding from the FA to run our offices and our football development. We could not join the NF Board unless it was approved by the FA and FIFA. We have asked the FA for clarification. The problem is that certain member federations may not be recognised by FIFA and we would not be able to play them without sanction. For those member federations that do not belong to other associations the NF Board is brilliant, but we are all governed by the FA and have to abide by their rules.

"I have fully briefed Guernsey and the IOM on the meeting and the Football Association so they can discuss and advise us if we are able to continue. If the NF Board was just the likes of Monaco and Gibraltar, for instance, it would not be a problem. Some of the other areas do cause problems for us."

Those 'problems' are evident in the other places that have since swelled the NF Board's provisional membership: the Roma, South Lower Saxony, Occitània, Sealand and Saugeais, a faux breakaway state from France situated near Switzerland comprising 11 communes that appears reminiscent of 'The

Mouse That Roared', the 1959 Peter Sellers film about a European micro-state that declares war on the United States hoping to lose and get some aid.

***********

Another four new provisional members of the NF Board then meet at the end of June in a double-header at The Hague in the Netherlands. Staged by the Unrepresented Nations and Peoples Organisation (UNPO) - a sort of UN for countries that don't exist - the first tournament with the NF Board's involvement was not an auspicious affair.

The UNPO was formed in 1981 and has 69 members (see appendices) from independence movements like the delegation from the tsunami-torn Indonesian province of Aceh to tribal peoples such as the Maasai in Africa and the Buffalo River Dene Nation from Canada. Although Tatarsan in Russia has skirted around the outskirts of international rugby league, the only FIFA member in the UNPO and a definite wannabe member of the UN is Taiwan.

The promotion of half-a-dozen former members - Armenia, East Timor, Estonia, Georgia, Latvia and Palau - to the Premier League of the global community, the UN, has not helped UNPO and the organisation is struggling for funds. That may explain the desultory nature of the first UNPO Cup, which was staged as a curtain raiser for the UNPO's seventh congress in the Dutch capital of The Hague between June 24 and 26.

The tournament featured just four teams: South Moluccas, a group of islands that is part of Indonesia which boasts its own football league, set up in March 2002, despite being troubled by conflict between Christians and Muslims, the Chechen Republic of Ichkeria, West Papua, which was invaded by Indonesia in 1963, and Southern Cameroon, which was a British colony before being united with the French speakers to form the modern Cameroon. Each of these territories are involved in some form of struggle for independence that has overshadowed any football ambitions.

At club level, Chechen team Terek Grozny qualified for the 2004/05 UEFA Cup after winning the Russian Cup by beating Premier League side Shinnik Yaroslavl 2-1 in the semi-finals and then Krylya Sovietov, a team from Samara, 1-0 in the final.

Unable to play in Chechnya's battered capital Grozny, Terek played their UEFA Cup matches in Beshtau and beat Polish side Lech Poznan 1-0 home and away before drawing 1-1 with Swiss side Basel and losing the second leg 0-2 on September 30 to exit the competition.

There were no Terek players in The Hague for this rare moment in football's spotlight for the four aspiring nations. All the teams were accepted into the NF Board and Vice President Jean-Luc Kit made a speech before the matches kicked off, followed by an address from UNPO secretary general Marino Busdachin, who marked the tournament by citing Baron Pierre de Coubertin, founder of the Olympic Games. Busdachin said: "Never have so many nations cheered the dream of global oneness, awaiting a spiritual and physical renaissance powerful enough to unite the world."

Despite these grandiose claims, the tournament, held on a gloomy day at the Sportcomplex De Verademing, had an air of a kickabout. The semi-finals were not even full-length matches, but UNPO described both as "bitterly disputed" with the "robust" Chechens overcoming Southern Cameroons on penalties after a 2-2 draw, as the Chechnya goalkeeper proved too good for the opposition in the shoot-out.

Described by UNPO as "dynamic and technical", South Moluccas trailed by a single goal to a "persevering" West Papua side until a last minute strike. South Moluccas then went through on penalties to the final that began, according to a slightly tactless report from UNPO, "with a bang", though the nature of the "bang" was never identified.

The report continued: "The South Moluccas team dominated the first half, scoring two goals rapidly. The Chechens did not throw in the towel and pressed on with a physical strategy that paid off when they scored their first goal. Unfortunately for the Chechens, the South Moluccas late third strike of the game sealed the fate of the tough Chechen team."

To underline that participation is more important than winning, every team in the UNPO Cup received identical trophies - a trend that FIFA may find hard to explain to Brazil or any of the other leading contenders at a World Cup finals. Despite the low key nature of the inaugural event, UNPO wants to expand the tournament and has signed an official partnership with the NF Board so that the two organisations can help each other drum up more members. Kit explains: "This partnership consists in our help to their members if they want to found their own FA. In return, they help us to promote the NF Board to their peoples."

Following the tournament, the NF Board got in contact with a football association run by the Maasai tribesmen of Africa that came through the UNPO. The NF Board hopes that their partnership with UNPO will ensure that the proposed 2006 Viva World Cup has at least 16 teams. For UNPO, working with the NF Board makes sense - after all, both are forms of waiting rooms - but the UNPO Cup looks more like a kick-about for delegates and has some way to go before providing the form of intermediary competition available to some more seriously aspiring nations, such as Greenland.

Previous members of the UNPO may have graduated to full UN status as a nation, such as Estonia, but none of the NF Board members look likely to play in a FIFA organised game, even though Kit manages to secure a meeting with FIFA in July 2005. After that meeting, Kit says: "They don't want more affiliation for several years. In Zurich, we had a first meeting with Jerôme Champagne of FIFA with Christian Michelis, me and Gilles Clémançon as an observer for Observatoire Mondial des Foot-Balls [A French-based group of sports statisticians]. FIFA don't want more members because they have to give a lot of money for each member."

So, for the foreseeable future, maybe there will only be a door into the NF Board's international waiting room, but no way out. For the NF Board executive, this only makes them more determined to press on with their mission. What restricts the Board is exactly what FIFA has in bucket-loads: cash. For all their good intentions, Kit and Michelis cannot just get on a plane like FIFA supremo Sepp Blatter and visit the far-flung outposts that his empire has yet to conquer; like Greenland.

# CHAPTER FOUR

# Greenland On Tour

*"If we all just do what FIFA want then we are all doing nothing."*
**Jens Brinch, head of the Football Association of Greenland**

## 12 July 2005, Burra, Shetland Isles

AFTER TWO MATCHES unbeaten in the 2005 Island Games, Greenland's only real outlet for international football, manager Jens Tang Olesen's side are on course for their best ever finish in the bi-annual event.

After a 0-0 draw with the Welsh island of Yns Mon, the Greenlanders travelled to the remote Shetland isle of Unst. The trip was a rare moment of glamour for Unst, whose population of around 700 people is reeling from a Ministry of Defence decision to close a long-standing Royal Air Force base on the island. Around 70 RAF personnel and their family will leave Unst after the MoD's decision to close the Saxa Vord listening base, which was set up in the Cold War to spy on the Russians and has been the UK's most northerly listening post.

Now, a thousand years after the Vikings rampaged through Unst, the Greenlanders quietly pitched up, clinched a 2-1 win over a weak Orkney side and returned to their base in Burra later that day for two matches in two days that could secure their first ever medal in the Island Games

Playing for one of these 'nations' is hardly the kind of glamorous lifestyle that comes with a Premiership contract. The entire squad of 18 Greenland players are camping out on the floor of a relatively new village hall built adjacent to the pitch in Burra with money from the Shetlands' oil boom. Like Greenland's population of 55,000, the squad is predominantly Inuit, but also includes a number of players of Danish descent from colonisation of the west coast. To the rest of the team, they are all Greenlanders.

The team's vital third match at the Island Games is against tournament debutants the Western Isles and a crowd of around 200 people has slowly built up by kick-off time, standing around three sides of the pitch that looks out into a glorious view of the neighbouring sound. Sometimes shy around outsiders, Greenland are well supported by other athletes from the Greenlandic squad at the games including Kim Godtfredsen, who has just won silver in the men's athletics 10,000 metres race and has represented Denmark on a number of occasions. The most famous Greenlandic footballer chose to do just the same.

Jesper Gronkjaer was born in the capital of Nuuq in 1977, but left Greenland as a young boy for Denmark, where he joined Aalborg and would play a vital role in Roman Abramovich buying Chelsea. According to football legend, Abramovich was only willing to buy Chelsea if the club were in the Champions League and it was the Greenlandic winger/striker who secured this with a superb solo goal against Liverpool on the final day of the 2003 season.

Gronkjaer joined Chelsea from Ajax Amsterdam in October 2000 in a £7.8 million move and played in all four Denmark games at the 2002 World Cup finals as the side knocked out holders France in the group stage only to lose heavily to England in the first knockout round. After scoring seven goals in 88 appearances, Gronkjaer left Chelsea in 2004. He had spells with Birmingham City, Atletico Madrid and VfB Stuttgart before returning to Denmark and joining FC Copenhagen, where he would have again played in the Champions League in the 2006/07 season but for injuries.

Gronkjaer, perhaps not unreasonably, prefers playing for Denmark ahead of the land of his birth. At the time of the 2005 Island Games, four other Greenlanders were playing in Denmark, Rene Overballe and Aputsiaq Birchm at Jens Tang Olesen's home town club Frederikshavn and Anton Overballe at Aalborg. The other man playing club football in Denmark is probably the team's best player, and one happy to put his career on the line for Greenland.

"It's just tremendous to be on the team again and see all your friends as it's so difficult in Greenland and there are no roads and it takes ages to get anywhere," says Niklas Kreutzmann, who plays as a semi-professional at Aarhus Fremand in Denmark's third league, the Liga West.

In football terms, the next season is a big one for Kreutzmann as Aarhus Fremand are likely to challenge for promotion. The city's biggest club, AGF, are on a poor run. If they go down from the top tier and Fremand get promoted into the second level to join Aarhus' other club, Gymnastik Forening, for the first time all three of the city's clubs would be in the same division. Confident that Fremand can meet their side of the bargain, Kreutzmann has bet 100 Danish Kronar (about £9) on this scenario panning out and the winnings of £180 would be a help towards his seven-year long course to be a dentist.

In addition to training with Aarhus Fremand five times a week, Kreutzmann works up to 60 hours a week on his dental studies, but was never going to let Greenland's bear-like manager Jens Tang Olesen down by not playing. For Kreutzmann, football has been as big a part of his life in growing up as rituals such as killing his first seal aged 12 with his father. In Greenland, most locals learnt to speak Danish and Greenlandic through sport and football in particular.

# OUTCASTS: The Lands That FIFA Forgot

"We can only play football outside for three or four months a year and in the winter we play futsal instead. At home, I spoke Danish, but I learnt Greenlandic through sport," adds the bright-eyed defender.

When Greenlanders reach 11 or 12, many are sent to Denmark on an exchange visit with a Danish child for three months to improve their Danish. This is co-ordinated through Greenland Houses located in each area. This is how Jens Tang Olesen came across the Greenlanders, by taking in youngsters like Niklas Kreutzmann.

Kreutzmann adds: "I left Nuuk when I was 16 to do my exams. Jens Tang is brilliant guidance for young people and learning about the soccer world. When I came from Greenland, I had never lived on my own and Jens Tang told me how to live and to behave. We were introduced to a tough world [moving to Denmark] and it is still difficult, but now because of Jens I manage to play football, study and be young."

In the Shetlands, the articulate and personable Kreutzmann is suffering from a niggling injury that he puts down to the sand pitches that players train on in Denmark and play on in Greenland. Injuries at least provide him with rare opportunities to return home to Nuuk, but despite that problem and his hectic dental and football schedule, he was always going to play the Island Games.

***********

Apart from those handful of Danish-based players such as Kreutzmann, Greenland's squad is drawn mainly from home, taking players from isolated towns such as Uummannaq and giving them a chance to play football - and experience places - that would otherwise be impossible.

Playing football at all would seem impossible in Greenland yet the island's oldest club dates back to 1933. The game was brought to the island long before that by the crews of whaling boats and first played around Disko Island. The first championships were staged in 1958 and the Football Association of Greenland (FAG) founded in 1971. Today, there are 76 clubs with 5,000 players, of whom 2,200 are under 18.

Football is a major source of identity for Greenland, which won home rule from Denmark in 1979, but due to Danish subsidies of around £15,000 a year per head of the population cannot afford to be independent. Instead, Greenland sends two representatives to the Danish parliament in Copenhagen and forms a Danish commonwealth with easterly neighbours the Faroe Islands - themselves, of course, a fully fledged member of FIFA, despite having the exact same political standing as Greenland.

A flight from Greenland to Denmark - the only international link with the outside world - costs about £1,000 in high season, which effectively restricted the

Greenland national football side's matches to casual outings against the Faroes until the 1989 Island Games. Since then, Greenland has played in the football tournament at every Island Games, providing great experiences for isolated Greenlanders, but never doing better than a play-off for sixth and seventh place.

After a good start, an improvement surely looks possible this time. Against the Western Isles, winger Kassava Zeeb is running the burly Scots defenders ragged and Kreutzmann is dominant in central defence. Within a few minutes the Greenlanders are in front as Brian Thomsen steers the ball home. Despite the Western Isles having more of the ball, the shorter but stronger Greenlanders hold out and increase their lead. With half-time approaching, Leifeeraq Karlsen scores a second against the run of play, a goal that is met by terrifying Greenlandic whooping on the pitch and quiet smiles among their supporters on the sidelines.

Smoking a pipe, Jens Brinch is one of these supporters. Brinch is head of the Football Association of Greenland and the island's overall umbrella body, the Sports Confederation of Greenland. Born in 1946 in Esjberg in Denmark, he studied in China and the US in the 1980s and published two books, "A comparative study of sports in China, USA and Western Europe" and "The Psychology of Sports" in the 1980s. He went to Greenland in 1995, initially for a year or two seeking a new experience, but fell in love with the place and the people and has been in the job for a decade.

"We don't have a league as the infrastructure is such that you cannot drive between the cities," he explains, unaware that the idea of Greenland having a city at all seems odd to most people. "We play regional qualifiers and then meet up for a week to decide who is champion. It's not very good as they cannot play regularly enough and we can only play three months of the year because the ice does not melt until May."

Played a month after the Island Games, the 2005 finals of the Greenland club championship were staged at Uummannaq in the north of the island. This meant that some teams needed a week by boat to get to the tournament, where B-67 - the number relates to the year of the club's formation - from the capital Nuuk clinched the title beating Ilulissat 3-1 in the final. Local side Malamuk finished third. The week-long finals over, the players set off home with many, again, taking a week to get back by sea.

For Greenlandic footballers, merely getting to play the game is a battle; but a popular one. At the finals in Uummannaq, 2,000 of the 3,500 inhabitants were watching the semi-finals of the championships being played on a sand pitch near the coast when an iceberg floating by capsized. A large section of ice under the water had sheared off, making the iceberg top-heavy and forcing it to topple. Jens Tang Olesen recalls large sections of the crowd fleeing into boats to escape from the mini-tidal wave that ensued.

# OUTCASTS: The Lands That FIFA Forgot

That sort of difficulty is what makes football's survival and prosperity in Greenland so amazing. The biggest network of roads is the 15km around the capital of Nuuk. This even includes a couple of speed cameras - those administrators don't miss a trick - but none of these roads lead anywhere outside of Nuuk. So just getting to matches can be difficult; and even fatal in the most tragic part of Greenland's football history.

On 8 August 2004, Karl Olsen, 35, Martin Larsen 40, and Kristian Davidsen, who was 43, set sail from Aasiaat in the north across Disko Bay to play in a veterans' game in Qegertarsuag. The journey usually only takes an hour and after playing the game, the trio set sail back home again. But they never arrived. A massive search and rescue mission was launched including Greenland Air's helicopters, fishery inspections ships, a Gulf Stream search and rescue aircraft from Royal Danish Air Force and hordes of locals in their own small boats; but the men could not be found. On 16 August, the search for the three men, who all had wives and children, was called off.

As the summer closed in and Greenland's harsh winter descended, there was still no sign of the trio and all hope was abandoned. Then, on 10 June 2005, the players were all found - dead. They had seemingly got lost and their boat was stuck on the small, uninhabited Hareoe Island (or Hare Island in English) to the north of Disko Island. The three men had built a rough shelter from driftwood and even written SOS on the cliffs to try and attract attention from the search parties, but to no avail. The footballers had died either from starvation or cold during the winter, all for a game of football.

The incident led to massive soul-searching among Greenland's tight-knit but geographically fragmented community with many criticisms of the local police, whose chief Steen Silberg responded: "It is my belief, that the search has been carried out thoroughly and has covered a very large area. I firmly believe that the military and police crew, and also the volunteers, have done a tremendous job, but the sad story is that the search did not find the missing men."

Against this background, winning a football match seems pointless, but the harsh conditions on the world's largest island of 2,175 million square kilometres mean there is a bond between the Greenlandic players that other national teams will never have. Olesen explains: "All the players, they love to be together. Sometimes I forget and shout when they forget a tactic, but they love it, to be together and to be with each other."

Before coming to the Shetlands, the Greenlanders had a week playing practice matches in Denmark and against the Western Isles were in command at two goals up. Peri Fleischer scored a lucky third, the ball going in off a defender and, though the Western Isles pulled one back through Alasdair Mackay, Salomon Thomsen finishes off a good move to make the score 4-1.

# Greenland On Tour

For Brinch, who is considering a return to Denmark in a couple of years, a medal would be nice, but is not imperative. Earlier, on meeting up in the ugly utilitarian Shetland Hotel in Lerwick, he shrugged when asked how the overall Greenland team is getting on. "There's not many medals, but I don't care. I want people to enjoy themselves," he says. "The media always want to focus on the score because that's easy, but there's so many other more human stories to tell."

He is talking, in part, about Greenland's friendly against Tibet four years ago that caused an international furore. In 1996 the Sports Confederation of Greenland separated from the Danish Sports Confederation, but with the Island Games their only outlet for football, Brinch explored the idea of trying to join UEFA and FIFA. Membership had certainly benefited the Faroes since Denmark's other overseas territory began playing internationally in 1994.

Those first games were played in Sweden due to the facilities in the Faroes, where the old Toftir stadium pitch was poor and the capacity of 7,200 - many on benches - was slashed to just 4,700 due to requirements for internationals to be played in all-seater grounds.

With 10 per cent of the Faroes' population regularly attending matches, the Island's association decided to take advantage of FIFA and UEFA's largesse and build a second international standard ground.

Costing 20 million Danish Krona (about £1.9 million), the ground held 10,000 fans for a World Cup qualifier against the Republic of Ireland in 2005 and benefited from a 6 million Danish Krona (£540,000) grant from FIFA, with UEFA also loaning 2 million Danish Krona (£180,000) towards the project. Ísak Mikladal from the Faroe Islands Football Association explains: "It was not necessary to build a new stadium, but we are of the opinion that it is better to have two national stadiums if, in the future, we participate in World Cup and European Championship qualification with a Under-21 team."

Jens Brinch had no such grand ambitions for Greenland's international participation.

He explains: "We applied to UEFA in 1998 and were promised there would be some changes to their laws so we could be an associate member. We don't have the money to play in the World Cup and European Championship; we just wanted to play friendlies against teams like the Sápmi [Lapland] team and the Faroes' second team."

Brinch travelled to Geneva and met FIFA president Sepp Blatter on a number of occasions, which initially appeared to go well.

"They were very friendly to start with," Brinch adds. "They said they would help, but then they became very unfriendly and I was never sure why. I think it was to do with Gibraltar as, if they let us in, then they would have to let Gibraltar in too. FIFA realised that if we couldn't play they were the ones with a problem not us."

# OUTCASTS: The Lands That FIFA Forgot

UEFA agreeing to let Greenland join as an associate would surely not have offended anyone, but would, as lawyers around the world know all too well, have set a precedent that Gibraltar would have exploited. Neither UEFA nor FIFA wanted to offend the Spanish, so the Greenlanders were quite literally frozen out. But as this was happening, a young Dane called Michael Nybrandt was trying to organise a game in Europe for a team of exiled Tibetans, after visiting the Himalayan kingdom. Nybrandt needed opponents for his team and who better than the Greenlanders, who had been left in an impossible position, having seceded from the Danish FA, but been completely shunned by UEFA and FIFA?

What seemed like a good idea did not go down too well in Greenland after the Chinese government made threats about putting an embargo on their export of shrimps to China, one of the few industries in the island and worth about 250 million Danish Krona (£23 million) a year.

Pressure was applied first in Denmark then to Greenland's own political administration, who in turn tried to lean on Brinch and the Greenlanders' coach, Sepp Piontek, whose appointment had been a masterstroke in terms of publicity. Though German and previously manager of Haiti, Piontek was appointed manager of Denmark in 1979 and held the post for 115 games that included qualification for their first ever European Championship and World Cup finals in 1982 and 1986 respectively, a golden period in Danish football. He left in 1990 and coached in Turkey before returning to club fooball at Silkeborg in Denmark. Piontek remained massively popular in Denmark, but was slipping slowly into retirement when approached by the Greenlanders.

His appointment was a fillip for a fixture that was under severe threat. On 3 April 2001, a shot was fired across the Greenland FA's bows by the home rule government affairs office in a message saying: "The Greenlandic society has present and potential (sic) export-interests in relation to China and this should not be threatened by a sport event. The foreign policy of Greenland is a matter for the Prime Minister and not for the sports confederation of Greenland!"

Two weeks later, the Greenland sea fishery and export association pitched in with their contribution, in a statement that said: "Official contact from the People's Republic of China to Greenland's Office of Foreign Affairs and the Danish Ministry of Foreign Affairs stated that a realisation of the football match will have consequences for the trade between Greenland and China."

By May, the umbrella Sports Confederation of Greenland recommended not playing the match by a vote of 3 to 2, but, in a brave decision, left the final reckoning up to Brinch and the Greenland FA, who decided on 28 May that the match would go ahead. FIFA had also tried to pressure Brinch to cancel the match, but, as the Greenlanders had been exiled by Blatter's own organisation, there was little that he or anyone else at FIFA could do.

# Greenland On Tour

On 30 June 2001, the game that nobody wanted kicked off in Copenhagen, with more than 5,000 people turning up to watch at the local authority-owned Vanlose Stadium; the choice of which had been determined by a FIFA threat to take action against any sports club involved in the game.

The match was a final hurrah for Piontek and, although Tibet scored first, his new charges responded with four goals in front of cameras from the BBC and US broadcaster CNN. A second match followed for Greenland, also in Copenhagen, against the Sápmi, but Piontek's moment was over. The Laplanders routed his charges 5-1. With no political furore attached to this match, only 150 people turned up. For the friendly, handsome Brinch, that first game against Tibet was clearly a high-point of his time with the Greenland team. He says: "The most important thing is that we show football can be played in another way. If we all just do what FIFA want then we are all doing nothing. After the Tibet game, Sepp Piontek said it was one of his greatest experiences as it was football from the heart."

\*\*\*\*\*\*\*\*\*\*\*

Piontek stood down in 2003 leaving Jens Tang Olesen to take the helm. Olesen might not have coached at a World Cup finals like his predecessor, but he must have at least been thinking of an Island Games medal with his team completely in charge against the Western Isles. Confident of a healthy win, he substitutes the game's most influential performer, Zeeb, which proves a mistake.

With 20 minutes to go, Greenland are still 4-1 up, but the Western Isles are energized by the surprise substitution of their most problematic opponent. Attacking the Greenlanders with determination, the Western Isles hit a post then Gordon Morrison pulls a goal back.

Soon after, a fracas breaks out and Mackay picks up a yellow card, but both sides quickly calm down until Greenland keeper John Kreutzmann clumsily bundles over a Western Isles forward with two minutes remaining. The challenge marred an otherwise dominant performance from Kreutzmann, but Morrison crashes home the penalty to set up a stirring finale. Greenland return to defend in numbers, but are clearly unsettled and in the last kick of the game Murdo MacLennan thumps home a dramatic equalizer.

The Greenlanders meet the result with equanimity, shrugging off the loss of two points. After three matches, they are still unbeaten, but that does not seem to be that important to Brinch, as for him Greenland playing at all is the real success. He says: "If the board of non-FIFA members gets stronger, it can only be a good thing as FIFA will then have to do something. I think that creating a new body is also a way of regaining some realism. Football has become all about money."

Yet money is still important to the Greenlanders too, as the team need help. The sight of Coca-Cola's logo on an international side's shirts should be a surprise given FIFA's ban on the practice, but Greenland, unhindered by such legislation, have signed a lucrative deal. The all-pervading bubbly stuff only arrived in Greenland in 2001 and most Greenlanders prefer a lemonade-type drink called Faxe Kondi, which sponsors the overall sports confederation.

To try and sweeten Greenlanders into drinking their product, Coca Cola has a deal with the Football Association that some rumours have suggested is worth around one million Danish Krona over four years, which is more than £90,000. This is unconfirmed, but Jens Tang Olesen admits that the FA have a "very good agreement" with Coca Cola. As Greenland's outings are usually restricted to bi-annual Island Games appearances, that is a generous deal, but even with Coca Cola's help, Brinch knows Greenland could not play regular internationals for a concerted period of time. However, he is not giving up and sees reason for optimism in recognition by FIFA from other sports in Greenland.

Greenlandic federations for Taekwondo, badminton, volleyball, biathlon and table-tennis are all members of their respective world bodies. Like the rest of Scandinavia, handball is also popular on the island and Greenland, whose top player plays professionally in France, have qualified for the Handball World Cup through the North American zone.

"If we applied to CONCACAF we might succeed," says Brinch of the island's football ambitions. "Geographically, we are part of North America, but culturally we are part of Europe and there are no travel links to Canada, only Denmark."

Instead of maybe getting a two-legged play-off against somewhere like Cuba or Cayman Islands once every four years, Greenland want to stay part of Europe; even if geographically they are nothing of the sort. For now, that means the Island Games is likely to be their only outlet for international football.

***********

After the draw against the Western Isles, Greenland return to Burra the next day for a vital game against the 2003 winners and this year's favourites Guernsey, with Brinch driven there as usual by his attaché, a friendly retired local oil worker called Jim.

The Island Games provides five matches over six days, but the draw has been cruel to Olesen's team. Their day off came before the round of classification matches and they went into their final group game against the form team without a single rest day - and it showed.

# Greenland On Tour

After just eight minutes, Guernsey went in front through Dave Rihoy and three minutes later Neil Clegg finished off a cross from the ever influential Paul Nobes for a second goal. That regular pre-tournament training by Guernsey was paying off. They looked sharp and fit with Ryan Zico Black making an impression, though the best player on the day was captain John Nobes.

Greenland, in contrast, were poor. Fleischer dropped keeper John Kreutzmann after his disastrous final quarter hour against the Western Isles and put in replacement Knud Pedersen, who has none of his predecessor's command of the box. Greenland were on the rack early on with Paul Nobes going close twice before Pedersen fumbled a header by John Nobes. Guernsey went into the break three up. The second half was mostly one way traffic with the Greenlanders looking tired. Dominc Heaume scores a fine goal 12 minutes after the re-start, then good approach work by Black set up Joby Bourgaize on 73 minutes. Daragh Duffy completed the rout with six minutes to go.

Although Anders Petersen sent a fine shot crashing onto the Guernsey bar with minutes left, Greenland were thrashed by six goals to nil. The neat passing they demonstrated against the Western Isles was gone and the defence was left sadly wanting by an injury to the absent Niklas Kreutzmann. With a few minutes remaining, a friend of Brinch's driver Jim arrives and asks the score. None of the Greenlanders answer.

"Are we winning?" repeats the Shetlander.

"Yes," says Brinch confidently. "We are winning experience."

The result was to cost Greenland dearly in terms of the Island Games. They finished level on points with the Western Isles, but the pasting by Guernsey left them in fourth place in their group on goal difference.

The day's rest proved no help either and the Greenlanders lost their seventh-placed play-off with the Finnish island of Åland by 2-3. There is no time to ponder what could have been. The entire Greenland games team had to fly out of Lerwick at midnight that night on their chartered plane, missing the closing ceremony of the Island Games in order to catch a connection in Copenhagen back to their homeland.

For Olesen, Kreutzmann and the rest of the Greenland team, there is likely to be a two-year gap before their next chance of international competition at the 2007 Island games in Rhodes. With Michael Nybrandt away travelling, Brinch appears to have lost some impetus and had to miss the NF Board meeting due to other commitments, but on being told of their plans for an alternative World Cup for national teams that do not exist, mooted for November 2006, he is interested.

Flights to Denmark at that time can be as cheap as £300 and with living costs in the venue of Northern Cyprus inexpensive, the idea of the tournament appeals.

"We will aim for that," he says. "I think that it's important to have a tournament every year with this group of people. Not just for sporting reasons, but for political reasons, as it's sport without the money."

\*\*\*\*\*\*\*\*\*\*\*

Six months after the Island Games, Greenland gives up on UEFA and FIFA and applies to join the NF Board. But while all appears to be lost in terms of football, the International Olympic Committee (IOC) has had a re-think.

Both the Greenlanders and the Faroe Islands are to be given the chance to re-state their case for membership to the IoC. Neither Greenland nor the Faroes want to leap straight into the games proper, but would prefer a chance to compete in the European Youth Olympic Festival and the Games of the Small States of Europe (GSSE), which is for states with less than one million inhabitants. To get into both requires IOC membership.

The 2005 version of the GSSE was held in Andorra and, apart from the hosts, the tournament featured Cyprus, Iceland, Liechtenstein, Luxembourg, Malta, Monaco and San Marino. Although the GSSE features team sports in basketball and volleyball, football is not on the schedule, but Brinch thinks this is a step in the right direction and so does Sølvi Hansen of the Faroese Confederation of Sport, who says: "There is a very strong national identity in the Faroe Islands and it would be unnatural for our athletes to compete under the Danish flag at the Olympic Games."

A glimmer of hope had appeared - only to disappear all too quickly for Greenland's footballers: as Jens Brinch explains: "Nothing really happened. We had a discussion with the Danish Olympic Committee. We argued that Greenland should be able to participate with lower qualification demands than the Danish participants and that led to a solution that softened the demands for all participants coming from Denmark and Greenland. That could lead to Greenlanders qualifying for the Winter Games."

As football is not a sport at the Winter Games, Greenland's footballers remain stranded and isolated. Popular pre- and mis-conception has it that this isolation was because there is no grass in Greenland. Not so, although as yet no international standard grass playing surface. But with global warming eating away at the Antarctic around them, the Greenlanders may end up with a grass pitch sooner than people think. Already, football outdoors is sometimes possible in southern Greenland from late May until early October, but a grass pitch is not what is isolating the Greenlanders; it is politics.

With financial pressures making competing abroad increasingly difficult, no grass pitches at home, a commitment to remaining independent of the Danes and players literally dying just to play the game, only the big hearts of the likes of Jens Brinch, Jens Tang Olesen and GFA president Lars Lundblad and commitment of players like Niklas Kreutzmann is keeping the Greenland team alive.

Then in May 2007, Greenland's international football aspirations take another knock - albeit indirectly. Greenland joined the International Handball Federation (IHF) in 1999 via the Panamerican Team Handball Federation (PATHF). Membership of the IHF meant that the Greenlanders were able to enter the PATHF qualifying route for the game's World Cup and the Greenlanders appearance at the 2007 finals was the third time that they had qualified.

This is not a no-hoper team that would be scrabbling around hopeful of gaining a point, but one that has beaten the United States and Australia in competitive matches and after the 2007 championships in Germany was ranked 22 in the world. Then in May 2007, the PATHF downgraded the Greenlanders' membership to associate membership, meaning that the team could not play in the World Cup qualifiers. The precise reason for the downgrading was not made clear by the PATHF, but the move did provide an easier route to the World Cup for the likes of the US.

The path to international recognition for Greenland's footballers seems equally blocked.

# CHAPTER FIVE

# The Falklands Conflict

*"In late March 1982 I was playing for the Islands against HMS Endurance - we lost 5-3 - on the afternoon that she was called away unexpectedly to sail for the island of South Georgia where some Argentine workers had landed illegally. The rest is history."*
**Patrick Watts, General Manager, Falkland Islands**

## 12 July 2005, Whiteness, Shetland Isles

TWO HOURS AFTER the Greenlanders left the field after conceding that shock last minute equaliser to the Western Isles, one of the biggest ever surprises at the Island Games football tournament is on the cards.

"What a shock, incredible!" says Patrick Watts, the general manager of Falkland Islands Sports at the 2005 games. "They're hugging each other, who would have expected that?"

The moustachioed Watts is commentating on the Falklands second match in the 2005 Island Games football tournament against Saarema. His emotional commentary is being relayed back to the 3,000 people on the islands, which is mired in a dark South Atlantic winter, by mobile phone. Watts is providing vital commentary to live but silent pictures of the match streamed onto the internet by Scottish Media Group, the ITV franchise holder in Scotland that is providing media coverage for the games.

"It's very big down there," Watts says of the Falklands' participation in only their second Island Games football competition. Given that they only have 60 players, four clubs and - Watts insists - do not allow military personnel to play, that they have got a team together at all appears some feat, but football has been played in the Falklands since the late nineteenth century with regular matches against the Royal Navy Ice Patrol vessel HMS Endurance an annual highlight.

The Falklands first took part in the Island Games in 1993, travelling to the Isle of Wight, but without a football team. The first and only previous appearance by the Falklands' national team was in the Isle of Man in 2001, when in the play-off for last place the team thrashed the Orkneys 4-1. Until the Saarema game, that was the biggest moment in the history of Falklands football.

# The Falklands Conflict

"Traditionally the national team has always played against visiting Royal Naval vessels and these matches were the highlight of the season, which runs from October to March," explains Watts later on. "There was a time when you could only play soccer if you joined the local volunteer defence force and there was keen competition between the various platoons. From 1947 onwards the main games were against the visiting Royal Naval vessels and I can recall games against HMS Bigbury Bay, HMS Burghead Bay, St. Austell Bay and Veryan Bay, all names on the Devon coast I believe.

"In the late 1950s, the Ministry of Defence kept one ship, HMS Protector, in the South Atlantic as the Falklands guard ship for the summer months and this vessel would visit each year. When the national team played it was never known as the Falkland Islands playing so and so, it was always Stanley versus HMS Superb or whoever. Stanley used to win most of these games. The biggest match for many years was against HMS Britannia, when the Duke of Edinburgh visited the Falklands in January 1957. Stanley lost 5-2 and the result is still remembered. I ignored a party onboard the ship in order to watch the game as an 11 year-old, such was my liking for soccer in those days."

The present association was formed on 7 January 1947 and named the Falkland Islands Football League (FIFL). The league championship was originally three teams playing each other seven times over the season, but that was changed in the mid 1990s when the FIFL started to secure sponsorship, reflecting an upturn in the colony's economy. A local fuel retailer called Stanley Services stepped in and the championship became the Stanley Services Football League and a five match series for the Stanley Shield was introduced.

Watts had made his debut as a 16 year-old in a game against HMS Protector in the early 1960s. He recalls: "Occasionally other ships would call, so games would be arranged against these crews also. After HMS Protector was withdrawn from services, a similar series of matches was played against her successor HMS Endurance. In late March 1982 I was playing for the Islands against Endurance - we lost 5-3 - on the afternoon that she was called away unexpectedly to sail for the island of South Georgia where some Argentine workers had landed illegally. The rest is history."

After that incursion on the island of South Georgia, Argentine troops were to invade the Falklands on 2 April 1982 and Watts himself is part of that history. It was Watts' voice broadcasting over the islands' radio service that kept his fellow islanders updated on the invasion until Argentine troops entered the radio station and, waving rifles in his face, ordered him to stop broadcasting. He has since been made an MBE for his part in the conflict and his services to the islands.

# OUTCASTS: The Lands That FIFA Forgot

Popular myth has it that the UK government were on the verge of doing a deal over the islands before Argentina invaded. Argentinians were certainly no stranger to the islands before the invasion, as workers from the country lived on the Falklands for several months building fuel tanks in the 1970s. Back then, the only battle was on the football field. With British workers assisting Argentinians building an airport for the Falklands, a four-way tournament was held between the two sets of workers, the Royal Marines and the Islanders, who beat their Latin neighbours 2-1 in the final in front of around 500 people - still reckoned to be the Falklands' biggest crowd for a football match.

Since the British Army re-took the Falklands in 1982, the islands' national team has played many games against Army, RAF and Naval teams. These are mostly won by the Falklands, but the Armed Forces combine once a year for a tri-services game, which they usually win. A knockout cup is held with two teams from Port Stanley and up to 14 from the forces with the Islanders making the final on a number of occasions, but never winning, losing mostly to the Royal Engineers. Watts even recalls the Army drafting in players from overseas to ensure a win.

He adds: "So keen were the military to win that they actually flew good players all the way from Germany to play in the final. I can recall a tri-services goalie being brought in."

***********

In 1997, Falklands' football took a big step forward with Watts at the helm for the national team's first foray overseas. A three-game trip to southern Chile was organised by him to celebrate the FIFL's fiftieth anniversary, with sponsorship secured for tracksuits and playing kit. The Falklands drew 1-1 and lost 1-7 against local club teams, but the highlight of the tour was the Encuentro Internacional de Futbol trophy against the University of Magallanes, which finished 1-1 with the Falklands triumphing 5-3 on penalties.

Watts had taken over as league chairman in the 1970s and the league had expanded with Dynamos joining the three other club teams - Redsox, Mustangs and Rangers - and the tournament began working in a not dissimilar fashion to Major Soccer League in the US. Players were signed to the FIFL, which then tried to evenly distribute them. In the 1990s, the league changed again with the advent of sponsorship for individual teams and the FIFL also stopped allocating players, which, according to Watts, has not met with universal approval.

In 2005, Penguin News - named after the island's paper - took the league title. The competition now includes Deano's - named after a popular bar - and Sullivan Blue Sox, which won the league cup, beating the other club side,

54

Kelper Store Celtics, in the final 5-3. Until recently, the league also included a team known as All Saints, which was comprised of migrant workers from St. Helena and won the league cup once, but that side disbanded in 2005/06 and the players joined other clubs.

Players from St. Helena, another isolated UK possession in the South Atlantic, play regularly on the Falklands, but neither island has ever sent 'national' teams over to play each other, nor has there ever been a match with Tristan da Cuhna, another British colony inhabited by a few hundred people and stranded miles from anywhere in the South Atlantic. For the Falklands, the Island Games is the only chance to field a national football team.

The Islands have, however, managed to join the International Cricket Council, being welcomed in on 29 June 2007 as an affiliate member - giving the islands the same status as the likes of Guernsey and the Isle of Man at the ICC. Cameroon, Peru and Swaziland were also granted 'affiliate' status on the same day with unanimous votes, but the Falkland Islands' election proved more controversial. Argentina is a member of the ICC and abstained.

With the Falklands conflict still fresh in the minds of many living on both sides of the south Atlantic, there is no hope of the Islands ever attaining official FIFA status. Watts explains: "There has never been an approach to join CONMEBOL. The Argentines would object most strenuously anyway and say that any players from the Falklands are Argentine, as allowing us to join would give recognition to the Falklands as a country, which the Argentines do not recognize. But they cannot stop us playing in the Island Games or sending shooters to the Commonwealth Games."

The Falkland Islands, however, are regular participants in the Commonwealth Games. Under its constitution, the Commonwealth Games could feature football, but no organising committee has ever dared raise the idea of adding another tournament to an already crowded international football calendar. So the Island Games remains the only overseas outlet for Falklands' football and a win over Saarema - an Estonian island with a 40,000 population and one player, Victor Alonen, with 68 full caps for Estonia in their side - would be a pinnacle for Falklands' football. With 10 minutes to go the burly Falklanders are 2-1 up thanks to Martyn Clarke's soft penalty on four minutes after a Saarema defender ran across him. The Falklanders then gifteed their opponents an equally soft equaliser, keeper Chris Gilbert having an otherwise faultless performance marred when, unsighted, a shot whistled crept past him and in at his right hand post.

Saarema play tidy football and have far more of the game, but a poor clearance by their keeper Roland Kutt gifts the Falklanders the lead for a second time. Kutt's kick is nodded back into the path of Eion Anderson, who slots home and Watts nearly falls off the stepladder supplied to him for his commentary role by a friendly local from the host village of Whiteness.

"A draw at these Island Games would be wonderful, but a win would be quite amazing," says Watts down his mobile as he steadies the stepladder and turns to Tony Mercury for expert comment, handing him down the phone. Watts' friendly co-commentator is standing on the balcony of the Whiteness sports pavilion in a Guernsey 2003 Island Games jacket. When passed the mobile, Mercury offers the odd piece of commentary, which is usually followed with a self-deprecating smile.

Born in St. Helena, the genial Mercury left for the UK with his parents aged just five. He moved to Essex, where he played non-league football for a number of clubs including Dagenham. Today, he divides his time between Essex and trying to catch up with a mail boat plying the lonely route between the UK and Africa, stopping off at St. Helena and another British colony, Ascension Island.

Unlike St. Helena, Ascension has a runway to get the military personnel based there in and out, but the more popular route back to the UK for the Saints is to get the mail boat from the island's capital Jamestown to Walvis Bay in Namibia, which takes four days, then fly to Cape Town and another flight to the UK.

The total cost of that arduous trip then getting up to Lerwick has been a thumping £3,500, which even overshadows the £2,000 laid out to get each member of the Falklands' team to Shetland. Not surprisingly, St Helena cannot always afford to get a team up, but the Shetlands tournament is the fifth Island Games featuring Saints' athletes. Eight made the trip from the South Atlantic and were joined by another three living in the UK to play in a total of four sports.

St. Helena's population has dwindled from 5,000 to near 3,500 in recent years as youngsters go to the UK or the Falklands to work, but the island still has an eight team football league. The Saints have never entered a football side in the Island Games and, having lived on the Falklands for five years and fulfilled local qualification rules, two Saints are in the Falklands' team playing against Saarema. "That's the dream," says Tony Mercury, "To bring a football team to an Island Games."

The Saints do manage to field an international team at futsal, the short-sided form of football advocated by FIFA. St. Helena is even a member of the European Union of Futsal (UEFS), which is not linked to UEFA and features the Spanish region of Catalonia as a full-member. An exiled team of Saints even entered the 2007 UEFS championships in Catalonia using their own money with a strip supplied by Andrew Weir Shipping, which runs the mail ship to the island. That side managed two wins, two losses and a draw in five matches and managed to finish in seventh place - not bad considering that by May 2007 England has yet to win a single futsal match due to being forced to use non-league players for internationals.

The Falklands' team features some Saints and a few UK based islanders, but is mostly made up of players from the Islands. For Patrick Watts, who has all of the Saarema team's names and numbers detailed in front of him, the dream is coming true. Having been thumped 0-4 by the Shetlands in their opening match, the Falklands are exceeding all expectations: 2-1 up going into injury time, a famous victory beckons. Not that it's Watts' style, but legendary rugby commentator Bill McLaren might have said, "They'll be dancing in the streets of Goose Green tonight!" - and then disaster strikes.

It appears that the passionate commentary is falling on deaf ears. Unbeknown to Watts, the entire Falkland Islands has been blacked out by a power cut. He is still enthusing down the phone over the Falklands team's performance when he realises that he has lost his connection to Port Stanley. He phones Stanley only to find out that with just minutes to go, no-one back home knows about that equaliser or the famous win about to be secured.

As the only journalist there, lending him a tape recorder seemed the only decent option. Watts gratefully accepts and records his commentary of the final minutes. He is so overcome by the victory that he proves extremely reluctant to return the tape recorder. Watts charges onto the pitch at the final whistle to record sounds of typically stolid British celebrations among the burly Falklanders. During the revelry, there appears no division between the players and management, but with such a tiny football community in the Falklands, there is. These divisions are not about tactics, a botched pass or missing an open goal, but something deeper.

Watts appears to get on with team manager Chris Clarke, but is not convinced that his nephew Martyn, scorer of that opening goal, should be in the side. Later, Watts says: "[Martyn] played for the Falklands in the Shetlands as striker, but was a bit short of pace and fitness, and should have been left off, but his uncle was managing the team."

Clarke went on to score again for the Falklands, netting a header in a 2-1 defeat to Åland and for him, the Island Games was to prove a much-delayed return to doing what he wants to do more than anything else, which is play football.

Watts insists that his only reason for wanting Clarke off the team are football-related, but not everyone agrees, including Clarke, probably the most famous - or perhaps most infamous - football player from the Falklands. According to Watts, Clarke has not been "very helpful" to his footballing career and that has nothing to do with his fitness, but about an opportunity that few young men of his age would have ever turned down. In 1996, aged just

16, Clarke was offered a trial with Boca Juniors, probably Argentina's most famous club and the side that launched Diego Maradona into the footballing stratosphere. Clarke was spotted playing football on the Falklands by a visiting Argentine, Esteban Cichello, who was a friend of Maradona and once arranged for him to speak at the Oxford Union, where he famously juggled a golf ball on his foot.

According to Watts, Cichello asked four or five other Falklands players if they were interested in a trial at Boca, but only Clarke, who had also had a trial at Leyton Orient in London, took him up on his offer.

Clarke had gone to school in England and moved to the islands aged 13 with his Royal Marine father, who had served in the conflict. Clarke considered himself a Falklander and was concerned at how becoming the first person from the islands to work in Argentina since the war would go down with the tightly knit community he lived in. So he told everyone apart from his mother that he was going to work on an oil rig in Chile. When Clarke arrived in Buenos Aires, he received a big surprise.

Clarke explains: "Cichello had got into the Falklands on an Italian passport and told me that he was there to write a book. He had started talking about Maradona and I only half believed him, but he said if it was possible to go for a trial, would I be interested? There was not much competition there and you tend to stand out a bit on the islands. My Mum had paid for me to go to trials in the UK and when they said about Boca Juniors, I said 'of course'. I wouldn't care where it was, if you really want to play football you will go anywhere. I'd forgotten about it as a few months went past, then they got back to me and I went. It was my first real job.

"When we got there we went to Maradona's flat and all went together to watch Boca play Independiente and afterwards for a pizza and Maradona lent me his mobile to phone my Mum. He was one of the best footballers in the world and that was pretty cool. When he started talking about his goal, though, [the handball incident against England in 1986] I had to keep smiling. I couldn't say what I was really thinking."

Even a decade on, Clarke still sounds excited by the memory. Apart perhaps from a few Falklanders, no-one could blame him for that, but his dream was to go quickly and spectacularly sour.

He adds: "I lost faith in [Cichello] almost straight away as he was only in it for himself. They took me on to a chat show [with Argentine veterans from the war] and there was a translator and they asked me what I thought about having two flags in the Falklands."

Those images were relayed around the world and did not go down too well in the Falklands. Clarke never got past a trial with Boca before being loaned out to Second Division side El Porvenir and then had a brief spell with another lower league team, Defensore, before being forced to return home due to lack of money.

"I think that I was used by Boca, but probably not the other two teams," he later told BBC Sport on leaving the Falklands. The experience left its scars and after the 2005 Island Games, Clarke said: "People [in the Falklands] treated me like I was nothing, but they would never say it to my face. Some of the people over there are very narrow-minded. They don't want to let go, yet some of these guys weren't even born when the war was going on."

After the trials and still only 16, Clarke returned home to his mother, who then ran the Globe Tavern in the capital, Port Stanley, but found that his adventure abroad also had repercussions for other members of his family. He explains: "A few of them started on my brother [Dustin] when I was away in Argentina. They were effing and blinding at him and he ended up hitting them. When I went back, it's a small place, and I fell out with my team-mates. Everyone was looking down at me. Patrick [Watts] had phoned me up in Argentina to ask me how it was going, but I knew he hated my guts."

In February 2002, Martyn Clarke was to leave the Falklands, seemingly for good, but Watts insists there is no problem. He says: "The whole episode of him going to play with Boca Juniors was nothing more than a propaganda exercise orchestrated by Cichello, who was looking for publicity himself. Martyn's mother was in agreement as she wrongly believed that Martyn was going to be a star in the future and, as she was not on the Islands in 1982, was inclined to be a bit pro-Argentine.

"Every photograph and TV picture saw Esteban upfront with Martyn. I actually felt rather sorry for Martyn, who did not realise what was going on. There were at least four to five better players here in the Falklands, but they wisely wanted nothing to do with the plan. But Martyn fell for it.

"The subsequent story that he was ignored and shunned by his friends here and left out of the national team when he returned was not true. He was picked and played as soon as he returned. Martyn showed promise as a 17 year-old and I took him on the tour of Chile in 1997 and he looked as if he could play in a higher class of football as he had skill, good crossing ability and was a good header of the ball. Unfortunately, he was always too lazy and this reflected not only in his football but his everyday life too."

That suggests some schism still exists. After leaving the Falklands, Clarke had a trial with the Connecticut Wolves in the US, only to suffer an injury. Having married an RAF girl, he moved to Essex in the UK, where his mother had already moved, but the Falklands football conflict was certainly not over.

The story rumbled on as Clarke's father sold his 'story' over his dissatisfaction with his son to the tabloids. Martyn and his mother were then approached by two scriptwriters, Dominic Morgan and Matt Harvey, who wanted to write a film about his story. The writers travelled to the Falklands for research and saw an obvious villain.

"Our take on Patrick is that he's Martyn's key antagonist," says Morgan. "The story we saw in Martyn's life was how sport became a lightning conductor for conflict. The best sports movies are about something else, as sport either brings people together or tears them apart.

"A lot of people who criticised Martyn didn't realise the situation he was in and the pressure he was under. There were fights in the pub and he was called a traitor. The feeling against the Argentinians there is almost like Northern Ireland or Bosnia. It's split between those who want the peace process and those who want nothing to do with it. The Falklanders have good reason to fear the Argentines as they can't help cheating. There's a long history of antagonism out there and no wonder there's some bad feeling towards Martyn."

The two writers agreed an option with Clarke and his mother and a script called 'Playing for the Enemy' was completed. An actor to play Martyn Clarke was even lined up with Martin Compston keen to take the part. Born in 1984, Compston grew up in Greenock, Scotland, and was playing in the Scottish league for his local side Morton when he landed the starring role in Ken Loach's well-received film Sweet Sixteen, which premiered at the 2002 Cannes film festival.

'Playing with the Enemy' was to stall, though, and Clarke's mother Julie was never entirely sure of the script. She said: "Overall it's not a bad script, though I'm not happy with the ending."

Clarke's brother Dustin, who has represented the Falklands at shooting, but is, by his own admission, not good enough for the football team, remains in the Falklands. A decade on, for him life has improved. He says: "Things have calmed down regarding Martyn's trip to Argentina and most of us get on now."

With his uncle in charge, Martyn Clarke represented the Falklands in the Shetlands, but a change of manager looks to have ended his international career. At the 2006 annual general meeting, Chris Clarke, despite surely achieving the best result in Falklands' football history, was voted out of the manager's seat. Chris Clarke had also spent time helping the team raise sufficient funds to go to the Shetlands, along with introducing new tactics, and the move was a blow for some players.

Was it another blow against the Clarke family in revenge for Martyn's trip to the Islands' would-be conquerors? No-one is saying, but Jimmy Curtis, Chris Clarke's replacement as team manager, is certainly no friend of Martyn Clarke, who does not expect to be chosen for the Falklands team with Curtis in charge. Clarke explains simply: "I had a fight with Jimmy Curtis before I left." This schism runs deep.

# The Falklands Conflict

Whether he would have made the Falklands' team for the 2007 Island Games in Rhodes will never be known as the team decided not to enter due to a combination of lack of funds and the tournament involving an even longer trip from the South Atlantic than usual, due to extra time needed to acclimatise to the extreme Mediterranean heat.

Back home, the Falklands manage a game against HMS Edinburgh, which sees a star performance from Phil Stant, who scores two goals in a 5-4 win. For Stant, a former Football League professional striker with seven clubs from Hereford United to Fulham and a stint as manager at Lincoln City, his 'international' debut is part of an emotional return to the Falklands. The term hero is often lightly used in football, but Stant was a real one in the Falklands when he served in the Army. As part of an ITV documentary to celebrate the twenty-fifth anniversary of the war, Stant returned to confront his memories of his experiences as an 18 year-old on one of the war's darkest days - the Argentine attacks on the British navy vessels Sir Galahad and Sir Tristram that saw 48 service men killed and more than 100 seriously injured.

Whether Martyn Clarke returns to the Falklands remains to be seen. He has since moved to Yorkshire, but plagued by injuries for years, he only began playing five-a-side in late 2006. Still in his twenties, he retains his enthusiasm for football and has not given up hope of playing semi-professionally in England. Whether the Falklands' football conflict is finally forgotten and Clarke is chosen to play for the national side at the following Island Games in the Swedish-speaking Finnish island of Åland in 2009 remains to be seen.

# CHAPTER SIX

# The Island Games

*"I think the games do support local identity which you could call nationalism. All islands are made to feel doubly insular."*
**Brian Partington, Island Games Association**

For isolated political oddities such as Greenland and the Falklands, the Island Games remains one of the few places that national teams that will probably never exist as far as FIFA are concerned can get a game. Every two years, the games offer a chance for these places that FIFA has so conveniently forgotten to be a real national side. Two decades after the formation of the Island Games Association (IGA), what began as a mainly British inter-island competition in the Isle of Man has grown into an association with members from Iberia to Scandinavia, the Mediterranean to the Caribbean.

Every two years, the games bring around 2,000 athletes and plenty more officials to its host island for a week, but the event remains ignored by the major media. That number of people might not exactly be the Olympic Games entourage, but is still a big fillip for small isolated economies such as the Shetlands. Now, with the membership roster full up, the IGA has to decide what it wants to be.

When the games were first held in the Isle of Man in 1985, as part of a Manx year of sport, football was not even included. The world's most popular game was not on the schedule in the second event in Guernsey two years later either, but when the games moved out of British territorial water, in came football. The Faroe Islands hosted the 1989 games, when football made its debut, and the home side won that event and retained the title in Åland two years later before moving on to bigger football tournaments, such as World Cup qualifiers, having joined FIFA in 1988.

As the Faroes won their debut competitive international - a 1-0 win over an Austrian team that had recently been at the World Cup finals - and have never really been humiliated at home or away since starting to play internationals, the Island Games was obviously not a bad place to warm up. The Faroes no longer play in the men's football tournament in the Island Games, but still enter the women's event and romped to the 2005 title. Their 3-0 win over Bermuda was the first Island Games match recognized by FIFA as a full international. Ironically, neither of those two teams are a country in terms of the United Nations, but recognition by FIFA was a big fillip for the Island Games in terms of prestige.

With a 22,019 population, the Shetlands is the smallest IGA member to stage the games, but crowds of between 2,000 and 3,000 attended the home team's football matches. For the final between Guernsey and the hosts in the capital of Lerwick - population 9,016 - an amazing 6,000 people turned up. If two thirds of London's population turned up for an England game, you would need a stadium with a capacity of around five million.

Staging the 2005 games involved plenty of investment by the island's council, including a £9 million extension to the main Clickimin leisure centre, which was funded by the estimated £500 million in oil money that has flowed into the islands from BP's Sullom Voe terminal.

"We'd never have had the games here without the oil money," says Jens Brinch's driver, Jim - a view shared by nearly all the locals, but one that was surely worth it judging by the welcome that the islanders gave the games.

The Shetlands event was the eighth of 11 Island Games to be hosted in the British Isles. The increase and geographical expansion in IGA membership has led to calls for the event to stop being a sort of mini-Commonwealth Games and evolve into something more multi-national. At the 2005 games, the IGA had 24 members and all but Frøya, a tiny Norwegian island with a population of just 4,100, sent sporting representatives to the Shetlands. The Norwegians did send some committee members to the IGA general meeting in Lerwick, though, when a membership that began at 15 islands at the Isle of Man event in 1985 was raised to 25 with the inclusion of the Spanish island of Menorca.

Iceland were once members, but pulled out to concentrate on their Olympic programme, as did Malta, although the Maltese have since tried to rejoin the IGA. This has proved impossible as new members must have a population of 125,000 or less. The Canadian island of Prince Edward and the Isle of Wight exceed this but, like UEFA, the IGA is happy not to make this rule-change retrospective, so these two members stay in and Malta stay out. Rather like FIFA and UEFA, the IGA has had some funny ideas on membership criteria and Gibraltar were admitted in 1989. With the British colony's only border with Spain closed, the IGA decided Gibraltar was effectively an island anyway and admitted the Rock.

"I think around 30 members is about our limit," says IGA chairman Brian Partington, relaxing in his pale blue IGA sweatshirt over lunch with James Johnston, a Shetlander and fellow IGA executive.

The former Archdeacon of the Isle of Man, Partington is also an OBE and was executive chairman of the Isle of Man Sport's Council for 11 years until 2002. Having retired as the Manx archdeacon, he is devoting more time to the

# OUTCASTS: The Lands That FIFA Forgot

IGA and took over as chairman at the 2005 AGM, after Bo Frykenstam of Gotland retired. A seemingly unlikely sports politician, Partington, who was born in Manchester in 1936, is a big fan of the football tournament, which he thinks has changed out of all recognition since 1989. He adds: "In the past, the football from some teams was just 11 lads and a few beers afterwards, but I think that's changed and that's partly due to having outside referees."

This is a reference to an incident that shamed an event otherwise generally played out in the very best of spirits. At the 1995 games in Gibraltar, the Isle of Man football XI were playing the hosts and took umbrage at a series of decisions they perceived as biased towards the colony's team. After losing an unruly game, the Isle of Man side, who were staying in a barracks on the Rock, decided to console themselves with a few drinks. The resulting drunken spree led to the Manx men's football XI being barred from the next event in Jersey, although this proved a one-off suspension and they were let back in for the next event in Gotland.

***********

The initial Island Games in the Isle of Man only had seven sports and 700 athletes, but that has since expanded. By the 2003 event in Guernsey, there were 2,100 athletes that met the qualification requirement of being born in the island you represent or having lived there for the last year - the latter perhaps explaining why some athletes from the Isle of Man that sound distinctly like they have heavy Scouse accents.

At each Games, a maximum of 15 events are chosen. Some are dropped depending on facilities and demand perceived by the IGA and the host island. Basketball, triathlon, judo and tennis did not appear in the Shetlands, but archery, athletics, badminton, bowls, cycling, golf, gymnastics, sail boarding, sailing, shooting, squash, swimming, table tennis and volleyball all took place. So did football, which has never missed out since 1989, although only 10 teams entered in the Shetlands.

That complement is well down on recent Island Games in the Isle of Man and Guernsey, where 15 football teams took part in each event. Untimely withdrawals hit the 2005 football event with the Greek island of Rhodes pulling out late on. Some people in the Shetlands suggested that was related to another stormy encounter to do with a referee.

At the 2003 football tournament in Guernsey, the Rhodes team grew increasingly dissatisfied with a number of decisions by the referee, one of the Football League's most experienced officials, Wendy Toms. Unable to accept a female referee, Rhodes had five players sent off and Toms had to abandon the game.

# The Island Games

"Rhodes were very apologetic and suspended all the people involved," says Partington, adding: "We did wonder about having football in Rhodes."

The Rhodes players involved were all subsequently banned, but it wasn't that ill-discipline which caused the organising committee to opt not to include Rhodes in the 2005 Games' football tournament. It was because the Mediterranean island only has seven grass pitches and one artificial surface and the IGA prefers competing teams to have at least 10 pitches.

Rhodes were not the only team to sit out the 2005 football tournament. Gibraltar, winners in 1995, entered other sports, but the Rock's football association opted against sending a football side. Having witnessed some bad behaviour in his own back yard, Gib president Joseph Nunez was concerned about controlling a large group of young footballers on one of the two cruise liners that were docked in Lerwick, which would have been the accommodation as the Shetlands simply did not have enough room on terra firma.

This accommodation did not deter the Falklands, whose team slept on one liner, the Van Gogh, but lack of money was also a reason which kept the Gibraltar FA from bringing 18 players and 10 officials over. Similar reasons also deterred 1997 winners Jersey from bringing a side to the Shetlands, while the Isle of Wight also sat out the football this time.

Partington has big ambitions for football at the Games, but accepts that other islands might not have the enthusiasm that the British have for the sport. Having finished a light lunch, the trim-looking former archdeacon says: "Team sports are a massive problem as you increase your numbers dramatically with 18 players for soccer then officials on top. There's no limit on the number of football entries, but ideally we'd like to have a maximum of 16 teams. I think we will have closer to that number in the next event in Rhodes. We had a strong lobby for hockey, but that's not very popular in Scandinavia. We're looking for stability and any sport that came in would be international and I don't think that there will be any new British-orientated sports for a long time. Any new sports will need an appeal outside of the Commonwealth."

At the 2005 annual general meeting, a vote was held on who would host the 2009 event. Each island has two votes with the IGA's six person committee one apiece and Åland, population 25,000, won by 33 votes with 21 cast for the only other candidate, Yns Mon in Wales.

"Four of the last five events have been on British islands and there was a desire to move away and that counted against Yns Mon," explains Partington.

Bermuda and the Cayman Islands considered bidding to host the 2011 event, although the travel involved and higher living expenses for athletes and officials cost both votes as it reduced the number of sides able to compete in the football tournament. In the event, the Isle of Wight proved the winner.

The vote may appear insular, but the Isle of Wight's proximity to Southampton, where the airport is a hub for cheap flights and regular ferries across the Solent, was probably the real clincher that brought the Island Games back for the second time after a successful tournament in 1993, when Jersey won the football title.

**********

The Games are unlikely to have the effect on the Corkheads [a nickname derived from the ancient art of 'corking' the seals on boats] of the Isle of Wight that they did in the Shetlands, where the idea of a Shetland team brought out latent nationalism. The Islanders still celebrate their Viking heritage each winter with the Up-Helly-Aa festival involving the ceremonial burning of a longship, but the advent of the games brought out something different.

Not a single Scottish saltire was to be seen in the Shetlands during the Games. Instead, locals hung their island's pale blue flag with a white cross from their cars or painted the flag on the faces of their children. Despite the unfurling of Shetland flags, a triangular tournament has thus far been the extent of the Scottish islanders' football ambitions as IGA executive James Johnston wants to use the experience of the 2005 games to extend the Shetlands' 80 year-old annual derby with the Orkneys into a three-way competition with the Western Isles. That team's dramatic late equaliser against the Greenlanders helped secure a play-off against the Isle of Man for a bronze medal, which the Western Isles won 4-0 to complete a dream Island Games debut.

After a pause, Partington continues on the idea that the Island Games produces a form of nationalism. He adds: "I think the Games do support local identity, which you could call nationalism. All islands are made to feel doubly insular. First by their parent country and then if they have larger islands around them like Menorca does with Majorca. That's why we need to support them as we are about sports development.

"In the Menorcan application for membership they state they feel a double isolation - they are a small section of the Balearic region, which is a small region of Spain - yet they have an identity as Menorca. Many of our islands would say the same, hence distinct flags, though some like Saarema are proud to fly their national flag."

The Shetland Islands and Saarema - who were playing in a strip supplied by FC Kuressaare, the island's top side, which plays in the Estonian top flight, the Meistriliiga - cancelled each other out in a poor group match at a rainy Seafield in Lerwick.

# The Island Games

Åland is a regular participant in the Island Games football, but has no ambitions for a higher grade of football. A group of islands between Finland and Sweden, Åland sent an under-21 team to the games for the men's and women's event. The biggest club in the islands, IFK Mariehamn, plays in the Finnish First Division, but Åland is populated mainly by Swedish-speaking people. Åland itself was part of Sweden until the 1808-09 war, when Finland and the Åland Islands were seized by Russia. After Finland gained independence, the Ålanders started looking for a reunion with the Swedes that has never quite happened. An act of autonomy was passed in 1920 and the first elections to Åland's parliament were held two years later. Further autonomy acts were passed in 1951 and, after 20 years in preparation, again in 1993, but Åland remains neither independent nor part of Sweden, nor in many ways even part of Finland.

Åland has youth teams playing in Sweden and the 'national team' takes players from Finland and Sweden and has played matches against the Sápmi and the Faroes in the past but has given up hope of joining UEFA. Anders Mattson, chairman of the Åland Football Association, says: "We have never asked to be members of UEFA or FIFA. The information that we have today is that it is impossible because they just accept states."

Mattson had contact with the NF Board prior to their meeting in London, but is too entrenched with the existing football authorities to break away. Mattson qualified as Åland's first FIFA referee in 1969 and refereed at the 1980 Moscow Olympics. He is still a referee's observer for UEFA.

Åland finished the Games on a high, beating Greenland in a play-off for seventh place, while Saarema's draw in the rain against the Shetlands proved to be the only point dropped by the hosts in the entire tournament.

For Patrick Watts' Falklands team, Saarema represented a high point. The next day against the Isle of Man, the South Atlantic colony gave their second team a run out and capitulated 0-9, then lost the play-off for last place against the Orkneys.

Of the IGA's 25 members, Bermuda, the Caymans and the Faroes all play international football under FIFA's umbrella, but Brian Partington is convinced that the Games represents the only chance for the other 22 members to play what could loosely be seen as international football. He says: "A few years ago, the Isle of Man wanted to follow the Faroes into international football, but FIFA and UEFA have closed the gate and I don't think that the Isle of Man or Guernsey will ever play international football."

Oddly, though, the football tournament at the Island Games is sanctioned by FIFA because all the participating islands are part of a larger parent FA, i.e. Guernsey and the English FA, or Åland as part of the Finnish FA - except that is not true. Greenland is certainly not part of the Danish FA, the Falklands have never received a jot of help from the English FA and the Gibraltarian association certainly does not consider itself part of Geoff Thompson's dreams.

Like many other anomalies, Sepp Blatter's FIFA empire prefers not to dwell on the Island Games. Apart, that is, from handing down the honour of deeming a women's match between two overseas territories as the first 'international' to be played at the tournament.

Perhaps then, the Island Games is another waiting room with a locked exit door, but it is hard not to be charmed by an event where golfers get attacked by terns while trying to win a medal and some athletes, at huge financial costs, need to spend more than a week by boat and plane simply trying to get there.

The games certainly won over the Shetlanders. Every local appeared to be some sort of volunteer and young children were desperately trying to collect pin badges of all the 25 islands in the IGA before the week-long competition was over. With all the athletes wearing national tracksuits, many were routinely pestered by local children and responded with a mixture of surprise and pride, enjoying their brief celebrity. Many often turned to fellow athletes to find another different badge for the enthusiastic Shetland children. Sponsors were in evidence, particularly NatWest, which began sponsoring the games in 1999 and offers grants of up to £2,000 per island to bring athletes over to the games, but the high street bank's advertising did not blanket Lerwick. The most prominent stall was a largely neglected one giving away Gideon's Bibles outside the Clickimin leisure centre, which hosted many of the main events.

There is a lot to like about the Island Games, particularly an enthusiasm for sport that is largely uncorrupted by commercial pressure - probably because so few people have even heard of it. Yet the games brought 1,800 athletes and another 2,000 officials, fans and media into the Shetlands and undoubtedly proved a success for everyone involved, despite typically Scottish weather at times.

The next tournament in Rhodes in 2007 saw Menorca make their debut but did not feature the holders, the Shetlands, runners-up Guernsey, the Orkneys or the Falklands due to a combination of funding (or lack of it) and fears of the Mediterranean heat. Brian Johnston, who managed the 2005 Shetland team to victory but then stood down, says: "The single main reason [for the Shetlands not playing] is the climate and the proposed times of the fixtures. You would not even ask a professional outfit to travel to Rhodes in June and July to play five or six competitive games in seven days in over 100 degrees of heat. Kicking off around 10am means you would be mad dogs in the midday sun come the end of every fixture."

Instead of four or five qualifying games in as many days, the 11 sides in the 2007 tournament, which included Bermuda's U-23 side, were split into four groups. In their fifth attempt Gibraltar finally lifted the trophy, beating hosts Rhodes 4-0 in the final with four second half goals from John Paul Duarte, Joseph Chipolina and a pair from Lee Casciaro. Despite the football withdrawals, Rhodes 2007 saw a new record with nearly 3,000 competitors and more islands are now looking to join the IGA.

"There is no proposal at present to increase the number beyond 25 [but] we do have interest from other islands and a definite application from Lesvos (Greece) and a number of serious enquiries," explained Partington before the Rhodes games. "There is a serious concern that [some] 'islands' couldn't cope with hosting more competitors. We have had enquiries from some large islands like Bahrain and Crete and strange ones like Sealand and several, following Shetland, from other Scottish islands."

For most of the football teams, a return to some form of representative football is all that the next season has to offer. For the Isle of Man, that pasting in the bronze medal play-off with the Western Isles was a body blow to a faltering and mostly ignored campaign to drag the Manxmen onto the world stage, and the side do not travel to Rhodes either, but for altogether different reasons.

Despite a very inauspicious beginning, the season after the Shetlands games will be one of the most surprising and eventful in Manx football history - one that even the former Archdeacon of the Isle of Man could not have predicted.

# CHAPTER SEVEN

# The Isle Of Man In Europe

*"The problem is that there's just not enough quality on the island.
We need to be winning the Island Games before we can even think
of things like internationals."*
**Eric Clague, Manx football historian**

## 22 July 2005, Douglas, Isle of Man

The 2005/06 football season is warming up with many top teams playing friendlies against unfamiliar opposition. The Premier League's continued attempt to win over Asian fans - and their money - has taken the likes of Bolton Wanderers and Manchester City to Thailand for a four-way tournament also including the national team. In London that same week, Queen's Park Rangers are getting ready for a Championship season with a 3-0 win over Iran's national team. Only weeks after the 7 July bombs that devastated London, the Iranians' brief tour is terminated early with a final game against Millwall abandoned amid security concerns.

At the Isle of Man's football headquarters, a quaint little ground known as the Bowl, there is barely sign of a policeman on duty. The only safety concern is a flock of seagulls that appear with 10 minutes to go and provide more of a threat to Oldham keeper Les Pogliacomi than the entire Isle of Man's national team managed in the preceding 80 minutes. Just minutes before the seagulls arrived at the Bowl stadium, Pogliacomi's team-mate Adam Griffiths had showed sharp control and a good finish to put Oldham 6-0 up in the island's annual 'international' football tournament, the Steam Packet festival.

Sponsored by the island government and held every year since 1983, the Steam Packet has featured a number of sides now in the top flight of English football from Newcastle and Blackburn to Wigan Athletic. A veritable feast of 'international' football, there have been entrants from Scotland - St. Mirren, Motherwell and Dundee - and Irish clubs like Shelbourne and Shamrock Rovers and even Dutch side FC Cambur. The most tournament wins is the five titles held by Wrexham from north Wales.

These days, the Steam Packet is resolutely English. Supported financially by the Isle of Man government, teams mainly from the North West are invited

70

over in the hope of persuading some of their fans to stay for a holiday. In addition to Oldham, Port Vale and a Carlisle side warming up for their return to the Football League are the other visitors.

Once a week-long affair, crowds of more than 2,000 watched John Aldridge, freshly back from the World Cup with Ireland, lead out Tranmere as player-manager. Those days are long gone and instead of a week-long affair, the event has been downsized for the first time to just two matches in two days for 'financial' reasons.

The gate fee of £4 is not going to help those finances and hopes for a crowd of about 1,000 are way off the mark. Despite the lack of matches this year and distinctly English opposition, the event is still flagged up as an international purely because the teams coming over are all from England.

With its own parliament, the House of Keys, its own currency - pounds sterling, admittedly, but with Manx logos - and its own language, a form of Gaelic undergoing a renaissance, the Isle of Man has a form of nationhood. Run by the UK as a sort of colony, many of the Islanders sound slightly Scouse and often refer to themselves as offshore Scousers. Maybe their athletes in the Shetlands were not Scousers after all. Certainly, the team trying to take on Oldham are mostly Manxmen - not that it is doing them any good.

The Isle of Man responds to the sixth goal by quickly making an effort to trouble Pogliacomi's goal, but do not get a shot in and lose the ball far too easily. A silly free-kick is then conceded that Griffiths steers home majestically to make the score 7-0.

Oldham's new manager Ronnie Moore must be pleased with his team despite a lack of urgency from either side. The Isle of Man have tiredness as an excuse after five games in five days in the Shetlands, but even the official programme for the Steam Packet concedes that this national team is worse than previous incarnations. Prior to the Oldham game, the Isle of Man's long-standing manager Kevin Manning was bullish, saying: "They'll have enough in the tank for the first game against Oldham and then hopefully adrenaline will carry them through the second match."

For the Isle of Man, the match compounds a miserable run that has seen them let in 11 goals in two matches, having shipped four goals to the Western Isles eight days previously to lose out on a bronze medal in the Island Games.

"What blew it was for us the Falklands game," says Eric Clague, who also helps run one of the island's most successful teams, St George's, and was in the Shetlands reporting for the island's main newspaper, the Manx Independent. "The Falklands put out their second team to give them a game and we won nine-nil. We went into the next game against the Shetlands needing to win and that wasn't good preparation."

Clague is the Island's football historian and chronicled the fortunes of the Manx game since a league first started in 1896. The IoMFA initially joined the FA as a colonial association in 1907 and then became properly affiliated the following year. Clague's book, written with Colin Moore, traced a first 'international' played by Manx-born players against a team of players living on the island, but not born there, back to 1927 with 3,000 people watching. Two years previously, 7,500 watched the Manx FA Cup final between Peel and Rushen.

In 1928, Liverpool Collegiate Old Boys visited the island to provide the Isle of Man their first 'overseas' opposition. The Manxmen won 2-1. Two years later, the Isle of Man won their first game off the island with a 7-3 routing of Liverpool Collegiate Old Boys on Merseyside. Since then, the Isle of Man team has grown slowly. A regular entrant at the Island Games, the side has been losing finalists three times.

Eric Clague agrees with James Davis of Manx Radio, who dismissed the team's chances in the Steam Packet programme, that the current crop are not the best. Clague says: "I always liken the Isle of Man's performances in tournaments like the Island Games to England before a World Cup or European Championship. They look good before they go, but never achieve anything. The problem is that there's just not enough quality on the island. We need to be winning the Island Games before we can even think of things like internationals."

Unlike the Channel Islands and their recent crop of England - and Northern Ireland junior - internationals, the Isle of Man has no such pedigree. Johnnie Myers is supposedly the Isle of Man's best player, but was poor against Oldham and unlikely to be offered a professional contract on that performance.

Myers was a junior with Stockport County only to be released, although David Cole did make it in the 1980s with Torquay United and Justin Jackson was the most expensive non-league signing when Rushden & Diamonds bought him from Morecambe for £300,000 a decade ago, but that's about it.

"[Jackson] has never played for the Isle of Man because the clubs didn't want to let him go," adds Clague. "If we had a World Cup of sorts, he'd walk into the side, but the Isle of Man is a bit of a backwater and there's just not enough money here. We'd have to start taxing the clubs to play internationals and we don't want to do that."

Ann Garrett, the secretary of the Isle of Man Football Association, agrees. At the start of the summer, The Observer ran an article on watching football on islands and briefly mentioned a campaign for the Isle of Man to join UEFA that perplexed Garrett. She says: "We do not know how the comment in The

Observer arose, but the IoMFA is not considering the possibility of applying for membership of UEFA as a separate FA. We are enjoying an excellent relationship with the English FA, to whom we are affiliated, and we value their ongoing support."

Keen not to upset the FA or jeopardise their main source of cash flow, the IoMFA insist they have not applied to join FIFA or UEFA but that does not mean they have not looked into it. FIFA's Andreas Herren explains: "The Manx Football Association enquired regarding the requirements for affiliation, both with FIFA and UEFA. They were provided by our associations department with the relevant regulations and given the information that they would not be eligible for affiliation not being an independent country as required by the FIFA statutes. In that sense it is correct that they have not applied, they only enquired."

The idea of a UEFA or FIFA application may not have any currency at the IoMFA but there is support elsewhere. Ann Garrett may claim not to know anything about the mention in The Observer but finding out where that comment came from is not difficult. The internet provides the answer - literally. Manxfootball.com has been running a campaign for the Isle of Man to play internationals for some time and, according to Chris Blackburn, who runs the site, the reason the Manxmen do not is all to do with money.

Blackburn says: "Unfortunately there is a general lethargy on the part of the Manx FA to break away from the Football Association to make any moves in this direction. We are associate members of the FA with full county status and qualify for grants from Soho Square in respect of ground improvement, administration, football development, etc. This is the main reason why there have been no real efforts made to push things any further."

The sums doled out are large for an island where football is resolutely amateur. Apart from FA grants, there is also cash for stadia work from the Football Foundation, which distributes money recouped from a levy on pools money. Braddan side Union Mills, which has an estimated 200 players, secured £382,312 towards relocating to a ground with new changing rooms and full and junior-sized pitches. Some clubs do have backers, such as Rushen United, which is one of the better supported clubs on the island with crowds of about 100 to 150 people.

The club has links with Bolton Wanderers via Manx businessman Eddie Davies, whose backing has enabled the Premier League side to attract a roster of big names like Jay Jay Okocha and Ivan Campo and qualify for Europe. Davies' largesse is not restricted to Bolton, however, and he helped arrange a visit by the club to the island just before the Steam Packet kicked off.

Bolton fielded a full-side and thumped Rushen 10-0, which was a disappointing scoreline, but the match at the National Sports Centre did raise

£35,000 for the club and was watched by around 3,000 people. Despite being surrounded by a running track, the ground at the National Sports Centre is far more modern than the Isle of Man FA's tired looking headquarters at the Bowl. A pall may have hung over Manx football at the 2005 Steam Packet, but there was some enthusiasm for international recognition outside of manxfootball.com. That was mostly generated during a more successful period in the late 1990s and early part of this century, when Rick Holden was working with the national team.

A former Manchester City and Oldham Athletic winger, Holden settled at Peel in the Isle of Man in 1996 and became involved with Peel FC, one of the island's biggest club sides, eventually becoming manager, coach and player. This led to Holden linking up with the national team as Manning's coach and with some success.

The Isle of Man's record in the Steam Packet is dismal, but with Holden giving the squad some professional input, they beat Burnley 1-0 in 2000. The national team had also played in a tournament with the amateur national teams from Scotland, the Republic of Ireland and Northern Ireland. Known latterly as the Guinness and then Statoil Cup, the four 'countries' took turns to host the tournament and the Isle of Man even won the event on home soil one year.

After the Burnley game, Holden wanted the IoMFA to take the next step up and look into joining UEFA, but nothing happened. He eventually moved back into the professional game and helped Andy Ritchie get Barnsley promoted to the Championship in 2006, but retains his home in Peel. Holden says: "When we got to that stage of beating Burnley, we should have gone and got independent status, but the [IoMFA] weren't really interested. You need a mind-set to be professional and they don't have that. It doesn't matter if you're Burkina Faso or the Isle of Man, if you want professional status you go and get it, but the Isle of Man FA don't want it. The people here shout from the rooftops about how proud they are to be Manx, but when it comes to talking about joining UEFA, no-one at the FA wants to do it.

"When I was coach at Peel, we played in the cup final and 1,300 people left Peel, which they won't thank me for saying is a fishing village of 3,000 people. The people here love their football and will come out to watch it. There's Isle of Man rugby teams that play in leagues on the mainland and the cricket team has affiliate status at the ICC [International Cricket Council], but football, which is the most popular sport, is lagging behind."

Holden's involvement and the Isle of Man's success led to the campaign at www.manxfootball.com for the island to join UEFA, but even Blackburn, keen advocate though he is of the team, cannot defend the Manx performance against Oldham.

He says: "It was a very poor performance. To give them their due they had already played five games in five days the previous week and there were several regulars missing. But until they get a decent coach and regular higher class opposition I can't see an improvement. The team you saw over the weekend were several levels below the sides groomed by Holden when he was over here. There are also better players on the island, but the current set-up seem to have their favourites, which is not helping the situation.

"The second game [in the Steam Packet] against Vale was a little more promising, they managed to hold them to 1-0 for the first half, but the difference in both fitness and coaching told after the break and it ended 4-0. Let's hope this sends a wake-up call to the powers that be for the future."

\*\*\*\*\*\*\*\*\*\*\*

Although the Isle of Man compete internationally at other sports, such as cricket and even squash, and Holden suggests there is some political will to further the game, this does not appear apparent. The only official support for the international football lobby comes from the United Irish Party, which is surreal. The island has plenty of Irish people living there, but the political system is not supposed to be party political, so the UIP's very existence seems odd - even more so as the party proves impossible to trace. Even down to a link on Manxfootball.com that does not lead anywhere.

The international campaign has provoked lively debate on Manx message boards and Peter Halpin, secretary of the Isle of Man Referee's Society, says: "Some of the contributions to the discussion page on manxfootball.com seem to be well thought out."

The departure of Holden appears to have been a body blow from which the team has yet to recover. Even goalkeeper Mark Blair, who was not at fault for any of the seven goals against Oldham, admits the idea of internationals is not realistic at the present.

A player at Laxey and, during the day, an architectural technician with Dandara, an Irish-owned company that is the Isle of Man's biggest house builder, Blair says: "The international football situation, I would say is a bit of a far cry for the Isle of Man. At the end of the day we pay subs every season to play in the Manx League and don't actually get paid for playing. It would be a bit ambitious for the island to be involved in international football, as I would only see us as the whipping boys in the qualifying rounds unless we were to become a professional side and trained on a regular or daily basis as a squad. For me I see becoming a semi-professional outfit and playing in a semi-professional league more realistic than internationals. I think Guernsey are in the same situation as ourselves as we aren't the biggest of islands."

Blair and striker Callum Morrisey were born in Scotland, but the rest of the side are all from the island. Blair adds: "At the end of the day we have both lived there for a number of years, I have lived on the island for 14 years now. I do call myself Scottish, but am proud to play for the Isle of Man as I think it's gonna be the highest level I will ever play at."

As Blair trudges off the field against Oldham, the crowd of a few hundred fans quickly exit. All that is left are the flock of seagulls dive-bombing the Bowl's empty terraces to pick up discarded hot dogs and burgers, which they tear to shreds mid-air just like the Isle of Man were torn apart by Oldham.

Despite the baking sun, the Bowl is a jaded ground and like every other natural grass football pitch on the Isle of Man does not have floodlights. The Steam Packet appears jaded too and had none of the pre-match hype and ambition of the Muratti. But for the Manxmen, the Channel Islanders and other unrepresented regions across Europe a relatively new competition - the UEFA Regions Cup - is to offer some hope of international exposure.

\*\*\*\*\*\*\*\*\*\*\*

The UEFA Regions Cup grew out of an amateur competition set up by a dozen of UEFA's then 33 members back in 1965. Only 12 countries took part because all of the participants had to be strictly amateur, but come from a country with a professional top division, which ruled out all the countries in the communist bloc that were supposedly all amateur. After a series of group matches, Austria's amateurs beat Scotland 2-1 in a final staged at Palma in Majorca.

Spain won the next competition in 1970, Yugoslavia and West Germany shared the 1974 title. Yugoslavia then won the 1978 competition that only featured 10 teams and resulted in the competition being abolished due to lack of interest. Nearly two decades later, as its membership was ballooning, UEFA set up a committee to look after Europe's amateur footballers, who by then made up 95 per cent of the people playing the game. As a result, the old amateur tournament was revived in 1999 and titled the UEFA Regions Cup with national associations allowed to enter teams providing they are amateur, aged between 19 and 35 and never have been on any form of contract, and their country has a domestic championship.

This time the competition attracted a little more interest with a 32-team qualifying round leading to an eight-team mini-tournament held at Veneto in northern Italy, where the hosts beat Madrid 3-2 in the final. The English FA nominated the West Cheshire League for the inaugural tournament, but did not enter into the 2001 competition, which was staged in and won by a team from the Czech Republic.

# The Isle Of Man In Europe

For the 2003 tournament, the FA's league committee nominated the Kent County League, which was knocked out in a preliminary round in Estonia after finishing second to the Czech representatives. That tournament's finals were in Germany and won by Italian side Piemonte Valle d'Aosta with a 2-1 win against French side Ligue de Maine.

This was to be the last time that FAs could nominate teams, so the English National League System Cup was set up as a qualifier for the UEFA Regions Cup. Of 43 eligible English leagues, 22 entered the inaugural NLS cup - the first new tournament organised by the FA since 1975. The Mid Cheshire League beat Cambridgeshire County League 2-0 in a final staged at Cambridge United in May 2004. Mid Cheshire then won a UEFA Regions Cup preliminary round in Slovenia ahead of teams from the hosts, Northern Ireland and Malta and went on to finish second behind the Republic of Ireland in the next round. The finals at Krakow in Poland saw Basque team Vasca beat the South West Region of Sofia from Bulgaria 1-0 in the final.

Entrants may have to submit to wearing their national FA's kit, but that did not stop Vasca celebrating not with a Spanish flag but the Basque standard.

***********

Qualification for the 2007 UEFA Regions Cup saw, for the first time, entries from the Isle of Man, Guernsey and Jersey. Having sat out the Island Games and lost the Muratti Vase to Guernsey, Jersey needed some success, but their first round match in the NLS Cup against the South Western League did not provide it. Staged at St Blazey FC in Cornwall, Jersey went 2-0 down in 34 minutes and the South West League coasted home without scoring again.

The Isle of Man and Guernsey fared better. The Isle of Man won 3-1 away from home against the West Cheshire League and the Channel Islanders beat the Reading Football League 3-2 at Corbett Field in Guernsey. In the second round, Guernsey beat Dorset 5-3 away at Hamworthy Recreation Ground, while the Isle of Man faced the Northern Alliance. This was not a team representing George Bush's allies in Afghanistan, but a team of amateurs from northern England; and the Manxmen triumphed again.

The possibility of a tantalising final between the Isle of Man and Guernsey for a chance to play in Europe remained. That would have been an interesting final, as anyone good enough can move about and qualify for a County FA side, but playing for the Isle of Man or Guernsey actually involves a more permanent type of move. For the Channel Islands, there is that huge bank balance needed to be allowed in and people with that sort of money generally are too old to play football. On the Isle of Man, getting a work permit and moving there is easier, but still more difficult than shifting from Norfolk to

Cambridgeshire. The Isle of Man and Guernsey sides are officially league teams, but both generally field players born in the place they represent.

The Manxmen went on to win 3-1 away from home against the Anglian Combination to make the final of the English qualification for the UEFA Regions Cup. In the semi-final, Guernsey's dream is scuppered by the Cambridgeshire County league, who they lose to 4-2 on penalties after a 3-3 draw.

At the Abbey Stadium on 7 March, the Isle of Man take on Cambridgeshire, but neither side can muster a goal in the first half. After 60 minutes, Nick Hunt - later voted Man of the Match - scored first for the Manxmen followed by two from Morrisey. With 82 minutes on the clock, Myers surged into the box and his deflected shot secured a 4-0 win. A season that started so woefully has ended with the Isle of Man in Europe.

The IoMFA make no attempt to send out a team in Manx colours, but the fans that boarded special boats from Douglas put on by the Steam Packet Line and travelled down to pack out one end of the Abbey Stadium can, like the Basques of Vasca, wave the flag of their choice at the UEFA Regions Cup qualifiers in the Czech Republic. By sticking inside the English FA, the Isle of Man national team will now play against an overseas team.

That progress comes at a vital time, though, as the Statoil Cup appears to have been discontinued and the Steam Packet definitely is after a run of more than 20 years; just as the national team are on the verge of real success. The move seems strange, but tourism minister David Cretney explains: "While agreeing that the festival had helped develop the Isle of Man's reputation as a sporting island, it was felt the time had come to move on. We have certain criteria regarding the department's involvement based on the return of our investment. Unfortunately this criteria was not being met by the football festival in recent years and the decision was taken with a heavy heart to re-think our investment."

With the big clubs preferring the Far East and Premier League football everywhere on the television, the IoM government prefers to get involved with the local Vagabonds rugby club. The decision leaves the Isle of Man football team with no outlets for playing a higher class of football or even representing themselves as a 'national' team. For Rick Holden, back living and coaching at Peel after being let go by Barnsley in November 2006, the success hides a deeper malaise.

He says: "Losing the Steam Packet and the Statoil Cup is watering them down to a County FA status, which is a shame. I don't think a lot of people here [outside the FA] are impressed. That's not to take anything away from winning the NLS Cup, but it's a shame in my mind that they are representing England and not themselves."

Chris Blackburn agrees, saying: "We are now becoming so successful in other areas of sport that football seems to be taking a back seat. It's a very short-sighted view because although we have world class cyclists and a handful of other world and European competitors in other disciplines, they will never create the interest nationally that a representative soccer team would do. There is a real mood change among local players and supporters now."

But for the Isle of Man's amateur players, like captain Nigel Shimmin, the UEFA Regions Cup offers a chance to live their dream. Not only does he captain the side, but Shimmin also helped the Manx FA financially as their main shirt sponsor; insurers Canada Life are his employers and agreed to sponsor the team because of Shimmin's role. Shimmin's bosses will not get any exposure from the Regions Cup, though, as the Manxmen must wear England shirts; even in the warm-up games, which start with a 1-0 defeat to a Republic of Ireland amateur team. Games then follow against Unibond league sides Skelmersdale and Cammell Lairds, which produce a 3-1 win and a 1-1 draw, before a step up of sorts.

On 10 March, the Manx team in their guise as the England Amateur XI take on San Marino, where the population of under 30,000 is less than half that of the Isle of Man. The likes of goalkeeper Mark Blair were hoping that their opponents will be the same team that only narrowly lost 2-1 to Ireland the previous month and are disappointed this is the San Marino amateur team. But as the tiny mountain state only have one professional in captain Andy Selva, who plays in the Italian third league, this is not so disappointing.

The San Marino team could be better described as a B team with U-21 players and non-starters from the Ireland game in the squad. San Marino keeper Daniel Ceccoli is sent off only minutes after he comes on at half-time for punching Morrisey, who fires home from eight yards on 83 minutes. A bystander throughout, Blair is substituted after 88 minutes.

He says: "[It] was another good experience and a clean sheet into the bargain. We were told that the team we were supposed to be playing was the team that lost to Ireland recently, but it ended up being their amateur team. We were very comfortable, so comfortable that I had nothing to do whatsoever. The shots they had were from distance and were wayward. We still count ourselves as the Isle of Man, but have to play in England gear. Although I am Scottish I'm still quite proud as it's quite a big achievement."

Manning is pleased that, despite much provocation from the Sammarinese team, no-one is sent off. The match provides the final rehearsal for the UEFA Regions Cup matches the following month in the Czech Republic.

On 17 April, the Isle of Man start the competition with a game in Trutnow against a Slovakian side from Bratislava played in burning heat. The Slovaks nearly scored twice in the first half hour, but then broke through on 32 minutes when a Patrik Kretter cross deflected off the head of Peel FC defender Nick Hurt, leaving Blair with no chance. Morrisey, who plays for St.

George's FC, came to the rescue again after 68 minutes, ramming home a shot from a Chris Bass corner after his first effort was blocked. Manning's side pressed for a winning goal, but Bratislava broke away and their most impressive player, Jan Bician, scored the winner six minutes later. In the dying seconds a powerful Hunt header hit the underside of the crossbar and appeared to cross the line, but not according to the Lithuanian referee. The score stayed 2-1, but Manning was not downhearted, saying: "This is in our own hands."

Two days later, the IoM took on host side Hradec Králové and were ahead on 16 minutes, Ross Williamson of Laxey heading home a Bass corner. The Manxmen piled on the pressure and almost extended their lead ten minutes later, only for a fine four-man passing movement to end with Jan Lemfeld equalising for the hosts. The excellent Sean Quaye, also of St. George's, headed the visitors back in front on 54 minutes from another Bass corner. Then a double whammy: Daniel Lace of Peel FC was sent off on the hour and on 73 minutes the lead vanished. Substitute Stanislav Horac fell over in the penalty area and Petr Makovsky sent Blair the wrong way from the spot. Facing certain elimination at 2-2, the Manxmen piled forward. A Bass piledriver was tipped over superbly by Jan Stastny, while Blair made an equally fine save from Horac. With eight minutes left, Bass swung in another excellent corner and Morrisey nodded home. The dream was still alive.

*************

The crunch match for the Isle of Man's inaugural European campaign came on 21 April against the third and final side in group four, a selection from the eastern side of Northern Ireland. The Isle of Man had fervent support from 'Kevin Manning's Barmy Army', a group of students from Walsall University, who followed the team through the NLS Cup campaign and then to the Czech Republic. Manning's side were reliant on Hradec Králové beating Bratislava to progress, but went out guns blazing. Bass fired over the bar when well-placed early on, but after 15 minutes a hammer blow; Northern Ireland score through Liam Bradley's over-head kick. Another boiling day took its toll, the game stagnating, but with the other game level, the Manxmen needed to push for a win. Hurt was clear on goal after 53 minutes, but volleyed wide. The same player had another good chance to level shortly after, but over-elaborated. The Manxmen pressed forward, but there were no more clear-cut chances. Hradec Králové won 2-1 but Northern Ireland went through to the eight team finals in Bulgaria. Slow starts in the two lost matches ultimately cost Manning's team, but he praised the experience as "unbelievable". He was not alone.

NF Board secretary-general Jean-Luc Kit goes in search of new members on his computer at home in France.

The members of the NF Board outside the La Mort Subite bar in Brussels after their inaugural meeting in December 2003. Jean-Luc Kit crouches in front of then Northern Cyprus FA secretary Taner Yolcu.

Shetlands striker John Montgomery converts a 61st minute penalty in the final of the 2005 Island Games football tournament against the holders, Guernsey.

The Shetlands celebrate in front of their home fans after completing a 2-0 win over Guernsey, the second goal coming from Duncan Bray four minutes after Montgomery opened the scoring.

Former New York Cosmos striker Edmond Rugova,
now the coach of Kosovo.

The Falklands team from the 2005 Island Games with Martyn Clarke in
the back row, fifth from the left.

The founding fathers of the NF Board at an early meeting.
(From left to right) FIFPro lawyer Luc Misson, Tibetan footall organiser
Michael Nybrandt, NF Board President Christian Michelis and
secretary-general, Jean Luc Kit

Isle of Man goalkeeper Mark Blair makes a save in training ahead of a
game against the Irish amateur international  side

The Monaco international side line up before their match against Kosovo, 150 metres across the border in France, where the team has to play matches because they are barred from the Monégasque national stadium just behind them

Isle of Man captain Nigel Shimmin in action during the 2007 Regions Cup in the Czech Republic.

The Sápmi team with (extreme left) their manager in national dress.

NF Board President Christian Michelis in action.

Igili Tare (R) and Altin Raci (10) of Albania fight for the ball with Faruk Statovci (L) of Kosovo during the friendly between Kosovo and Albania in Pristina on 6 September 2002. Albania won 1-0 in the first game since 1946 at the city stadium packed with fans waving national flags.

The Tibetan national team, with Michael Nybrandt (centre of middle row, in red top) and manager Kalsang Dhondup immediately to his right.

The North Marianas national team that was created by
US soccer Dad, Peter Coleman.

Vince Stravino (left) in action for North Mariana against a local All-Star
side ahead of his team's EAFF qualifier against neighbours Guam.

Hummel's 2007 Tibetan national shirt begins to pay its way.

A player from Gregoriana's De Paz Dino of Brazil pauses for breath at the St. Peter's Sporting Centre in Rome during the 2007 Clericus Cup, an international tournament for catholic clerics.

North America college in red take on Pontificio Collegio Urbano in the 2007 Clericus Cup at the St. Peter's Sporting Centre in Rome.

Dorjee Tsawa of Tibet (far left) watches as his team-mate Pablo Lobsang is tackled by Gibraltar captain Colin Ramirez during the 2006 FIFI Wild Cup in Hamburg.

Burger King girls keep the St. Pauli team occupied at the Wild Cup.

Greenland captain and dental student Niklas Kreutzmann (left)
in action against Zanzibar in the Wild Cup

Gibraltar took on hosts St. Pauli (left, in brown shirts) in the Wild Cup's opening game, which finished all square at 1-1

St. Pauli push forward to try to win the game
in front of their home crowd.

Tibet's goalkeeper is helpless as he lets in one of seven goals against St. Pauli at the Wild Cup.

There were plenty of Tibet supporters in the crowd...but all they saw was one way traffic.

Tibet kept the score down to 5-0 in their final Wild Cup
Group A match against Gibraltar.

German comedian Elton briefly in action during a guest appearance for Northern Cyprus against Greenland in the Wild Cup.

Captain Hüseyin Amcaoglu leads out the Northern Cyprus team
for their Wild Cup group match against Greenland.

Zanzibar goalkeeper Salum Ali Salum makes a save
against eventual champions Northern Cyprus.

# The Isle Of Man In Europe

For keeper Mark Blair the experience is one of a lifetime, but not without a few glitches. He says: "[The] Regions Cup was superb, very physical and demanding. The first game we played against Slovakia was played in 35 degree heat. We felt very hard done by in the tournament; although the officials were FIFA referees we thought they were very poor. One of our boys was booked for jumping and winning a header against a Northern Ireland player from a standing start. We also had a goal denied against the Slovaks which apparently was a good yard or so over the line."

Nigel Shimmin had to leave his seven month-old son behind to play in the Regions Cup, but senses the competition will bring about a change in IoM football. He says: "The trip itself was brilliant, we've been extremely fortunate to experience what very few get to achieve, representing England. When you play for the Isle of Man, people will treat you as an underdog, with England you sense that you are never the underdog, and that beating England is what it's all about.

"In terms of where does the Isle of Man go now, well it looks like this competition will be the main objective for years to come. The problem we have is that there are few competitions for us to enter. The Manx FA have yet to find a suitable means to raise funds to support the Manx national sides. The Manx FA decided not to send a men's side to the Island Games as they had hoped that we would be representing England in June. However, although there was still the option to enter the Island Games if we got knocked out of the UEFA Regions Cup, they chose not to.

"The question has been a hot topic on the Island in relation to the Isle of Man becoming UEFA affiliated. Obviously there are pros and cons, but I think the Manx FA have the appetite to seriously consider an application now. Recent years have seen a dramatic change in the way club/youth football is run on the island; this is backed up by the fact that a number of members of the squad have in excess of 30 caps, even though they are only 22. This is largely attributable to the school of excellence, run for the most talented youths on the island, which results in young players being coached properly from an earlier age. Where does the Island go now? [It's] difficult to say. The Manx FA need to decide what their ultimate goal is. If they are happy to enter competitions here and there, then no need to change. However, if it is to produce a Premiership player, then we have a long way to go."

***********

For the Isle of Man, the UEFA Regions Cup was a high point, but involved missing out on the 2007 Island Games in Rhodes and therefore does not initially appear to be a stepping stone to anywhere.

Then, after a two-year absence, the Statoil Trophy is revived. The event, it appears, had been only postponed rather than cancelled due to the IoM and Northern Irish both playing in the Regions Cup. The tournament will re-start in April 2008 and be played every two years, giving something for the Manxmen to aim for. With the Steam Packet Festival gone, the next Island Games in Åland was to be the next big outing for the team. But Manning wants to retain the NLS Cup and a successful defence would ultimately mean missing out on Åland too. To develop Isle of Man football, the national team was starting to regress to a county side until the announcement - after the Regions Cup performance - that the Statoil Cup would return.

Ironically, despite the reluctance of the IoMFA, the Manxmen and the Channel Islanders could find themselves in UEFA if the United Kingdom ever decides to join the European Currency Union. The tax implications of EU monetary membership for the Channel Islands and the Isle of Man could mean that a move for full independence was the only option to retain their distinctive set-ups. That is why Liechtenstein, for example, has never joined the Euro. If the UK government did embrace the Euro and the parliaments in St. Helier, St. Peter Port and Douglas had to seek independence, their respective football associations would have to pursue UEFA membership, as supporting football there would surely be impossible politically for the English FA. It's a situation which could occur in the near future, particularly given the change of leadership from Blair to Brown in the summer of 2007. Would it be the death or the making of UK island football?

# CHAPTER EIGHT

# Between A Rock And A Hard Place: Gibraltar

*"Spain's behaviour has so far been very unsportsmanlike and it is a terrible shame that decisions about international football have to get politicians and courts involved."*
**Neil Parish, conservative MEP for Gibraltar**

## 18 January 2006, Gibraltar

"GIBRALTAR DOESN'T have a national team," says the long-haired assistant in the Sports City sportswear shop on the main drag in the British colony.

The assistant shrugs and turns away, passing rows of football shirts: club ones for Newcastle United, Chelsea, Barcelona and Malaga, along with international shirts for Spain, England and Morocco, just across the Straits of Gibraltar from the British colony; even shirts for Paraguay but not a single Gibraltarian top.

"There is no Gibraltar shirt," adds the bulky assistant, cheerfully. "There's a team, a squad, but they don't play anyone. There's a local league with Gibraltar in it, but that isn't the Gibraltarian team. There isn't one. There used to be a team in the Island Games, but they never had an official shirt. Most of the players play in Spain now, it's just dwindled. Who would [an international team] play against anyway? There isn't a team, so there isn't a shirt. Not an official one anyway. You could probably buy some cheap one, but that isn't the official one."

Armed with that confusion - a squad but no team? - a trip to the other Sports City outlet produces the same result: no Gibraltar shirt. But at the far end of the strip near the Royal Gibraltar Regiment offices, a small stall, Super Sports, sells the red and white strip of Gibraltar in adult sizes for £29.95. Passing Super Sports, a youthful soldier parades outside the Royal Gibraltar Regiment offices as a local policeman, old enough to be his father, has to ask tourists to move on so that the lone parade can continue.

The Royal Gibraltar Regiment's origins date back to 1755; 42 years after the Rock overlooking the Straits of Gibraltar was reluctantly ceded to Great Britain by Spain in the 1713 Treaty of Utrecht. The three sides, Britain, Spain and Gibraltar, have been almost continually at odds over the colony ever since. A 1967 referendum saw a landslide vote in favour of remaining a British dependency and a constitution drawn up two years later ensures that sovereignty of the 6.5 square kilometres of Gibraltar cannot pass to another state against the wishes of the residents.

After New Labour came to power in Britain in 1997, talks over joint sovereignty ran for five years and produced some benefits. The border crossing, once barricaded, has been speeded up, Spain has allowed more phone lines into the colony and Britain has agreed to pay pensions to Spaniards employed in Gibraltar before the border was closed. In 2002, Gibraltarians held their own unofficial poll on sovereignty and 99 per cent of respondents still wanted to remain part of Britain - but they still want to play international sport as Gibraltar.

That might appear strange, but the Gibraltarians are far from alone in being content with their status as a colony. A United Nations committee for colonies listed as in need of liberation was blasted by a number of its members for meddling in their affairs. A 2001 UN conference on decolonization left many of the 17 territories represented, including the US dependencies of American Samoa and Guam, and Gibraltar, voicing vociferously their desire to be left alone. But both Guam and American Samoa play international football under the auspices of FIFA and attempts by the Gibraltar Football Association (GFA) to join them have led to one of the longest running and potentially most controversial legal battles in the world of football.

***********

Sitting in his office on the tenth floor of the ICC Tower in Gibraltar, the Gibraltar FA president Joseph Nunez sighs on hearing about the shirt saga, saying that the real reason is that he would not agree an exclusivity deal with Sports City, so they now insist there is no national team. The slight, bespectacled Nunez, also the commissioner of oaths in the colony, has been doing lots of sighing, raging and fuming over the last decade as he tries to keep football in Gibraltar alive.

The GFA's origins lie in a civilian football association formed in Gibraltar in 1895, making the GFA one of the world's oldest FAs. In 1901, the locals took on the British military in their first representative match and a league started six years later. After World War Two, football in Gibraltar enjoyed what is widely regarded as its golden period between 1949 and 1955. During this time, many big overseas club teams visited the colony, including top Austrian sides Wacker and Admira and FC Malmo of Sweden, to play against the 'national' team. Years ago, even Spanish club sides, such as Real Valladolid, came over and the highlight of Gibraltar football remains a 2-2 draw between the local XI and Real Madrid in 1949.

The 1950s were to be turbulent times for Spain and Gibraltar. In 1956, Spain granted independence to its territories in Morocco, but, crucially, retained two enclaves on Moroccan soil in Ceuta and Melilla - a distinct parallel with Gibraltar, but not one seemingly apparent in Spanish political circles. The previous year, Spain's Delegacion Nacional de Deportes had decided that all Spanish sports clubs needed written permission to play in Gibraltar. Teams without this permission were turned back at the border, including Real Madrid, Valencia and Sevilla - and so started what many in Gibraltar see as the slow death of football in the colony.

***********

Gibraltar only has one pitch, at the Victoria Stadium, which has a 3,000 capacity that is doubled for big occasions and has played host to larger crowds for concerts by the likes of Elton John. The Victoria Stadium is situated by the airport runway between the actual base of the Rock of Gibraltar and the border with Spain. Using just that one pitch, the GFA runs three men's leagues, but in 2006/07 the senior First Division had just five sides. Newcastle United and Manchester United are named after their more famous British counterparts, a Gibraltar tradition that has encompassed other famous British clubs, such as Celtic. The top flight also includes Glacis United, Gibraltar United, who were created in 1943, and the colony's oldest club side, St. Josephs, which dates back to 1912.

The Victoria Stadium has floodlights, which are necessary as the pitch is used from seven in the morning until late in the evening, particularly by local schoolchildren. In one of those anomalies that crops up regularly around the outskirts of international football, the artificial surface at the Victoria Stadium is a FIFA-approved pitch even though the GFA are not in UEFA, let alone FIFA.

In the late 1990s, Nunez and the GFA, seeing football in Gibraltar dwindling away as players increasingly used the relaxations on border controls to play in Spain, sought to change that situation. Many other sports in Gibraltar are members of their respective world bodies, including some Olympic sports. Gibraltar's athletics association secured membership of the International Association of Athletics Federations in 1954, as did basketball, gaining entry to the Federation International de Basketball (FIBA). To back up an application to join UEFA in 1999, the GFA pointed to Gibraltar enjoying membership of 23 other world sporting bodies. In the complicated, murky world of sport, being a member of a world body does not mean that a team can play in a world championship, as Gibraltar found out when it tried to send a team to the 2001 Badminton World Championships.

The Gibraltar Badminton Association joined the International Badminton Federation (IBF) in 1986, but an attempt to play in the 2001 Sudirman Cup - the sport's world championships - ended up in the International Court of Arbitration for Sport (CAS). Gibraltar wanted to send seven players to the tournament, which was, unfortunately for the Gibraltarians, in the Spanish city of Sevilla. The IBF ruled that Gibraltar could only participate if they did not fly the Gibraltarian flag or display the word 'Gibraltar' on any of their kit. The colony objected. The case went to CAS, which ruled in favour of the Spaniards. The Spanish café au lait culture may allow the Basques and Galicians their own international teams, but this would not stretch to Gibraltar at any sport if the Spanish could help it.

By this time, Nunez was already well aware of the workings of CAS and what it meant for Gibraltarian football. Badminton is one thing, but when the GFA applied to UEFA in 1999, Nunez was making the first play in a game that could see the Spaniards facing the ignominy of having to play a place they insist does not exist at the sport they love above all else. Neither Spain's government nor the Royal Spanish Football Federation (RFEF) could allow this to happen and the Spaniards threatened to pull its representatives out of all international and club competitions run by UEFA if Gibraltar were allowed in.

Nunez, sitting back in his office and looking out of the window towards Spain, takes up the story, the dates ingrained into his legal mind. He says: "We applied in April 1999. In May 2000, UEFA and FIFA came to Gibraltar and did site inspections. In July 2000, UEFA administration issued a report approving our membership, but restricting it to amateur and junior competitions, futsal and ladies competitions. We were perfectly happy with that. I don't want to play in the World Cup. You have to be reasonable. The World Cup or the Champions League is not realistic in the immediate future.

After that decision, UEFA's executive committee then said different because of Spanish objections that, as we are a colony, we are not entitled to membership."

The problem for UEFA was that its membership criteria were then woolly enough to perhaps allow Gibraltar in and possibly lead to a melt-down in European football. Understandably preferring to see Real Madrid and Barcelona regularly in the Champions League rather than Gibraltar playing futsal, UEFA decided to shift the goal-posts. UEFA sat on Gibraltar's application until 7 September 2001, when its executive committee decided to indefinitely postpone its decision. This gave UEFA chance to come up with some new entry criteria, specifically designed to exclude 2.5 square miles of rock.

UN membership was proposed on the condition this was not retrospective and accepted. The following year UEFA showed it was not averse to new members as Kazakhstan was admitted to the European federation after transferring over from the Asian federation.

Out-manoeuvred and shunned by UEFA, the GFA - like the colony's badminton association - sought solace at the Court of Arbitration for Sport, which is football's (indeed all sports') ultimate legal arbiter. Although essentially private members clubs, UEFA and FIFA are not legally obliged to stick with CAS and routinely threaten any national FA that is interfered with by its government with suspension. This makes both bodies pretty safe from meddling.

Many commentators saw Gibraltar's application as a political stunt, but Nuncz and the GFA were convinced that something had to be done to save football in the colony. Nunez cites the example of Tony Macedo, a Gibraltarian who played more than 300 games for Fulham in the 1960s and represented England at Under-23 level before moving to South Africa, where he ended his career. Those halcyon days when Gibraltarian players could make their mark at the top level are long gone. Tim Buzaglo's international career was restricted to cricketing appearances for the colony, which is an associate member of the International Cricket Council. Between 1982 and 2001 Buzaglo scored 681 runs in 30 innings for the colony. But he remains far better known for football and the hat-trick he scored for non-league Woking in a famous 4-2 FA Cup Third Round win over then second tier West Bromwich Albion in 1991.

Since then, apart from winning the 1995 Island Games football tournament as hosts, Gibraltar football has had little to celebrate. A bright spot on the horizon could be Jason Pusey, who was handed a three-year contract by La Liga giants Atletico Madrid in the summer of 2006 after finishing his GCSEs. Gibraltar may still be the subject of a form of sporting embargo by Spain, but that did not stop Pusey being selected for the Cádiz regional representative side.

The captain of the Gibraltar national side has also played professionally in Spain and Colin Ramirez knows that without some sort of support from UEFA or the English FA, the future for football in Gibraltar in the long-term is not good. Ramirez says: "The standard in Gibraltar at club level is pretty low and we have to give the kids a reason to compete. The only way we can compete is with teams from abroad. We need to compete as a national side."

Now in his mid-thirties, Colin Ramirez played in Spain in his teens before moving to Northern Ireland and playing professionally for Glentoran. He then moved back home and played in the Spanish Third Division for La Real Balonpedica Linense. Without a hint of regret, the slim, easy-going Ramirez adds: "I chose my wife over football and that's why I came back from Northern Ireland. I had no problems playing in Spain. I'm the same colour and got the same insults, which you don't hear anyway. Now we play friendlies against club teams from Spain and the UK. When we play the Spanish teams it can get a bit tense, but only because we're a physical team and the Spanish teams have a tendency to go to ground a bit easy, but that's the only reason."

***********

With his local players and FA behind him, Nunez took his case to the CAS headquarters in Lausanne and then even had the support of the English FA, although this was to change. Whether the English FA supported UEFA's change in entry criteria to specifically bar Gibraltar is not known as the FA will not comment on this, but England were initially supportive of the GFA application.

Sitting up in his chair seemingly galled by the very mention of the England FA, Nunez adds: "We only said we would apply for UEFA membership if the FA said 'OK'. I saw Graham Kelly [then England FA chief executive] in 1997 and he thought we were a member of the FA at the time. Something has happened since then. I don't know what, but it suits me better not to be involved with them. We were part of the FA, but then unilaterally thrown out. We've had all sorts of problems with Geoff Thompson [current FA president] and his cohorts."

According to Nunez, the UEFA executive committee was ignoring approval of Gibraltar's application by their own panel of three judges from Switzerland, Belgium and Germany. This panel had ruled that changing the criteria after an application was made was not on, so proceedings against UEFA started at CAS in 2002. This ruling also went in favour of the Gibraltarians, but UEFA, worried about those Champions League euros, simply ignored it. Nunez explains: "CAS has always acted on the basis that the party ruled against will comply. This time they would need to be forced."

The GFA was literally stuck between their own Rock and a hard place not of their making. There had been some initial contact from the NF Board and, although Nunez was to attend that London meeting in 2005, he did not initially want to do anything to jeopardise the GFA's application - like playing a friendly against an unrecognised state such as Northern Cyprus.

So, as the GFA set out on another lengthy appeal to CAS, Nunez went looking for 'internationals' of his own. A game in Monaco in 2002 led to the foundation of the Gibraltar Cup in 2004. Keen to avoid potential 'international flare-ups', initial entrants included the Isle of Man and the Isle of Wight. Monaco pitched up on the Rock the following year, along with a team from the Amateur Football Alliance, an English body formed back in 1907 and representing 420 amateur clubs. The first two Gibraltar Cups were won by the hosts.

88

As this was going on and the legal forms batting back and forth between Lausanne and Gibraltar for the second appeal, the colony's football received a fillip with the recruitment of Jeff Wood as a development officer and coach. A former goalkeeper for Charlton Athletic, Wood moved to Spain to run the Addicks' European Soccer School. Concerned by what he felt was lack of support from Charlton, he split off to run his own school with bases across southern Spain and Gibraltar staffed by the likes of Terry Gibson, a former top flight player with Spurs, Manchester United, Coventry City and Wimbledon.

Wood, who also played for Brighton & Hove Albion and Sliema Wanderers in Malta, started out taking two coaching sessions a week with the Gibraltar national team and admits that the situation is "pretty odd". Wood now coaches youth teams in the colony and a boy's side won its category at the prestigious Holland Cup amateur youth tournament in 2004.

The GFA also managed to get into the Straits Games and in 2005 was invited to play in the Wild Cup in Hamburg, a tournament specifically for non-FIFA teams in which Gibraltar finished third (see chapter 13). To play in the Wild Cup, Nunez had to bring the Gibraltar Cup forward. Seemingly unnoticed by the Spanish government, the competition included a club side from San Roque in Spain, as Nunez steered a course away from the NF Board and its potentially explosive members.

Gibraltar did try and enter a team in the 2005 Mediterranean Games, but, as it was held at Almería in southern Spain, their application received a predictable response; the GFA did not even get a reply. As the Spanish football federation has to object to anything that would lead to any form of international recognition by political decree, the period between the first and second appeal saw furious objections and manoeuvring. Months and months passed with Gibraltar sitting on the touchlines and Spain desperate to keep them there before CAS finally made a decision.

\*\*\*\*\*\*\*\*\*\*\*

On 6 July 2006, the CAS ruled in favour of Gibraltar - again. The CAS decision has been known about by the GFA and the Spanish FA for months, but the pair are prevented from publishing the ruling by UEFA. Eventually, the ruling is leaked to a Spanish newspaper, Mundo Deportivo, and UEFA relents, allowing the GFA to publish the ruling three months after it was made.

In August 2006, then UEFA president Lennart Johansson, candidly revealing his feelings on the subject, is reported as saying: "It is something that we cannot do anything about, in the congress of Düsseldorf next January, Gibraltar will in reality be a new member of UEFA and consequently also of FIFA. It is a matter that goes beyond sport and becomes political. Personally, I believe that at this time this is more an issue for the Spanish government than for the Spanish football federation. Gibraltar will be a member by right, with a voice and vote and now it will be necessary to study in what competitions it can take part."

Even fellow UEFA executive Lars Christer-Olsson admits the "sports route is exhausted. Now it is already a political problem for not only Spain, but also England and the rest of the federations of Great Britain."

Gibraltar, it seemed, had won. But the Spanish federation was not about to give up yet and had until a UEFA executive meeting between October 4-5 in the Slovenian capital of Ljubljana to find a way to keep Gibraltar out.

As the sporting negotiations rumbled on, the UK government was involved with other delicate negotiations over the colony's future. Spain's new socialist government, which replaced the right-wing government of José María Aznar that had been toppled following the Al Qaeda terrorist bombings of Madrid in 2004, has adopted a more conciliatory tone. It wants to offer carrots not sticks to the Gibraltarians and the British government. They are not prepared to relinquish their stance on Gibraltar, but, on 18 September, an agreement involving both governments and Gibraltar allows direct flights from Spain and the rest of Europe into the colony's lone airstrip right alongside the Victoria Stadium.

A fortnight later, UEFA's executive committee met, but are again unable to make a decision on Gibraltar in Ljubljana. This gave Spain vital extra time to find grounds to object and the airstrip duly provides one. Ownership of the land that includes the airstrip and the stadium is, apparently, still a subject of debate centuries after Britain took control of the Rock. So, while the land can cope with international flights, it cannot cope with international football according to FIFA, which ruled that because of this Gibraltar can never join the world body.

The New Labour government struck a political bargain over the airstrip, but carefully kept out of the UEFA decision. This did not stop the Liberal Democrats and the Conservative Party from voicing support for the GFA. In a strange political anomaly, Gibraltar's interests at the European Parliament are included as part of a constituency that stretches from south west England all the way down to the Rock - but handily missing out France and Spain. Gibraltar's two MEPS are Liberal Democrat Graham Watson and Neil Parish, a Tory.

Parish, a Somerset-born farmer, took time out to write to UEFA's chief executive Lars Christer-Olsson and issued an impassioned plea that said more about political researchers than anything else. Parish said: "UEFA must ensure this decision is about football and not politics. Spain's behaviour has so far been very unsportsmanlike and it is a terrible shame that decisions about international football have to get politicians and courts involved. All I am asking for is a fair hearing. If the Faroe Islands and Greenland can be members, why can't Gibraltar? The way Spain has been playing lately, they could face a drubbing up against the Rock in Euro 2012. UEFA must not be hoodwinked into a decision that may cause fewer waves in Madrid, but that would be unfair on Gibraltar."

Despite this ill-informed missive, Spain's FA president Angel Maria Villar was sounding resigned to losing and in October admitted: "All I can do is vote against."

On 8 December 2006, Villar did so to no effect. UEFA caved in, but provided a significant get-out clause for the Spanish. In a statement, UEFA said: "The UEFA executive committee has duly taken notice of the CAS award of 6 July 2006 and had no choice but to admit the GFA as a provisional member. Furthermore, the UEFA executive committee has also taken note of the FIFA executive committee, according to which the GFA 'does not meet the statutory requirements to become a FIFA member'."

***********

On 17 December 2006, a Spanish-owned Iberia Airbus 319 swoops round the cloud-capped 1,300-foot high Rock over the Bay of Algeciras to land on Gibraltar's airstrip. The first scheduled service from Spain since 1979 touches down. On board is Bernardino Léon, the man charged by Spain's socialist Prime Minister, José Luis Rodríguez Zapatero, to negotiate with the Gibraltarians.

Gibraltar has international contact with Spain in the air and perhaps soon on the pitch. The GFA's battle for UEFA membership seems over, but it will have to be ratified by a vote at the next UEFA congress in Düsseldorf and they will still be barred from FIFA because no-one seems to know who owns the airstrip that the Iberia flight touched down on. The decision to let UEFA members decide, yet again, provides the Spanish FA with some extra time that they will keep playing vigorously through, but for seven weeks, the GFA has its foot on the touchline of international football.

## 27 January 2007, Düsseldorf, Germany

At the UEFA congress in Düsseldorf, Montenegro's ascension to Europe's top table as its 53rd full member is waved through, but not Gibraltar's. Joe Nunez has been expecting as much. Before Christmas, he had warned: "It will be a very uphill struggle. This is the best example I have ever seen of politics in sports. No-one has ever raised any sporting objections to our application."

To do so would surely be hypocritical in the extreme. Gibraltar's only playing surface, albeit artificial, is FIFA-approved and the Victoria Stadium is surely the equal of the Serravalle Olimpico Stadium in San Marino, a fellow UEFA member. The Serravalle holds 5,400 fans; the Victoria Stadium's capacity is 6,000. This does not seem to matter and before the Düsseldorf congress, UEFA chief executive Lars Christer-Olsson tells the Play the Game newsletter: "We will see. Opinions are very divided. Some believe that UEFA's congress is independent of CAS."

At the congress, Spanish FA President and UEFA Vice-President Angel Maria Vilar Llona urges fellow members to block the colony, saying: "In Spain, this subject carries a huge social and political sensitivity. We don't want to bring political problems in soccer. We want politicians to solve political problems."

England, Scotland and Wales come out in support of Gibraltar, but they are the only supporters for the Rock's application out of UEFA's 52 members. With the politicians on their back, the home nations' FAs probably had little choice to avoid creating a media back-lash, although a Department for Culture, Media & Sport spokesman insists: "Gibraltar FA's recent application for membership of UEFA was and still remains a matter entirely between the GFA and UEFA. Therefore, the Government has no locus to intervene as UK football is represented in UEFA by the Football Association (and their Scottish, Welsh and Northern Irish counterparts)."

All the English FA's Adrian Cooper would say is: "The Gibraltar FA was once affiliated to The FA, but that has not been the case for several years. The FA voted in favour of full UEFA membership for Gibraltar at the recent UEFA congress, but was in a small minority."

Curiously, Northern Ireland went against the other three home nations and did not vote for Gibraltar. After a long protracted attempt to find out why, all Sueann Harrison, the IFA's communications manager, would eventually say is: "Decisions of this nature are the private business of the IFA."

Joseph Nunez knows the answer though and is left raging in the Mediterranean winter light at the successful Spanish lobby to stifle football in the colony, saying: "With regard to the Northern Ireland FA, I suspect that as [Jim] Boyce, the President, is a member of a UEFA Committee, his views on the subject may well have been coloured by his desire to continue his future association within UEFA Committees.

It's true our application was rejected after the [UEFA] executive committee strongly recommended to delegates that they do so on grounds which the CAS had held were unlawful. We will be consulting our lawyers, but the probability is that we will be going back to court. The behaviour of the executive committee was shameful."

Gibraltar's two MEPs do not miss a chance to fire off brief broadsides across Spain's bow. Graham Watson says: "It is abundantly clear that 11th hour sabotage by the Spanish authorities has resulted in the delay of what would have been a proud day for all Gibraltarians. Since July, UEFA has been legally bound to accept Gibraltar as a member. Its decision to not formally do so is a depressing set-back for Gibraltar and its citizens."

Neil Parish chips in with: "Spain has acted like a jealous spoilt child over the application. It should settle its differences on the football pitch, not the legal and political arena."

***********

Spain, it seems, has won again and Gibraltar will not be allowed in. Joe Nunez is left fuming in the office he shares with his brother. The GFA are pursuing UEFA for legal expenses for the entire carry-on through the Court of Arbitration again and also starting another application based on what they see as UEFA's unlawful actions. It's déjà vu, all over again.

Gibraltar did their case some good by winning the gold medal for five-a-side football at the World Firefighter Games, beating the cream of Venezuela's fire service 2-0 in the final, Ramirez and Ivan De Haro scoring the goals.

That is the kind of competition at which Nunez must go looking for matches. After the UEFA decision, he returns to organising the 2007 Gibraltar Cup and completing plans for the 'national' team that UEFA refuses to allow to exist to travel to the Island Games in Rhodes, where they win the title. GFA vice president Albert 'Bubi' Buhagiar says: "We are there, where we are supposed to be, at the top of football in the Island Games family."

Perhaps that is where Gibraltar must stay. In the 2007 Gibraltar Cup, the Spaniards of San Roque played again, along with Yeading FC, of the Football Conference Southern Division. The embargo against Spanish club sides playing in Gibraltar seems well and truly over. But any idea that Jason Pusey may have of pursuing an international career with the place that he grew up in are dead.

But if Joe Nunez has anything to do with it, Spain hasn't won yet.

# CHAPTER NINE

# The Turkish Republic Of Northern Cyprus

*"How and in what ideology does a human not have
the right to compete with another nation?"*
**Ahmet Esenyel, Çetinkaya SC**

## 23 February 2006, Monaco Consulate, London

A CROWD OF around two dozen Turkish Cypriots gather in freezing weather outside Monaco's consulate at Cromwell Place in south Kensington. A slightly bemused male member of the Monegasque consulate emerges and politely takes a football covered in graffiti and letters of protest from the leader of the protestors, Ipek Ozerim. The Turkish Cypriots carry banners with 'Monaco: play fair' and 'Keep politics out of sport' and brandish red cards with 'Non' printed on them. A song strikes up, twisting a well-known terrace chant into "North Cyprus, we're by far the greatest team the world has never seen" to the bemusement of passers-by.

The latest stunt is to protest about the Monaco government caving in to international pressure and forcing its amateur national team to cancel a match against a team representing the Turkish Republic of Northern Cyprus, one of the world's true pariah states. Ozerim's campaign has attracted some support from the British political establishment in Baroness Ludford, but the Liberal Democrat member of the European Parliament is unable to make the Monaco protest due to a prior commitment in Brussels.

Two months later and the cheerful Ozerim, a Londoner from a Turkish Cypriot family and co-founder of the UK-based Embargoed campaign aimed at ending sporting embargoes on Turkish Cypriots, is on the case again. A demonstration called 'Gagged' is planned for outside the Council of Europe's offices in Brussels to coincide with the second anniversary of the CoE's decision to end the isolation of Turkish Cypriots, who have been in virtual limbo since declaring independence from the rest of Greek-dominated Cyprus in 1983 - a move still only recognised by Turkey.

# The Turkish Republic Of Northern Cyprus

The independent Republic of Cyprus was formed in 1960 after a long battle for independence from Britain led by the EOKA activists. A treaty of establishment created what most people know as Cyprus, but the Turks and Greeks who inhabited the island were not split up in that grand colonial tradition of arbitrarily drawn lines.

Prior to independence, there had been unrest between Greek and Turkish Cypriots and in 1955, according to the Turkish side, their most famous football club, Çetinkaya, was barred from playing a match against a Greek-Cypriot side, Pezoporikos, in the capital Nicosia. Çetinkaya Sporting Club had won the all-island league in 1952/53, but when the Turkish Cypriot clubs were expelled from the Greek Cypriot FA in 1955, their clubs formed their own association, the KTFF.

The tensions between the Greek Cypriot majority and the Turkish Cypriot minority continued after independence. A number of intercommunal clashes came to a head in December 1963 with a violent battle in the capital of Nicosia. United Nations peacekeepers were deployed the following year, but the violence continued and Turkish Cypriots retreated to enclaves throughout the island. In 1974, an attempt sponsored by the government of Greece to seize control of the island prompted a Turkish invasion. On 20 July 1974, Turkish paratroopers landed on the northern coast. After a 25 day battle that left around 6,000 people dead, the Turkish troops had seized a third of the island, including a large section of Nicosia - or Lefkosa, as the Turks call the island's capital. Thousands of Greek Cypriots retreated to the south behind a hastily drawn line between the two communities, losing their homes in the process.

Soon after independence in 1960, records show a team representing the Turkish Cypriots playing odd matches against Turkey. In 1975, the KTFF claimed that former FIFA general secretary Dr Helmut Kaser agreed that the Turkish Cypriots could play friendlies against FIFA members, but not official competitions. Ad-hoc 'internationals' continued with Northern Cyprus playing matches against not just Turkey, but also Saudi Arabia, Libya and Malaysia. This all came to a sudden end in 1983. That year, attempts at resolving the conflict were sent spiralling into retreat, when the Turkish-zone declared itself as the Turkish Republic of Northern Cyprus (TRNC) led by nationalist president Rauf Denktas.

The Greek Cypriots already had to put up with one section of their island being under foreign control. Under the terms of the 1960 treaty, Britain retained sovereignty over two areas in Akrotiri and Dhekelia to the south west of Limassol that comprise a total of 254 square kilometres and house a large number of British military personnel. Having a second area sectioned off was too much and, in protest, international embargoes were placed on just about anything in what Greek-Cypriots refer to as "the occupied area", with any institutions therein, sporting or otherwise, always referred to officially as "self-styled".

\*\*\*\*\*\*\*\*\*\*\*

After 1983 and the declaration of independence, Northern Cyprus continued to have a national team, but it was a fairly pointless exercise as no-one would play them. During a large part of this time, the would-be captain of a national team that did not exist was Ahmet Esenyl. Apart from a year with Dogan Turk Birligi during his national service, he spent his entire career with Çetinkaya SC, still the strongest Turkish Cypriot club, before recently retiring at 31.

Esenyl recalls trips abroad when the team had games called off as soon as people found out what they represented. He says: "I have been chosen for the national team, but never had the chance to play with a European team because of the embargoes. As a team also, we visited some countries like Belgium, Germany, Hungary, but the teams never accepted to play eventually because of Greek embargoes. Nobody can feel what I have gone through seeing how unfortunate the European teams have been when they were actually resisting to play. They were very keen in the beginning, however, when they found out that they will be fined, they had to change their minds and every time our real dreams have turned into a misery."

Esenyl's father was a famous Turkish Cypriot player. After retiring, his father managed and coached Kucuk Kaymakli FC in Turkish Nicosia, had two spells as KTFF President between 1987 and 1990 and 1992 and 1995 and helped build a 28,000 capacity stadium in the Turkish side of Cyprus' divided capital. Ahmet Esenyl adds: "During [my father's time as KTFF president], teams like Xamax from Switzerland, Trabzonspor, Sariyer, Aydin from Turkey [came over], also many youth teams from England and Germany. The team Genclerbirligi from Turkey first time played with the national team and they played legally without thinking about the fines they would be getting and it was really fantastic to see a lot of interest to this game. He also brought Fenerbahçe and Sariyer to do the opening of the [new] stadium. These are some of the things I remember, probably there are many more he has obviously done as President."

Esenyl trails off thinking what could have been, then adds: "I just remember now, Çetinkaya has beaten Dinamo Bucharest [of Romania] in the north in 1985. This was a very big event for the whole island. This would be every football player's dream in the north to play as a professional. However, since there are such embargoes it is an impossible matter. A joint national team at this stage is not possible yet, as Greeks do not recognize the North and they believe there is only one Cyprus and they are Greeks. With such understanding, how could anyone expect to have a joint national team?

# The Turkish Republic Of Northern Cyprus

"My last words would be to cry out to all the authorities of the sports' world: how and in what ideology does a human not have the right to compete with another nation?"

The problem for Esenyl and the rest of the Turkish Cypriots is that more than two decades after declaring themselves a country, no-one but the Turkish administration in Ankara agrees. And Turkey's football association is so scared of punishment from FIFA that they will not help either. When the TRNC seceded, Turkey was a far weaker side than the one that made the 2002 World Cup semi-finals and now regularly has top clubs in the group stages of the Champions League. Back then, the Turks gave discreet support to the KTFF, but nothing overt. During one of Fenerbahçe's summer training camps in the TRNC, the Turkish giants proposed a game against a local side, but FIFA warned of severe sanctions if it went ahead. The game was never played.

\*\*\*\*\*\*\*\*\*\*\*

When Cyprus was granted independence, the Turkish Cypriots insist this enshrined the right for separate sporting institutions, but only the Republic of Cyprus, the Greek partition, is recognized by UEFA and FIFA. In 1996, the KTFF applied to join FIFA, but were rejected, although some clubs managed to tour abroad. Çetinkaya visited Bavaria in 2000 for a two-game tour despite concerns voiced by the Cyprus embassy in Berlin.

Players from Northern Cyprus are not helped by rules in the Turkish football league. As the TRNC is a separate state according to the Turkish government, players from Northern Cyprus have to be treated as overseas players. For ambitious players from TRNC that want to play a higher standard of football, the obvious place to go - Turkey - is one of the hardest to break into. Mete Adanir played in the Turkish top flight a decade ago, but died in a car accident. Another, called Kenan Özer, is on the books at Besiktas, but plays only sporadically. The most famous Northern Cypriot players today are actually two that played in the Greek Cypriot league.

Sabri Selden left the TRNC in 2002 to play football and found himself branded a "weak character" by North Cyprus president Rauf Denktas, as his departure was seen as a public relations coup for the Greek Cypriots. After crossing over to the 'free state', as Greek Cypriots call their part of the island, Selden responded: "I passed over to the South to play football. In some newspapers unfounded articles have been published. I am bored of these. I will talk when the day comes. I will play in southern Cyprus, in Greece, but the most important in Turkey, if I am given the permission."

A number of teams in the Greek Cypriot league, which is professional and has attracted many eastern Europeans and Africans, sought Selden's signature, including AEK Larnaca and Omonia Nicosia. Eventually, he signed a deal with Nea Salamina and was subsequently followed south by his brother Raif.

The departure of the brothers was a cause célèbre, but as relations eased slightly between the two sides, a move by another Turkish Cypriot player to the Greek Cypriot league proved less controversial. In April 2005, Denktas was ousted in elections and replaced by the more moderate and younger Mehmet Ali Talat. Relations eased between the two sides and crossings through a border hidden away in Greek Nicosia became a daily occurrence. Around 4,000 Turkish Cypriots cross daily to work in Greek Cyprus, where per capita income is estimated at ten times higher than in the North.

Like Selden, Coskun Ulusoy just wanted to play a higher standard of football. A strapping, muscular midfielder well over six foot tall with distinctive fair hair, Ulusoy does not even look particularly Greek or Turkish. When Greenland's Niklas Kreutzmann came up against Ulusoy, the Greenlander said it was obvious that he had played a higher standard because of the way he used his elbows. Ulusoy had studied in Istanbul between 1994 and 1999, but could not find a professional club because of the rules treating him as an overseas player.

"Everyone asks me what is your nationality and I say the 'Turkish part of Cyprus' and everyone has the same answer: 'that is a problem'," explains Ulusoy. In Northern Cyprus, he played for Girne - or Kyrenia as the Greeks know the pretty harbour town - but in 2004 was offered a £9,000-a-year contract with Nea Salamina, which has a left-wing fan-base. Every day, he travelled back and forth across the border to training. Though he received some abuse, Ulusoy has mostly good memories of his two years with Nea Salamina. The easy-going Ulusoy explains: "I was always very friendly with the other Greek players, there were no problems. A lot of the Salamina fans know Turkish and they are to the left. Sometimes the right side teams shout at me, but nobody hit me or nothing."

Ulusoy returned to the TRNC when his mother-in-law fell ill and took a job at the interior ministry. Instead of joining his former club, he signed for Lapta and is keen to bring some professionalism of sorts to football in the North. Ulusoy adds: "I chose my family over football, but that is only right. When I cancel the contract, they [Nea Salamina] are very sorry. I never forget they said to me they lose a friend and I said that I lose many more friends.

"Here in North Cyprus, all the players want to play professionally, but that is too much for the top league, so we try and make some contracts and get insurance for the players. We want a system in football. I train maybe three times a week, but before I trained twice a day. I played two years as a professional and after that I believe that there are other players here that can play professionally, but we don't have the chance. Sometimes I think I am in prison because everyone says 'no' all the time. Everyone in the world says that football is friendship and peace, but we don't have the chance to play because of the embargoes."

Ulusoy's move to the south came during a time of big change in the isolated territory's status in political and football terms. Talat took over as President, but a two-year series of talks between the leaders of the two communities brokered by the United Nations failed to reach an agreement to reunite the divided island. The Turkish Cypriots had supported the EU plan, but it was rejected by the Greek Cypriots in an April 2004 referendum. The following month the entire island of Cyprus joined the European Union. This entry only applies to the areas under direct government control and not parts of the TRNC, but Turkish Cypriots are eligible for Republic of Cyprus citizenship and can enjoy the same rights as other EU citizens. What the Northern Cypriots want is a system modelled on the UK in political and sporting terms. Not too much to ask?

Ferdi Sabit Soyer is probably one of the few Prime Ministers to hand out business cards to journalists, but then politics in the TRNC is not quite like everywhere else. The dusty streets in Lefkosa on the Turkish side of Nicosia show little of the investment evident on the Greek side. There is security at the parliament, but it is relaxed. Soyer sits up pertly in an office featuring another image of Kemal Atatürk, who founded the modern Turkish state that succeeded the remains of the Ottoman empire in 1923. He thinks that the Greek Cypriots have "lost their enthusiasm" for a solution since gaining EU membership, but ambitiously thinks that if one can be found, this could even help instill a sense of peace in the nearby Middle East.

Soyer adds: "Our name is Northern Cyprus, but I think sometimes people think we are North Korea, but we are more isolated than North Korea. Maybe people think that we have an atomic bomb.

"Greek Cyprus is a Christian community, Turkish Cyprus is an Islamic one, but very secular. If we can find a solution under the EU, this can give a good atmosphere and feeling across the Middle East and for the relationship between Turkey and Greece. Under the UN solution, we want a federal common government and, under that federal centre, two federal states. They would share powers and give their powers to the central government. Both sides can have elections together and make a selection for a central government."

Since the EU admission, border crossings have become routine. Not only were Turkish Cypriots such as Ulusoy crossing regularly, but so were Greek Cypriots back to the north, where the only industry is tourism, subsistence farming and a construction boom providing hotels and holiday homes. Those holiday homes are increasingly being bought by British holiday makers - the only problem is that some of these homes have been built on land seized from Greek Cypriots, who remain their legal owners in the eyes of the EU.

Some Greek Cypriot restrictions remain in place, but appear more to do with mainland Turkey than their fellow Cypriots at the top end of their island.

In July 2005, Reporters Without Borders, a lobby group that defends press freedom, slammed the Republic of Cyprus for refusing to allow Turkish journalists based in the TRNC to enter the country to cover a competitive football match between Greek Cypriot side Anorthosis Famagusta and Turkish side Trabzonspor. According to Reporters Without Borders, Turkish nationals wanting to travel to Greek Cyprus for professional reasons need to seek permission two days in advance. Reporters from the TRNC are not subject to the same restrictions and were allowed to cross the border by the Greek Cypriot police. But any Turkish journalists that tried to get into the game on 25 July were refused entry. This time, the Northern Cypriots were not the ones being isolated but their sponsors.

Reporters without Borders said: "We are dismayed at this decision by Cyprus, a new EU member since 2005, which is a clear violation of free access to information. The Turkish journalists were coming simply to cover a popular sports meeting between teams from Cyprus and Turkey. It is unacceptable for journalists to be targets of political blackmail, fomenting confrontation rather than reconciliation between the Turkish and Green communities."

The game was to be a great night for Cypriot football and the closest a team from Cyprus had got to the Champions League group stages. Having eliminated Dinamo Minsk of Belarus in the first qualifying round, Anorthosis Famagusta routed Trabzonspor 3-1 and went through 3-2 on aggregate to the third and final qualifying round, where they lost to Glasgow Rangers.

***********

The problem for many visitors to Northern Cyprus is that the place appears rather like an outpost of Turkey itself. Not just because of the thousands of Turkish troops still posted there - along with some bored-looking Argentine UN peace-keepers - but because of signs of Turkish support like the constant images of Kemal Atatürk that pop up everywhere. Even the flag is merely the Turkish standard with the colours reversed, as is the Northern Cyprus football strip. There is not even a TRNC currency. Visitors to the pariah state can spend Turkish lira, Cypriot pounds, Euros, even English pounds, but there is no Northern Cypriot denomination. There is investment, but due to the lack of recognition this is mainly from Turkey, although also occasionally by the

Israelis. The post boxes are still the blue ones put in decades ago by the British colonial authorities, but all post has to go via mainland Turkey.

To the Greek Cypriots, Northern Cyprus remains a part of their country that has merely been sectioned off and their people driven out after the war. Despite the EU negotiations, the TRNC is at the heart of the stalled EU application by Turkey, which insists on recognition for Northern Cyprus and the establishing of direct trade and economic links to support reunification. The Republic of Cyprus are not having any of this and are blocking any attempts that would lead to the TRNC being recognized as a country in its own right in any way.

These frustrations lead the TRNC to try and secure a different form of national recognition - on the football field. Soyer adds: "There is a big isolation for Turkish Cyprus, not just culturally but sporting. That is why we are trying to destroy the blockade. The Olympic flame came to Cyprus [on its journey to Athens in 2004], but only the Greek Cypriots could take the fire. No-one in Europe asks the question, 'Why does the fire not go to North Cyprus?' They just close their eyes. The UN solution has an idea for a common national team and a separate one. If we can have a common team that is good, but maybe we follow the UK plan. We can decide this at the table."

The KTFF and the TRNC government decided that rather than wait, an international side would be launched for the 250,000-odd residents of Northern Cyprus, who were more used to watching the likes of Galatasaray on television in the Champions League than their own home-grown players. Taner Yolcu, secretary of the Northern Cypriot Football Federation, had already eagerly signed up to the NF Board initiative, although some at the KTFF suggest he did so without universal approval from their association. In the summer of 2004, the KTFF assembled a side that was taken to Norway to play the Sápmi team representing ethnic Laplanders. That was followed up by a tournament hosted in Northern Cyprus to celebrate the fiftieth anniversary of the founding of the KTFF. The Sápmi were invited for a re-match. Kosovo, a UN protectorate and still part of Serbia to the Serbs and Russia, also took up an invite. Monaco were also invited, but could not afford to travel. Christian Michelis did visit Northern Cyprus to represent the NF Board - a visit that was picked up on by the Greek Cypriot media and almost certainly started the pressure that would lead to the game in Monaco being cancelled.

Played in the 28,000 capacity stadium that Ahmet Esenyl's father helped build in Lefkosa, the matches were beamed live back to Lapland and Kosovo, but only a few hundred locals scattered the stadium. Mehmet Ali Talat was presented to the teams before games and the national anthems were played. In the case of the Sápmi they had their own, but Northern Cyprus had to make do with the Turkish anthem.

# OUTCASTS: The Lands That FIFA Forgot

Northern Cyprus won both matches and the tournament even prompted coverage in the Greek Cypriot media. In the Cyprus Mail, Simon Bahcelli wrote: 'One could not ignore the enthusiasm with which the organisers took on the project. Sport and politics are not supposed to mix, but in Cyprus - as in many problematic places around the world - nothing is inseparable from politics. And this tournament, although refreshingly devoid of political dogma, either deliberate or inadverted (sic), sends a political message to those who will acknowledge it. As a Greek Cypriot friend told me after the match, "People shouldn't laugh at this. In a few years you people could surprise us."

"What about reunification?" I asked. She smiled wryly, but did not answer.'

**\*\*\*\*\*\*\*\*\*\*\***

Dubbed the Peace Cup, the tournament is the start of a new beginning for the KTFF. After that NF Board meeting in London, Taner Yolcu, who did not look too healthy then, stepped down after a heart attack. Elections were held at the KTFF and a new sheriff was in town. The KTFF needed someone with a good command of English and willing to take the idea of a proper national team forward. Cengiz Uzun was their man.

Born in Paphos in 1964, he and his family had to leave their properties after the invasion and move to Guzelyürt in the TRNC, where he finished his schooling before going to Turkey for an English language course. Now a deputy headmaster at a secondary school in Guzelyürt, Uzun, who has played and coached football and futsal since the age of 12, is also studying for a PHD in international terrorism and took up the challenge of trying to organize regular fixtures for a national side in the TRNC, which has three leagues of 14 teams each and 4,000 registered players. As the only NF Board member with this sort of structure and some reasonable stadia, Northern Cyprus was an obvious venue for the first World Cup for nations that do not exist.

Uzun, who also has a Greek Cypriot passport, argues that Northern Cyprus is very different to mainland Turkey and far more relaxed - something the holiday atmosphere and preponderance of betting shops and a shortage of mosques backs up to some degree, although perhaps not the thousands of Turkish troops.

**\*\*\*\*\*\*\*\*\*\*\***

A couple of months after the Northern Cyprus team had visited Lapland, the Embargoed campaign was set up by Ipek Ozerim, who had been a PR adviser to President Denktas. The plight of the Northern Cypriot footballers was a good stepping point for Embargoed. After the Monaco protests, a 'Balls to Embargoes' poster was launched with half-a-dozen mostly London-based Turkish Cypriot players asked to strip for a poster, including former Crystal Palace player Kerem Bashkal. Put out before the 2006 World Cup, the idea was to shame FIFA into embracing the Turkish Cypriots.

Yasin Kansu of Çetinkaya, top scorer in the Northern Cyprus league in recent seasons, also took everything bar his socks off for the poster. He explained: "Stripping off was a laugh, but there's a serious point too. We Turkish Cypriots have been forced to live under embargoes for 42 years. We voted for the solution in Cyprus and still we can't play football with the rest of the world. In a few years, I will be retiring and if this situation continues, I will never get the chance to play against first class international opposition and know just how good I am."

Embargoed were handed an even better PR opportunity in February 2007, when Arsenal decided to ban flags from the club's new Emirates stadium after some fans complained about a TRNC flag being waved at the ground by a Gunners' fan, northern Cypriot Mete Ahmed. The ban followed the launching of a petition by north London Greek Cypriots signed by 9,899 people in just a few weeks that led to a meeting between Arsenal managing director Keith Edelman and Ahmed. The petition included comments such as 'Death to the Turkish dogs' and 'F*ck the Koran', but Arsenal initially agreed to let Ahmed wave his flag after consultation with lawyers and the Home Office. Mass action by Greek Cypriots followed and Arsenal, understandably concerned about any trouble at the ground, decided to ban all international flags with the FA's blessing.

For Embargoed, this made Arsenal and the FA easy targets. Campaign chairman Bulent Osman, a former investment banker taking a sabbatical to help Embargoed, said: "A few weeks ago, calling an Indian a 'poppadom' caused an international outcry. Here we have a lifelong Arsenal fan, Mete, the victim of racial bullying simply for taking pride in his ethnic roots. He displayed the North Cyprus flag - which is his legal right - and it has resulted in verbal abuse, including death threats, while racist comments on the Greek petition have offended us all. Yet neither Arsenal nor the FA seem interested. It makes you wonder how serious they are about stamping out racism in football. Clearly this is not a concern if it targets Turks or Turkish Cypriots. They should hang their heads in shame."

Embargoed and the team at the KTFF are trying to find a solution to a conflict that few of the generation they aim to help can remember. Since the invasion in 1974 football has changed out of all proportion in terms of popularity and commercialism, as using the world's most popular sport as a tool to reinforce the idea of a nation was an easy option. The KTFF must also notice with some degree of envy the improvement in the football in the south. Unlike clubs from most small nations, the professional Greek Cypriot teams always manage to get through at least a couple of rounds in European football, although no club has qualified for the Champions League proper yet. The national team is also improving and in 2007 managed to thrash the Republic of Ireland 5-2 and draw 1-1 with the previous year's World Cup semi-finalists, Germany.

Relations are softening. The KTFF have met with the Cyprus FA in the south, but the meeting had to take place in a Hilton hotel, not in the Greek Cypriot association's offices, or else it could have been deemed a formal affair and given some credence. There were some constructive talks over youth football, but the KTFF did not like the suggestion that they become part of the Cyprus FA. What they want is a new FA set up, following the British model. The KTFF invited the Cyprus FA to the north, but they have yet to take up an invite to cross the eerie border, where empty buildings full of bullet holes remain just as they were when so suddenly abandoned three decades before.

So far, the idea of a Northern Cyprus national team has yet to stir much interest among the locals. The Turkish league on television remains more popular and crowds for national team matches are very low. But for Cengiz Uzun, the future lies most definitely in a Northern Cyprus team. He explains: "It will take a little time for the people to love their national team, but we are not terrorists. We have peaceful feelings towards our neighbours, so why should FIFA put bans on our players? These are questions to be answered by the Greeks.

"If we are given the chance to play internationals, we think in a couple of years we can reach the same level as the Greek Cypriots. If we are able to play internationals, we can transfer players abroad and this will motivate the players that are at home and will create a circle. The people here complain about the embargoes and people should do something and come and support their team, but they are not used to this. Instead, they go to watch the big league matches from Turkey. We have good players and a good national team. We are better than the other non-FIFA teams and we think we could be among the top 100 teams in FIFA."

For Uzun, his personal quest is to launch the Northern Cyprus team at an unsuspecting sporting world with a series of games culminating in a World Cup for nations that does not exist in his own homeland. But his plans and those of the KTFF are about to clash in spectacular style with the ambitions of Jean Luc Kit, Christian Michelis and the internet enthusiasts of the NF Board.

# CHAPTER TEN

# The Language Of Football: Occitània

*"The victory has already been won, as the victory is sport."*
Pèire Costa, President, Associacion Occitana de Fotbòl

## 15 April 2006, Vendargues, France

A FEW HUNDRED supporters mingle around the small municipal stadium at Vendargues, several kilometres outside of Montpellier in southern France. A drum is being noisily beaten, one man sports an accordion that wheezes away and a handful of red flags showing the ancient Occitan cross flutter in the wind. By the pitchside, a table sells Occitan football shirts alongside a pile of deflated footballs and pin badges for the NF Board that Jean Luc Kit has brought along. Kit sits up in the stand with his file of potential members, all colour-coded depending on their status. Alongside him is Christian Michelis and the delegation from Northern Cyprus, which includes Cengiz Uzun and the TRNC's Minister for Sport.

"Some people back home have criticised us for bringing such a big party," sighs Uzun, looking resigned to this sort of criticism. With KTFF officials, ministers and three journalists, the Northern Cyprus party includes 36 people, but they have at last made it to the southern Mediterranean coast for an 'international' football match. While Northern Cyprus is a relatively new creation, too new and problematic for FIFA or UEFA to consider, their opponents are a team from a 'country' that has not existed for centuries - Occitània.

Occitània occupied large swathes of what is today southern France and was controlled by various factions from Dukes of Aquitaine, the Counts of Foix and Toulouse and the Catalan kings up to the thirteenth century. From the thirteenth century to the seventeenth century, the French kings conquered Occitània and started to enforce the French language on its inhabitants. Even before the French invasion, Occitània was never united politically. What glued the country together was its language and its culture. The French had started trying to get rid of Occitan as far back as 1539, when Francis I issued an ordinance insisting that French instead of Occitan be used in political administration. The language remained in common usage for centuries, but the French stepped up their attempts to eradicate Occitan in 1881, when children speaking the language at school began to be punished due to a government order from a minister, Jules Ferry. Amazingly, the language survived and Occitan writer Frédéric Mistral won the Nobel Prize for literature in 1904, but French slowly gained the upper hand in the twentieth century.

Still the language survived and a campaign to keep the Occitan language and culture alive continued through literature, music and - from 2003 - through football with the help of the Associacion Occitana de Fotbòl (AOF) and its president, Pèire Costa. Costa played briefly for Châteauroux in the French Second Division before a broken knee ended his football dreams. Still slim and only in his thirties, Costa looks like he could still manage a game, but after his professional football dreams were over he was increasingly radicalized by the idea of keeping alive the Occitan culture that he grew up with. This led to his taking a rare job at an independent foundation aimed at doing just this. The AOF is part of this brief, but very much Costa's idea.

Before the kick-off against Northern Cyprus, Costa makes a short speech in Oc to the couple of hundred people present, saying: "The victory has already been won, as the victory is sport."

Costa has been offered jobs by the French state to promote Occitan, but suspects this is simply to neuter activities such as the nascent football side. Along with the rest of the activists at Vendargues, Costa is convinced that the French government are still trying to eradicate the Occitan tongue.

***********

Occitan is a Latin-based language similar to Spanish, Italian and French and there are half-a-dozen variations of the language. In geographical terms, Occitània today is best described as the southern part of France comprising Provence, Drôme-Vivarais, Auvergne, Limousin, Guyenne, Gascony and Languedoc, a name which translates literally as the language of Oc. But Occitània also comprises the Occitan valleys of the Italian Alps, where the language was given legal status in 1999. Occitan is spoken in Monaco, alongside Monégasque, and in the Aran Valley in Spain, where the language was also given official status as part of a statute to guarantee the status of the Catalan language.

There are an estimated fourteen to fifteen million inhabitants in Occitània today, but, according to a 1999 census, native speakers of the language number only 610,000 - mostly of the older generation - with another million people exposed to the language in some form. Unlike Italy and Spain, there is no protection for Occitan in France, but activists like Costa are trying to counter that.

Role models for would-be Occitanians tend to be from the past, such as ancient seer Nostradamus. More recent influences include philosopher Albert Camus - although he was actually born in Algeria, whose national team he featured for as a goalkeeper - and cartoonist Daniel Goossens.

Musically, Occitan cultural influence has grown in recent years. Popular French reggae group Massilia Sound System and the Fabulous Trobadors of Toulouse were espousing Occitan back in the early 1980s, and are still pushing the message. François Ridel, who goes under the stage name of Tatou, was the leader of Massilia Sound System and went on to form another popular French-based band, Moussu T, which is still spreading the Occitan word today. Ridel told Songlines magazine: "We don't write Occitan lyrics for the sake of erudition. I'm part of a new generation who speaks the language from choice... I'm against the centralised French state... France is way behind the rest of Europe in the recognition of minority languages and it's getting worse."

The fans at Vendargues, which is supported by Occitànian businessmen, tend to agree with Ridel. The backers are older, but most of the fans are younger activists that are part of this new breed that Ridel is talking about. People that want to speak Occitan instead of French. What Costa wants to achieve with the team is to provide another outlet for Occitan culture outside of literature and music.

The excitable, friendly Costa says: "We say that Occitània is not a region, but a nation without a state, which is delimited by the Occitan tongue. There would not be Occitan country if there would not be the Occitan tongue. We wanted to promote a new way for the Occitan identity and we loved football. Before, Occitan was always promoted through literature and poetry. Now with the football, we always have a party afterwards. We call this the third period of the match."

In terms of sport, Occitània is mainly rugby territory. The most well-known footballers to come from this long-dead country are eccentric former French national keeper Fabien Barthez and another international for Les Blues, Gilles Grimandi. Neither are likely to be pulling on an Occitanian shirt as Costa has to step carefully around the French Football Federation by only selecting amateur players. He explains: "We have not had any connection with the French federation, but I know that they know about us. Our players are all amateurs; one does not want problems with the FFF. A few years ago, Brittany wanted to play pros in a game and that was stopped."

In a country that has, throughout its history, been shot through by racial conflicts, the idea of a team resembling a nation long gone could sound like a template for white nationalism. Costa insists this is not the case and, indeed, Occitània field a black player against Northern Cyprus.

"The whole world could play for us as long as they could speak Occitan," says Costa. "The only criterion of selection is of speaking the tongue. Our selector is a Guyanese woman. She has lived in Montpellier for five years and learned the language. It must be the only case in the world of a female trainer in a male selection."

The AOF regularly puts out beach football and futsal sides, but first fielded an eleven-a-side 'national' team in 2005, when they took on Monaco's amateur side at Sauclières à Béziers. That game came about through the NF Board and contact with Christian Michelis. Another NF Board enthusiast, Thierry Marcade, a school teacher from Marseille, tried to bring over the Tibet side based in India for a game, only for the Tibetans to be refused visas by the French government. Politics at play again.

The French government allowed the Northern Cyprus party visas, but insisted to the AOF that no flags should be on show. That proved pointless as the teams are led out by two young girls holding an Occitan flag and a Northern Cyprus standard - a potent image that underlines how powerless remote legislators such as FIFA are. Like the Greenlanders when they took on Tibet, the AOF needed to play the match at a municipal stadium, as hosting a pariah team such as Northern Cyprus would involve sanctions for any club team involved.

***********

There are also larger sporting events aimed at preserving a language. Ironically, one of the biggest is the Francophone Games. Held every four years, the Francophone Games features teams from the 56 members of the Francophonie. Essentially a French Commonwealth Games, the event involves three teams from Canada: one for Quebec, one for New Brunswick - the only officially bilingual Canadian province - and another covering the rest of the country. Belgium's team, though, is restricted simply to the French-speaking part of their country with the Flemish area not invited. Staged five times since the first event in Casablanca in Morocco in 1989, the most recent games was in Niamey in the African country of Niger. Unlike the Commonwealth Games, football is a fixture among the Francophonie, but was restricted to under-19 teams in Niger, where the Ivory Coast emerged as the winner. The next Francophone Games will be in the Lebanese capital of Beirut.

# The Language Of Football: Occitània

The success of the Francophone Games, which has seen between 1,500 and 3,000 athletes entering, also led to an attempt to keep the Portuguese language alive outside of Portugal by using sport. Football was again high on the agenda. The first Lusofonia Games were staged in 2006 in the former Portuguese colony of Macao, now a special administrative region of China. Entrants ranged from Portugal and Brazil to the tiny African island state of São Tomé and Príncipe. India also took part because the island of Goa was a former Portuguese colony and the language is still spoken there. The football event featured mainly under-23 teams and Portugal won the gold medal, beating Angola 2-0 in the final, with another former Portuguese colony in Africa, Cape Verde, taking bronze. There was also a futsal event that featured a few bizarre scores. Eventual winners Brazil beat East Timor by 76-0. Some achievement in two halves of just twenty minutes each and probably not a match that East Timor will want to remember.

The game at Vendargues, which is being broadcast live on local radio, is proving a far closer and testy affair. Occitània are holding their own in the first half against Northern Cyprus. Coskun Ulusoy makes his presence felt despite recently breaking his nose in a Federation Cup match back home. An early shot for the home side flies wide before Julian Cambon is shown the yellow card for a clumsy foul on a Northern Cyprus player. The Occitan number five, Ciril Campos, follows Cambon into the referee's book soon after, when he is also shown a yellow card for a rash challenge. Northern Cyprus have the better touches. Pony-tailed midfielder Erdinc Börekci looks the best player on the pitch, but Northern Cyprus are not troubling the Occitan goalkeeper, Guillaume Daumond, who lives nearby and was instrumental in bringing the match to Vendargues.

Towards the end of the first half, Daumond is exposed by his defence and Ayhan Demir is put through with only the Occitan keeper to beat but fails to control the ball properly. The best chance for the visitors is lost. Daumond then appears to handle the ball outside of his box. The handful of Northern Cyprus fans in the stand bang their seats noisily, but the referee eschews a red card, awarding only a free-kick which Dervis Kolcu drives straight into the Occitan wall. That proves the last threat to Daumond's goal and the teams go in level at half-time.

In the second half, Börekci starts to impose himself more on the game and the fitter Northern Cyprus team take control. Ali Oraloslu opens the scoring for the visitors with a superb goal, driving a shot from the right hand side of the goal into the opposite corner past Daumond. Occitània respond by substituting forward Yves Niabia Mokuba, but Northern Cyprus remain on top. Kemal Uçaner misses a good chance straight after Mokuba goes off. Northern Cyprus hit the post again before Oraloslu chests the ball down skilfully and drives an excellent volley towards Daumond, who spills the ball into his net to put the visitors two up. Kolcu then finishes the game off with an excellent run and shot for a third in the seventy fifth minute. Northern Cyprus make a flurry of substitutions to give their large squad a run-out, while only a good stop from Daumond with his feet prevents a fourth before the game ends.

Northern Cyprus captain Hüseyin Amcaoglu throws his jersey into the crowd in the style of Reading goalkeeper Marcus Hahnemann as the two teams traipse off. Despite the defeat, no-one is downcast. Behind the cheerless concrete stand, wine and crisps are on offer to everyone, drums are beaten, the accordion squeezed and Occitan flags waved. Jean Luc Kit and Christian Michelis talk with Thierry Marcade, all pleased that the NF Board is moving from an idea being debated on the internet to one that provides real football matches.

Kit is again dressed in black with his trademark sunglasses despite little threat of the sun appearing in the chilly April of southern France. Getting into his car, he removes his keys and out pops a souvenir key ring from the cult 1960s television series, The Prisoner. The series starred Patrick McGoohan as an un-named spy always dressed in black, who is kidnapped and taken away to a village where no-one has a name, simply a number. Inside Kit's small car, the sun visors are all stuffed with road maps and a tube of cigars lies close to hand. For Kit, the match clearly means a great deal. The NF Board is starting to move from a fairly amateurish website and reams of files identifying and categorising potential teams to a reality. "This is the real football for me, football for the people," says Kit excitably.

With the crisps and wine hoovered up, the fans and team all head back into the centre of Vendargues to a small community centre, where seemingly everyone at the match from the referees to the players and sponsors, sit down for the obligatory third period; a banquet. At the table, in true football fashion all the Çetinkaya players sit together at one end of the table with the players from assorted other Cypriot clubs at the opposite end. In the middle, Cengiz Uzun sits down with Michelis and Kit. Bread, red wine and rosé are spread out over the tables. A traditional Occitan fish dish is served up. As the wine flows, the accordion appears again. The good-natured Coskun Ulusoy gamely gets up to join in the dancing with the Occitanians, watched nervously by the rest of the Northern Cyprus party.

Perhaps this was how international football started out, as some form of cultural exchange, although the idea of roast beef for everyone, English folk songs and Ronaldinho up dancing in a local village hall after the England vs Brazil international curtain-raiser at Wembley seems a little hard to visualise.

# The Language Of Football: Occitània

Before the game, the Northern Cyprus party had been shown the local sites by the Occitanians. For Cengiz Uzun, the trip has been a success and he is able to relax after the match - even if he cannot stomach the Occitan food. For Uzun and the Northern Cyprus party, a policy of keeping the match details quiet beforehand has proved a success; Northern Cyprus have played another game abroad. Another step to what the KTFF and the Turkish Cypriot politicians hope will be some form of recognition.

The NF Board members are happy to see their dream a reality, Costa pleased to have played a part in this. Kit and Michelis talk of their plans, of other teams that could be drawn into the world of the NF Board. The discussion turns to the Falklands team that played at the Island Games and their lack of opponents.

"There was once a team on South Georgia too," says Kit excitably. Michelis rolls his eyes then starts to do what initially appears to be an impression of a mouse before saying something in French.

"I say to Jean Luc 'who could South Georgia play?' Maybe the penguins from the Kergulen Islands," says Michelis with a smile, referring to another remote South Atlantic island claimed by France.

"But there is a pitch in South Georgia," insists Kit. "There is proof on the internet."

Michelis smiles, obviously used to this sort of undimmed enthusiasm, but Cengiz Uzun looks on baffled, unsure quite what he and the KTFF are getting involved with in the NF Board.

By ten o'clock, the third period of the match is over and the Northern Cyprus team return to their hotel. The Occitanians get into their cars, big Occitan flags hanging from the windows and drive away into the night sounding their horns, pleased at another successful day in keeping the idea of Occitània alive.

# CHAPTER ELEVEN

# Monaco

*"We are caught between a rock and a hard place. If we existed sportively,
some people maintain that we would put the Monaco AS in peril,
susceptible of being excluded from the French championship,
by virtue of our mere existence."*
**Blaise Giffoni, President, Fédération Monégasque de Football**

## 22 April 2006, Cap D'Ail, France

A WEEK AFTER Costa's Occitànians took on Northern Cyprus, another NF
Board fixture kicks off further along the French coast as Monaco host
Kosovo. Unlike Occitània, centuries of deal-making have enabled Monaco to
maintain their independence, first secured in 1419 under the House of
Grimaldi. Prince Rainier revived the slumbering principality in the latter half
of the twentieth century after marrying the American film star, Grace Kelly,
adding a sprinkling of showbiz sparkle to the trendy Med. Today, Monaco is
a member of many international organisations, including the United Nations.
After Prince Rainier died, Prince Albert succeeded his father as head of state
on 6 April 2005 and continues to rule as a hereditary monarch, choosing a
Minister of State from three candidates presented by the French government.
There is a National Council with 16 members elected by a majority system
and another eight by proportional representation. The Monégasque compete
in the Olympic Games and at sports such as tennis; Monaco provided the
opposition for Greg Rusedski, when he had his Davis Cup debut for Great
Britain in 1996. Could it be more of a country?

As the youthful Prince Albert is a renowned football fan and Monaco is in
the UN, an application to UEFA would appear a formality, surely. Yet Thierry
Petit's national side are not even welcome in their own land and must play
matches 150 metres inside France at Cap D'Ail.

The only stadium in Monaco is the 18,500-seat Stade Louis. The ground is
home to the principality's only professional club, AS Monaco (ASM), who
play in the French league and regularly, in recent times, the ground has hosted
the European Super Cup match at the start of each season, which pits the
winners of Champions League and UEFA Cup in a battle for supremacy.

# Monaco

Monaco are still one of French football's strongest clubs - they reached the Champions League final in 2004 - but by the end of the 1990s, some Monégasque football fans felt that the club no longer represented the principality. Native Monégasques playing at or near the top level in France or anywhere else have been rare and hard to recall in recent years. Olivier Lechner reportedly had a trial at Aston Villa, but was not invited back. That is not much for Monégasque football fans to hang on to. But by the end of the twentieth century, the idea of the NF Board had taken root in the minds of the Monégasque Christian Michelis and his French friend, Jean Luc Kit.

NF Board president Michelis works in the tourism industry in Monaco and helped organise a league between teams from companies operating in the principality. There are about 800 players in 24 teams such as Monaco Télécom, Grimaldi Forum and Carrefour Monaco. Though mostly non-Monégasque, this was a good basis for helping start a national team that would provide at least one NF Board member and make contact with other potential affiliates. So in 2000, Michelis and a group of Monégasques formed a national team with Andre Brezzo as the initial president of the Fédération Monégasque de Football (FMF). The team made its debut on 14 July 2001, after trooping off to Freiburg in Germany to meet the touring Tibetan team, fresh from their recent encounter with Greenland in Copenhagen. Monaco won 2-1 with Damien Choisit registering the principality's first international goal.

In 2002, the FMF invited Gibraltar up the Mediterranean coast for a match in the principality only to find that their initiative did not go down too well with AS Monaco or even the Monégasque government. Home matches at the Stade Louis stadium were out of the question. Michelis explains: "In Monaco, they are afraid they will throw [ASM] out of the French league. When Monaco have a good season in the French league, there is a lot of noise from the other French clubs like Lyon and Marseille. Without the guarantee of the French federation, they will never approach UEFA. The idea is not even to create a league, but just to have a national team."

For Monaco's government, the FMF is accepted but not encouraged, and after the Northern Cyprus game was cancelled, rumours abounded that players employed by the government were put under pressure at work not to play. All Paul Masseron, Monaco's government advisor for the interior, would say is: "The FMF was freely formed among Monégasques in 2000 by simple declaration to the authorities and is consequently open exclusively to nationals. In order to allow this federation to join the (sic) UEFA, it would be necessary to be able to regroup all of the players of this discipline in the principality and that discussions be held with the French Football Federations."

113

# OUTCASTS: The Lands That FIFA Forgot

So far, no-one in Monaco appears keen on having that 'discussion'. The reason given is that AS Monaco looked at places such as Wales, where clubs such as Cardiff City, playing in the English league pyramid, have been excommunicated and barred from once regular forays into European competition via the Welsh Cup. With UEFA's help, the League of Wales was set up and only clubs playing in that league can now qualify for Europe to represent Wales. In theory the possibilty remains that Cardiff, Swansea or Wrexham could win the Carling or FA Cup and represent England. Not even Welsh clubs playing in the lower echelons of England's non-league pyramid, such as Merthyr Tydfil or Newport, can be offered a place in UEFA competitions unless they renounce all links with England. For Monaco, the 2005 Champions League runners-up, this is a nightmare scenario - not least because if a Monégasque league was formed there would only be one club in it.

Even with these concerns over protecting their unique situation, AS Monaco have still used the principality's independence for its own ends. French league regulations bar non-French internet betting activities, as gambling is a state monopoly in France. In 2006, Monaco put this to the test by signing a sponsorship with Austrian online betting firm bwin.com Interactive Entertainment. AS Monaco tried to cite the principality's independence and refused to take down hoardings until the league refused to sanction a match against Le Mans and the Monégasques eventually caved in. That sort of carry on is what agitates the other leading French clubs.

With an amateur side, the FMF even explored trying to enter the UEFA Regions Cup, but that was not acceptable to the principality's government as it would have meant playing as part of France. In 2005, the FMF regrouped and Blaise Giffoni took over as president, Michelis was Head of Logistics, which presumably meant finding opposition, and Christoph North took over as General Secretary. North says: "Our difficulty for being recognized is the Association Sportive de Monaco Football Club. There is a danger from government that ASM FC would be excluded from France League if Football Federation of Monaco exists. We tried to have some discussions with France Federation and French league, but actually unsuccessfully to get a written response that AS Monaco FC will not be excluded. Despite all [these matches], we still don't have recognition of our government as a real federation, but some sponsors and organisations are with us."

Despite that lack of recognition, the Monégasque government still managed to force the cancellation of the match against Northern Cyprus. The theory among some seasoned watchers is that the 'Wales excuse' is just a cover. After all, Liechtenstein has no league and their top club, Vaduz, play in the Swiss second tier. One local football journalist, who preferred not to be named, says: "AS Monaco is so powerful and has such an image that they didn't want any shadow on it."

\*\*\*\*\*\*\*\*\*\*\*

Experiences such as the Monaco national team's trip to play a club side, FC Marsa in Tunisia, when some of the opposition seemed to think they were playing against AS Monaco, will do nothing to endear the FMF to the principality's club side. For the average Monégasque, AS Monaco is likely to stay as their 'national team'. The FMF do not expect to triumph against such overpowering institutional opposition, but Giffoni insists that the national team is not about being a rival to AS Monaco. Giffoni told Onze Mondial magazine: "That is really not what motivates us. Simply, for amateurs born in Monaco it is the only means of existence. For it has been a long time ago since a native Monégasque has taken part in the AS Monaco. Our final goal is, one day, to be affiliated to FIFA. But, we are caught between a rock and a hard place. If we existed sportively (sic), some people maintain that we would put the Monaco AS in peril, susceptible of being excluded from the French championship, by virtue of our mere existence.

"It's Utopia… I simply know that Jean-Louis Campora (former president of the ASM and member of the Monégasque parliament) is not for it. The idea doesn't come from him; so he has done everything possible to block the situation. However, Prince Albert supports us, but he can't get involved, at the risk of putting himself in a conflict with respect to the club."

So, Monaco must soldier on, a national team seemingly unloved by anyone with the power to approach UEFA.

At Cap D'Ail, a crowd of about 150 people - mostly Kosovars from nearby Nice - prepare for a rare opportunity to watch their 'national' side. The game is something of a mismatch as Kosovo, which has been run under a United Nations mandate since the Serb Army was forced out of the province, have around two million people to choose from. Monaco has a population of real Monégasques - as opposed to overseas tax exiles - of around 8,000 people. Thierry Petit, Monaco's coach and an assistant to then AS Monaco manager Didier Deschamps, has fewer than 100 Monégasque players to chose from for his squad.

The Kosovars took 17 players - all from their local leagues - to Cap D'Ail with the party flying to Milan, then getting a bus to the French coastline. The Monégasque team is over-run by superior opponents. The Kosovans score three goals without reply in the first half through Haxhi Zeka, Uliks Emra and Dukgijn Gashi. In the second half, Monaco manage to score, but the Kosovans make a rash of substitutions and score four more goals to complete a 7-1 rout. Kosovan captain Arben Zhejci says: "We have reached our goal in Monaco. We are pleased with the performance and we have also pleased the coaching staff and the federation. This win gives us hope to build a strong team."

For Kosovo and their federation, membership of UEFA and FIFA remains the ultimate goal, but the Monégasque must continue to tiptoe around international football, with the NF Board seemingly their only option.

The Kosovans set off on a long, complicated journey back to their homeland with all of the 17 players selected for the trip by their coach, Muharrem Sahiti, happy at getting a run-out. Sahiti says: "I am very pleased with the team's performance even though we had predicted a stronger opponent. However, I want to emphasize that our players have been fantastic. The fact that we do not play many international matches may have inspired the players to give their all this time."

As Kosovo set off home, Sahiti is unaware that, despite having secured a resounding win, the match would prove to be his last in charge of the Kosovan team, who are about to welcome home a hero.

# CHAPTER TWELVE

# And Then There Was One: Kosovo

*"Despite riots, revenge killings, limited electricity and water, racial hatred, cluster munitions everywhere, we did a great job and helped kick start football in Kosovo."*
**Scotty Lee, football coach**

## 23 May 2006, Montenegro

CROWDS CELEBRATE in the street as Serbian president Boris Tadic accepts the preliminary results of a vote for independence in Montenegro that severs ties between the pair. Yugoslavia is all but a memory. From the terrible wars that led to Croatia and Bosnia-Herzegovina breaking away, through the less violent departure of the Slovenians and Macedonians, the peaceful vote in Montenegro is a successful endgame. The former Yugoslavian republic set up by General Tito after the war has been disbanded.

On the football field, the creation of a Montenegro national team could not be simpler. By the start of September, the newly formed Football Association of Montenegro (FAM), led by president Dejan Savicevic, is welcomed into FIFA's offices by Sepp Blatter to discuss their entry. The Montenegrins' admission is then formally discussed a week later at a FIFA congress. At UEFA's January 2007 congress in Düsseldorf, the FAM is officially welcomed into the European fold. Simple when the will is there.

Entry to UEFA competitions for the 2007/08 season is confirmed and the Montenegro national team kicks off successfully with a friendly against Hungary in March 2007 that produces a 2-1 home win. But Montenegro's peaceful arrival as a European state and a national team is watched carefully in Kosovo, where the break-up of the Yugoslav republic is most certainly not over.

What was the heart of the Serbian empire until the fourteenth century was over-run by the Ottoman empire in 1389 before the Serbs regained control in 1913. Kosovo later became - and remains in the eyes of many Serbs - a

117

province of Serbia. Kosovo had always enjoyed a level of autonomy, but that was stripped away by Slobodan Milosevic when he became Serbian president in 1989. This escalated rising tensions between Slavs and Albanians, who had lived side-by-side in Kosovo since the eighth century. This blew up after Milosevic made a speech in 1991 to hundreds of thousands of his people celebrating the defeat that had heralded the Ottoman occupation. Milosevic likened the problems in Yugoslavia to those endured by Serbs in the fourteenth century.

Increasingly disenchanted at Serbian repression, an Albanian resistance movement was formed. Its leaders declared unilateral independence and the Kosovo Liberation Army began attacking Serb targets, which led to a crackdown. Milosevic refused to call off this repression and the United Nations launched air strikes against Serb targets in Kosovo and Serbia. Milosevic eventually backed down, losing his grip on power and ending up at a war crimes tribunal in The Hague, which was 50 hours from delivering a verdict when it learnt of Milosevic's death, from a heart attack. Ever since Milosevic was banished, Kosovo has been a political anomaly effectively run by the UN. Tensions still remain between the 2.1 million Albanian Kosovans and the 175,000 Serbs that stayed behind after the fighting stopped.

Into this volatile void stepped Scotty Lee, an ebullient and enthusiastic football fan. Lee had driven truckloads of aid during the earlier Yugoslav conflict in Bosnia. Distressed by the suffering he had seen, in 1996 Lee set up Spirit of Soccer, a hugely successful initiative that involved him travelling around Bosnia-Herzegovina in a van with footballs and cones offering training sessions. The only proviso was that if the kids wanted to join in his training sessions, then they had to listen to his mine awareness courses.

"What do you need to be a professional footballer?" Lee would routinely ask his charges. He got a wide range of responses, but rarely the one that he would reply with: "These," he would say, tapping his thighs, "a pair of legs."

\*\*\*\*\*\*\*\*\*\*\*

After Bosnia, Lee went to live in the United States, but returned to the former Yugoslavia for a second Spirit of Soccer campaign in Kosovo. Like his earlier visit, this was documented in a Channel Four film. Lee isn't on anyone's side and simply loves football, loves training kids. After pitching up in the Kosovan capital of Prishtina, Lee gave football coaching sessions to more than 2,000 children and says: "Despite riots, revenge killings, limited electricity and water, racial hatred, cluster munitions everywhere, we did a great job and helped kick start football in Kosovo."

# And Then There Was One: Kosovo

After Kosovo, Lee moved on to do just the same in Cambodia. Since 1996, Spirit of Soccer has re-equipped 450 schools and clubs with more than 7,000 footballs and distributed 2,000 books combining football coaching and mine awareness in Bosnia, Kosovo and Cambodia. It is an inspirational undertaking.

Lee usually travels with an English-speaking local. In Kosovo that person was Afrim Toverlani, a stalwart of Kosovo's biggest club, Prishtina FC, which dates back to 1922. Toverlani made his Prishtina debut in 1979 and played in the old Yugoslav First Division between 1983 and 1988, when Prishtina were relegated. Toverlani also played 15 times for Yugoslavia's under-19 and under-20 sides and stayed with Prishtina until retiring in 2003. By then, the Football Federation of Kosovo (FFK), which was formed in 1946, had seceded from Yugoslavia. An amateur three-division league was running and the people in the province, seeing the likes of Bosnia making it into the UEFA fold, began dreaming of their own national team.

In a country where organized crime is prevalent, even football has had to endure some scams and that has hit the reviving football scene. Toverlani helped expose a training session held in Kosovo by Swedes claiming to be providing people with UEFA licences. Even Swedish national team coach Lars Lagerblack became involved to confirm to the participants that the licences were not from UEFA at all. Football is not easy in Kosovo and getting a national team together is even more problematic.

The Albanian Football Federation put out a team against Kosovo in Prishtina in 2002 and squeaked past the home side 1-0. The same year, the UN helped the Kosovans send a junior national side to the Dana Cup tournament (the world's biggest annual youth international football competition) in the Danish town of Fredrikshavn, home to Greenland's coach, Jens Tang Olesen. Like Scotty Lee, Juan Pablo Covacich turned up in Kosovo as a volunteer in spring 2001, but was charged by the UN with helping to organise a boy's team. He explains: "Football doesn't care about different ethnic groups or countries and it makes people happy, regardless of their social, environmental or whatever situation."

Covacich selected a 30-boy squad with as many different ethnic backgrounds as possible and took his team training twice a week in Janjeve, a small village in the mountains south east of Prishtina. Covacich adds: "This is very important. In a professional football team you seldom only have one ethnic group because the players all come from different parts of the particular country. So they have to be able to get along with each other. These boys all come from all the different ethnic groups. They are Roma, Ashkali, Albanian and Croatian and they play football together every day. They are very eager to learn and some of them are really good players. At least they are the best example for a multi-ethnic football team."

# OUTCASTS: The Lands That FIFA Forgot

Held in July 2002, the Dana Cup featured hundreds of different teams at various age groups and Covacich's team were to finish second in their group. After the Dana Cup, he left the organisation to the locals to concentrate on women's football in Kosovo, which had been in its infancy before the war and was almost wiped out by the conflict. The momentum for a full national team was lost to some degree. Until, in 2005, the FFK was invited by Cengiz Uzun to send a team to Northern Cyprus for the Peace Cup and matches against the hosts and the Lapland side. This provided some impetus and the match in Monaco followed a few months later only for the idea of an organized national team to wither again, foiled by lack of opponents.

"For now, we don't have an organized national team," sighs Toverlani, now the sports editor at the local Express newspaper, a role he combines with coaching the under-19 team at his old club. "FFK doesn't want to be a member of the non FIFA nations. They have had contact with UEFA and do not want to play against non FIFA teams because we are waiting for the status of Kosovo to be decided and then to apply for membership in UEFA and FIFA. If we join UEFA, we will have greatest supporters in [the] region because our people love very much football."

Attempts at resolving the issue of Kosovo's independence (or not) under UN mediator and former Finnish president Martti Ahtisaari have not produced much progress. An independence plan has been unveiled and Kosovo's Prime Minister, Agim Ceku, said: "Ahtisaari's document made the future of Kosovo very clear and opens the way to Kosovo's independence."

His counterpart in Serbia, Vojislav Kostunica, refused to even attend the meeting when this document was unveiled in February 2007. Even the Serb's president, Boris Tadic, a pro-western liberal, said: "Serbia will never accept the independence of Kosovo. An imposed independence would represent a dangerous and political precedent."

With Russia, still a key political player in the region, and its President, Vladimir Putin, particularly concerned that Kosovan independence could herald a domino effect which would topple the troublesome 'Federal Subjects' such as Chechnya into nation or republic status, Russia uses its membership of the UN security council to put the Serbs' case. The stand-off looks set to continue. This means that the FFK has to tread warily around the politics. But on 21 February 2006, two FFK representatives, Fadil Vokrri and Fazil Berisha, were accepted by FIFA in Zurich for talks, a move that probably did not go down well with the Serbs, or the Russians.

Kosovo's international aspirations were discussed at the meeting, but top of the agenda were problems faced by local players trying to transfer to clubs outside of Kosovo. After the meeting, FIFA issued a statement saying: "Mr Erzik explained that, according to article 10 of the FIFA statutes, any association which is responsible for organising and supervising football in its country can apply for membership, pointing out that the expression 'country' refers to an independent state recognised by the international community.

"In this context, FIFA indicated that it would follow the discussions opened by the United Nations in Vienna regarding the 'final status' of Kosovo. The delegation from the Kosovo football community understood and accepted this explanation, and stated that they only wished to discuss football-related matters and problems faced by Kosovo players. Both delegations considered the meeting as positive and fruitful and agreed to await the results of the discussions initiated by the international community regarding Kosovo."

\*\*\*\*\*\*\*\*\*\*\*

Having decided to shun the NF Board, the Kosovo team was grinding to a halt after the victorious Monaco match - until the man who could well turn out to be the saviour of the Kosovo team turned up for work in September 2006. Like Toverlani, Edmond Rugova also played for Prishtina FC, but in 1984 he left what was then Yugoslavia and signed up for the New York Cosmos in the hey-day of the National American Soccer League. A strong forward, Rugova left the Cosmos and moved on to the Kansas City Comets before retiring and moving into coaching at youth level at the likes of Rockhurst University. He stayed in the US for 22 years, but was tempted back to his homeland by the idea of taking a national team that did not exist into the international arena.

The solid-looking Rugova explains: "The FFK has survived since 1946, even through the 80s and 90s, the most difficult and horrific times of persecution and war, thanks to individuals and private donors who kept the leagues, teams and players active from funding out of their own pockets - and still do. I have come to Kosovo specifically to run the national team as well as to organise the other and develop other age groups. The programme that I have submitted [to the FFK] includes short-term, mid-term and long-term goals for the development and identity of the national team of Kosovo. That includes a series of games and consistent and sustainable schedule.

"We are indeed in a very strange situation [in] finding teams to play against, but we are working hard to make sure that changes. We have contacted and are in the process of establishing relations with many federations, especially with the neighbouring countries as well as [the] US soccer federation."

Making friends with the Kosovans is a sure way to make enemies of the Serbs and the Russians, as Rugova admits, saying: "[There is] no direct help from any federation so far, but a lot of well-wishers and a lot of moral support.

# OUTCASTS: The Lands That FIFA Forgot

A lot of work is ahead of us, under very difficult circumstances, with problems of infrastructure, finances, etc. My ambition is restructuring the youth system and [to] develop the talent that is abound in Kosova, which I believe is crucial in having a competitive and successful national team. My ambition is also to build a Kosova team that every Kosovar and Albanian will be proud of, that will compete for a spot in the World Cup in 2010."

Rugova's first match in charge on this long and seemingly impossible quest was on 28 November 2006 against an all-star selection of Kosovans playing professionally abroad. The match proved a massive draw with 15,000 people cramming into the dilapidated Prishtina FC stadium to see an exciting 3-3 draw, with Ahmet Jonuzi, Ilir Nallbani and Fisnkik Gashi netting for Rugova's team and Fitim Kasapi, Njazi Kuqi and Debatik Curri for the all-stars.

Many of that team, like Marseille midfielder Lorik Cana, are not just earning a living abroad, they have already decided to further their international ambitions elsewhere. If Kosovo does gain independence and acceptance into UEFA and FIFA, the national team of neighbouring Albania could take a hammering.

"More than half the Albanian team are from Kosovo. The main reason for this is that they are unable to play international games with Kosovo," explains Toverlani.

For the Kosovans, denied their own national identity, many would rather see themselves as Albanian than Yugoslavian or Serbian. The ties between the Kosovans and the Albanians on the sporting field were best demonstrated at an international match between Albania and the Ukraine, when the Albanian fans unveiled a giant Kovosan flag across an entire stand in a message of support for the Kosovars.

Kosovans turning out for Albania include Anderlecht's Besnik Hasi, Anorthosis Famugusta goalkeeper Arian Beqaj, Debatik Curri and Armend Dallki of FC Vorskla in the Ukraine, striker Bekim Kastrati of Eintracht Braunschweig, and Besart Berisha of Hamburg. Other players that would be eligible for Kosovo and that Rugova fancies in his squad include Besijan Idrizaj of Liverpool, Shefki Kuqi of Crystal Palace and Perparim Hetemaj, who plays in the Greek capital of Athens for AEK.

Kuqi's story is typical of the Kosovan footballer left searching for a game. Born in Kosovo, he was raised in Finland, where he broke into football with HJK Helsinki and then FC Lokerit before a £300,000 transfer brought him to England and Stockport County in 2001. A £1 million fee took him to Sheffield Wednesday before he moved on to Ipswich, then played briefly in the Premier League for Blackburn, netting seven goals in 15 games. His spectacular, belly-flopping goal celebration soon brought him lots of attention on Match of the Day. Competition for places at Ewood Park intensified with the arrival of South African international Benni McCarthy and Kuqi transferred to Crystal Palace for a reported £2.6 million in August 2006.

"I have had a conversation with each of these three [Idrizaj, Kuqi and Hetemaj] to share my thoughts about the future of Kosovo's football. These lads are included in my future plans," adds Rugova.

Kosova's potential new status brings an added dimension to the dilemma for Kuqi as he has, since 1999, been playing international football for Finland, for whom he has played 43 times, scoring five goals to the summer of 2007.

Valon Behrami of Serie A giants Lazio is another player that Rugova would like to bring into the Kosovan squad. There is also a large Kosovan expat community in Germany as a result of a guest worker programme instituted by the German government in the 1960s and 1970s. Rugova is going to spread his net wide, but whether all these players would all fall into line behind him remains to be seen. But with some degree of confidence, he says: "Combining these players that I just mentioned and the players and talent that exists in Kosova's super league with hard work I believe we will have one of the more competitive teams in the world. I have never been more excited about a project as I am now. It is a tremendous challenge that I gladly and proudly accept and I know that with better organisation, hard work and commitment Kosova will be [on the] international stage, where it belongs."

\*\*\*\*\*\*\*\*\*\*\*

For the time being, this dream remains distant. Rugova cannot call on these players as he has nothing to offer them bar the occasional friendly game for his Kosovo national team, which is usually against a team from the Kosovo top flight. This has proved an arduous process. On 14 March 2007, Rugova's team took on FC Kek and were stuffed 0-3, but he is not about to give up and wants to arrange a game a month against sides from the 16-club Kosovo super league.

That programme could all change if the UN mediators win a breakthrough. A decision on independence was originally scheduled for 2007, although at the time of writing that looks unlikely. If the Kosovans do win their independence and a place in the UN, then UEFA would have to accept the Football Federation of Kosovo (FFK) as a member.

A UEFA spokesperson confirmed: "UEFA has had some contacts with the Kosovo federation. If Kosovo meets all criteria to become a UEFA member, and if a hypothetical application for membership is accepted by the UEFA congress, the players who have played for the national team of Albania and others would be able to choose which country they would like to represent."

At that point, stars like Cana and Kuqi will have to decide if they want to carry on playing for their adopted countries or play for the newly created nation that they were actually born in. With Rugova in charge, this could be one nascent national side that has a FIFA-legitamised future. It is certainly a story beginning, not ending, both from the point of view of international competitive football and providing kids with hope through schemes such as Spirit of Soccer.

**\*\*\*\*\*\*\*\*\*\*\***

Then, on 15 June, Kosovo got their big break. The Saudi Arabia squad were in the middle of a training camp in Turkey and offered to play a game against Rugova's team in Ankara. The Saudis played in the previous year's World Cup finals and, although a few stars were missing, a strong side pounded Rugova's Kosovans, who held out until the 86th minute, and then broke out to win a penalty. Kristian Nushi stepped up to score and the Kosovans held on to register a shock win. Rugova says: "Of course we defended like heck the whole time against their best side. It was a great experience for my boys, who got a real taste of an international match. We got a national heroes' welcome back home. This was just a friendly but it was historic. In a sense this was the first time Kosovo national team played an international match against a side with World Cup experience. It was truly awesome."

Rugova's Kosovans are up and running. Don't expect that this is the last you'll hear of them.

# CHAPTER THIRTEEN

# The Wild Cup

*"Sometimes I think FIFA forgets it doesn't own football. It's supposed to be a World Cup, but FIFA doesn't want to share it with the world."*
**Jens Tang Olesen, Coach, Greenland**

## 29 May 2006, Hamburg, Germany

A HANDFUL OF teenagers wander down the streets near the northern German city's train station into the commercial district wearing football shirts of the Ukrainian national team. In a month, the Ukraine, a country barely fifteen years into its independent life from the yoke of the Soviet Union, will make their World Cup finals debut, finally giving Andrei Shevchenko a chance to play on football's biggest stage. As the teenagers disappear down a side street, three more young men appear wearing international football gear.

The black and red tracksuits of Gibraltar will not be seen at the World Cup, though. On the opposite side of the street, unnoticed by the three Gibraltar players, a handful of Zanzibar squad members head in the opposite direction. International football has arrived in Hamburg a month before FIFA's biggest event, but this has nothing to do with Sepp Blatter's private members club: this is the Wild Cup.

With the World Cup coming up, fans and officials at St Pauli, Hamburg's second club, decided to do something to mark the occasion. Turkey played Estonia in a friendly at the club's run-down Millerntor stadium, but this is not the average St Pauli fan's idea of how to mark the 2006 World Cup finals; far better to wind up the establishment and provoke a row with authority.

The whole concept of what St Pauli stand for is probably a bit alien to fans of top flight football in England. Perhaps only Manchester City in years gone by compare to what is Germany's most anti-establishment football club. Based a football's throw from Hamburg's infamous Reeperbahn strip stacked full of prostitutes and night clubs, St Pauli fans are made up of anarchists, socialists and anti-establishment fans, perhaps exemplified by Andrew Eldritch, lead singer of the Sisters of Mercy.

Supporting St Pauli is not just about supporting Hamburg's second biggest team, or indeed any of the other sports played by this sports verein, or sports union/club, but making a public statement about who or what you are. St Pauli fans pride themselves on tolerance, but a club logo of a skull and crossbones, which appears on fashion items across Germany, also shows up a darker side. When German clubs from the old East Germany visit Hamburg, pitched post-match battles between their often notoriously right-wing fans and the followers of St Pauli are frequent. Not so long ago, property developers were proposing a major redevelopment of part of the Reeperbahn. After a league match, St Pauli urged the near capacity crowd to head down town after the match to protest over the proposals and the impromptu demonstration turned into a pitched battle with Hamburg's police. It's anarchy - football-style.

*************

Despite having a history of insubordination, St Pauli was in the top flight of the Bundesliga just a few years ago, but by the 2005/06 season, the club had slipped into the third level of German football and faced the ignominy of playing against the reserve sides of big German clubs, which often also play at this level. Importantly, in the mid-1980s, St. Pauli became the first team in Germany to officially ban right wing, nationalist activities and displays in its stadium in an era when fascist-inspired football hooliganism threatened the game across Europe. The club prides itself on having have the largest number of female fans in all of German football. In fact, in 2002 advertisements for the men's magazine Maxim were removed from the team's stadium in response to fan protests over the sexist depictions of women in the ads. The club is also active raising funds for charity and in 2005 St Pauli, the team and its fans initiated the 'Viva Con Agua de Sankt Pauli' campaign which collected money for water dispensers for schools in Cuba. Famously this renegade club has the only known openly gay club chairman on planet football, Corny Littman.

St Pauli fans are used to the club's yo-yo form and the average attendance at their crumbling 20,000 capacity stadium is around 18,000, even in the third tier. The club did make the German cup semi-finals in 2005/06, which provided a few problems for Hamburg's sex tourists. Many of the prostitutes on the Reeperbahn went on strike to attend the match, which St Pauli lost 0-3 to Bayern Munich, with England's Owen Hargreaves on the scoresheet.

By that time, St Pauli's management had already decided on how to end their season. They invented a bogus organisation called FIFI and decided to stage a World Cup for places which FIFA could not handle. FIFI is supposed to stand for the Federation of Independent Football Nations. That spells FIFN, but the St Pauli team don't care. What they wanted was a perversion of FIFA and FIFI also goes well with the little dog chosen as their logo. So, the Wild

Cup was born. "This was a concept that was basically thought up on a drunken night," admits Michael Meeske, the manager at St Pauli.

St Pauli turned to a sympathetic private media agency, Carat, to organise the Wild Cup. For FIFA and the German FA, the DfB, who had the world's biggest footballing event to deal with, this provided a convenient excuse to not get involved. The DfB warned St Pauli that the Wild Cup had to be a one-off in order for it to be tolerated. It knew that to provoke a row was just what St Pauli wanted.

Will Hink, head of amateur sports, referees and women's football at the DfB, said: "The FIFI Wild Cup is not organised through our affiliated club, but by a commercial agency. Our associated club St Pauli itself will not take part with their official team, but with a team combined out of former St Pauli players and youth players. The whole tournament is therefore an (sic) non-official private tournament of non-official teams and is therefore not explicitly covered by our DfB regulations.

"We have however informed FIFA about this tournament and received the answer that the tournament is not covered by FIFA regulations, so they have no obligations because of the participance (sic) of non-FIFA members. At the end its people who want to play football and there is also some social benefit. Let them play."

The only response from FIFA was through Head of Media Andreas Herren, who said: "We have heard about this tournament, but were never asked for an official approval by the DfB, so we do not have any other information or regulations."

Both responses were a disappointment to St Pauli, its organisers and its fans. Steffen Frahm, St Pauli's youthful-looking organiser, says: "The DfB called and asked if any current FC St Pauli players are playing. If they are, they will stop it, but not if only veterans and youth team players play."

Frahm knew of some non-FIFA teams like Greenland, but turned to Jean Luc Kit and asked for his bible of non-FIFA teams to find enough to contest a six-team tournament in which the host club were to participate as 'The Republic of St Pauli'. Gibraltar were so keen to play that Joseph Nunez moved the Gibraltar Cup - featuring Spanish side San Roque and English non-league club Yeading - to an earlier date. Jens Tang Olesen of Greenland was also eager to take part. He said: "Sometimes I think FIFA forgets it doesn't own football. It's supposed to be a World Cup, but FIFA doesn't want to share it with the world."

For all their anti-establishment attitude, St Pauli still needed money to run the event properly. They had a stadium with floodlights, but needed Carat to find a sponsor. Until Carat could do that, the Wild Cup could not go ahead. But with football fever growing in Germany ahead of FIFA's World Cup that did not prove a problem. An internet betting agency, My Bet, came on board, presumably because an invite to the Tibetan side meant they could use the slogan, 'Tibet, Your bet, MyBet'. To the delight of Frahm, this led to the Chinese Embassy phoning him up and asking him to rescind the invite to the Tibetans. With a laugh, Frahm says: "They asked me to cancel the tournament and I said 'obviously not'."

With sponsors on board, a German satellite channel DSF agreed to screen the games live and the St Pauli crew set about finding more teams. An attempt to persuade the Vatican to send a team got nowhere. Monaco originally agreed to enter then somehow forgot that the Wild Cup was on at the same time as the principality's Formula One grand prix. With a good number of the Monégasque players working during the race, they had to pull out and Northern Cyprus stepped in as a last minute replacement. In the space of three months since that drunken session in a Hamburg bar, St Pauli organised an alternative world cup. No wonder the NF Board were feeling threatened. Jean Luc Kit and Christian Michelis had first had the idea of a world cup for FIFA's outcasts in 1997, but by the time the Wild Cup kicked off nine years later they had still not turned this idea into reality.

***********

For two of the teams that would contest the Wild Cup, though, the tournament involved a sort of deal with the devil. A German comedian, Oliver Pocher, was 'coaching' Zanzibar and another German funny-man, known simply as Elton, was imposed on the Northern Cyprus team. Both sides even had to endure each comedian having a brief run-out at the start of their games. Neither nation seemed to object, taking the imposition of Germany's Baddiel and Skinner as the price they had to pay to play. Northern Cyprus probably got the better deal as Pocher could run about and actually wanted the ball in his brief appearance in their game against Zanzibar. In contrast, the portly Elton could barely struggle into a Zanzibar shirt.

The presence of the two comedians upped the profile of the Wild Cup and helped bring in other sponsors, but how much they were actually paying is debatable. Burger King provided 1,500 vouchers for free food, but whether they contributed in real Euros to the organisers was a mystery. What Burger King got in return was the chance to send a TV crew along for the opening match between Greenland and Northern Cyprus to film an advertisement. Both teams were led out by girls dressed in red hot pants, shivering away in the bitter north German wind.

The likes of Niklas Kreutzmann and Coskun Ulusoy were bemused by all this female attention, but amazed at the organisation. A fleet of Smart cars

The film *The Dream of Zanzibar* and the help of German comedian Oliver Pocher attracts interest in the Zanzibar team at the Wild Cup.

Zanzibar's fourth goal in a 4-2 win over Greenland clinches their spot in the last four.

Northern Cyprus celebrate defeating Gibraltar 2-0, thanks to a last minute own goal, to reach the Wild Cup final.

A pitch invasion of a higher quality during the semi-final between Zanzibar and St. Pauli!

Zanzibar celebrate reaching the final.

Gibraltar score the winning goal to clinch a 2-1 victory over St. Pauli and third place at the FIFI Wild Cup.

The third place medals are awarded.

Zanzibar say 'thanks' to their hosts before fighting out a tense final,
which ended in a goalless draw.

Extra-time meant cramp and another hard fought half hour,
but the influential Erdinç Borekci of Northern Cyprus (right in red)
could not break the deadlock.

The first FIFI Wild Cup goes to Northern Cyprus, 4-1 on penalties.

A poster advertises the Occitania national side's match against Northern Cyprus at Vendargues near Montpellier.

Nadeva Robinson, the Occitan trainer.

Patrick Watts, manager of the Falklands' national team, commentates on his side's match against Saarema via mobile phone over the internet for the 3,000 inhabitants of the Islands.

Leif Isak Nilut, resplendent in traditional Sami jacket and leather trousers, ready to 'yoik'.

Greenland coach Jens Tang Olesen.

Pelle Mortensen of Greenland (white shirt) in action against
Kyrgyzstan during the 1-0 defeat in the ELF Cup Group A match,
held in North Cyprus in November 2006.

The Kyrgz keeper shows how much finishing third in the ELF Cup means to the tiny Asian nation, after completing a 9-8 penalty shootout victory over Zanzibar following a 2-2 draw.

Hosts North Cyprus lifted the ELF Cup thanks to a 3-1 victory over Crimea in the final.

The 2007 Island Games football final saw a highly competitive match between hosts Rhodes (in red) and Gibraltar.

The Gibraltans emerged victorious 4-0 at the Diagoras Stadium thanks to a splendid second half performance.

The very expression of a dying tongue, the Occitània national team.
before their 2007 Viva World Cup tie against the Sápmi.

The Sami team en-route to a 7-0 win over Occitània
in their opening Viva World Cup match.

Occitania goalkeeper Guillame Daumond takes a drink during a pause
in the action in his side's Viva World Cup game against the Sami.

The Sami bench, including Hakan Kuorak (bottom right
with sunglasses on his head) watch pensively.

The Monaco team at the Wild Cup.

Occitània greet Monaco before their local derby,
which Monaco win 3-2

Tunnel vision: The trophy awaits as Monaco are over-run by the Sami 21-1 in the final of the first Viva World Cup in Occitania.

The Sami team rejoice with the Viva World Cup after their impressive victory.

Greenland's Pelle Mortensen (left) watches the airborne Coscun Ulusoy
of Northern Cyprus – one of only a handful of his countrymen to play
professionally in the Greek Cypriot league – in action.

Northern Cypriot players launch the Balls to Embargoes campaign in
an effort to gain official recognition which will allow them to play
international football.

Stil score a penalty against Guovdageainnu II in the final of the
2007 Sami Cup in the Norwegian Sápmi capital of Karasjok.

Stil celebrate their eventual 7-0 win over Guovdageainnu II
and winning the Sami Cup.

with the logos of each participating team on the door was available for players and management, while everyone was put up in some luxury at the Intercontinental Hotel. Lounging around the foyer of the Intercontinental, the hearts of a few players jumped when German footballing legends Karl-Heinz Rummenigge and Uli Hoeness walked through the door. Sadly, Rummenigge and Hoeness were not scouting the Wild Cup, but were at the Intercontinental to try and persuade Daniel van Buyten, a Belgian player on Hamburg's books, to sign for Bayern Munich, the club the pair now work at. For the Wild Cup players, that just contributed to the feeling of being part of something big.

The Tibetan team that struggles to get the funds to go anywhere was able to return again to Europe, led by Kalsang Dhondup, who took the team to Copenhagen to play Greenland in 2001. This time he rustled up a 25-man squad mainly from the Tibetan Diaspora in India and Nepal, but they were boosted by one Tibetan from Chicago and five players from Switzerland, including Dorjee Dsawa, who has spent 12 years playing in the Swiss top flight. All the teams put together the best teams they could.

"After this tournament, FIFA can see we are playing and that we have a talent to play. Then perhaps FIFA will let us in," says Zanzibar goalkeeper, Salum Ali Salum, a 26 year-old civil servant from Stonetown.

Colin Ramirez came out of retirement to captain Gibraltar, who were to play their first games on grass in two years in Hamburg. "You have to understand, there are only about 30,000 people in Gibraltar and this is the most prestigious tournament I've played in anywhere. I probably won't get to play in a tournament this professional again," Gibraltar striker Roy Chipolina told the New York Daily News.

That was to be one of the ironics of the Wild Cup. There was plenty of attention in Germany and the press seats were rammed due mainly to the involvement of the two German comedians. Elsewhere in Europe, the event was virtually ignored. The only mainstream media attention came from a newspaper in a country where football is not even among the four most popular sports.

***********

None of that matters to any of the players in the first match between Northern Cyprus and Greenland. Kreutzmann is enjoying the surroundings, but says: "We can just stay in a school hall. It's just tremendous to be on the team and see all your friends again."

Kreutzmann's presence at the event is amazing. The day after he is due to return to Denmark from Hamburg, he has crucial dental exams. The 40 to 60 hours a week that he has spent studying and training to be a dentist over the last three years could all be wasted if he fails, but Kreutzmann has no intention of letting Jens Tang Olesen down by not coming. Into his sports bag went his football boots and his books. Other players might be enjoying Hamburg's delights and the luxury of the Intercontinental. Not Kreutzmann. When he is not playing or training, the Greenlander is in his room, studying.

Against Northern Cyprus, Greenland have a real chance to make a winning start to the Wild Cup. Northern Cyprus look tired, but that is hardly a surprise. The Northern Cyprus league finished the previous day and the entire team then had to get a 5am flight from the military airport in the TRNC across to Istanbul and fly on to Hamburg. This could be Greenland's chance to get off to a flying start, but they cannot take advantage of the lethargy dogging the legs of the Northern Cyprus players. A lacklustre game is decided by a defensive error handing North Cyprus a 1-0 win in front of 1,400 people. In the next game, Gibraltar share a 1-1 draw with the St Pauli team.

Watching that game on the terraces with the Gibraltar squad is Joseph Nunez, seemingly immune to a harsh wind that even Jens Brinch finds hard to cope with. Prior to the tournament, both had contact from the NF Board and are a little puzzled at the communiqués flying across the internet.

"They wrote to me asking why Gibraltar are playing in this tournament," says Nunez, still wearing his tinted glasses and balancing on the balls of his feet like a bird. "I say to Jean Luc 'if we had joined, maybe I would ask you permission, but we have not.'"

Brinch had a similar experience, even though Greenland have joined the NF Board. Kit then emailed the pair back giving them permission that had never been sought.

For the NF Board, the Wild Cup is an unexpected challenge. Emails fly across the ether demanding to know who or what FIFI is. No-one seems to have the heart to explain that FIFI is just a cartoon dog. For Kit, there is no option but to visit Hamburg. Brinch has done the same to see his team play, travelling a relatively short distance down to Hamburg with Michael Nybrandt, the young Dane who helped arrange Tibet's game against Greenland in 2001.

The Greenlandic media that had covered the team's appearance in the Shetlands are not in evidence. The reporters are instead in South America, where the Greenland national handball team are playing in a world cup qualifying series that eventually sees the side qualify for the finals by beating (and eliminating) the United States. In the finals the following year, also in Germany, the Greenland handball team go on to beat Australia in front of 7,500 fans; an experience that Kreutzmann and his side can only dream of. But at least the Greenlandic football side are getting some more games.

So are Tibet, and Michael Nybrandt is back on the scene after taking in a cycling trip to Cuba and other projects. In Hamburg, he wants to catch up with some of the players he has not seen for five years. He also wants to meet up again with Kalsang Dhondup, who is about to start negotiating another shirt contract with sportswear group Hummel that provides the Tibetans with a vital source of income.

As the first two games play out, the Tibetan squad sit huddled in the cold, sending a chant of 'St Pauli' across from their empty stand to the opposite terrace, where the club's fans drink beer and eat pretzels. The St Pauli fans return chants of 'Ti-bet' as they watch a stranger game of football than even they are used to. After the matches, the Gibraltar squad lingers at the stadium to soak up the atmosphere. Joe Nunez still, at this time, waiting on a result from CAS, passes the time of day outside the changing rooms, again balancing on the balls of his feet, only to be forced back onto his heels in surprise as the match referee appears, strips off his top and reveals a fine site of chest piercings.

The following night, Tibet make their debut in front of 1,800 people and nearly emulate their performance in Copenhagen, when they scored first. This time the header from the corner flies over the bar and St Pauli's battle-hardened veterans soon take control. Dsawa is Tibet's outstanding player, constantly covering for his colleagues and almost keeping the opposition out single-handed. In the stands, Nybrandt winces as St Pauli score again and again. A landslide threatens. Eventually the Tibetans struggle off after 90 minutes, having conceded seven goals without replying. In the next game, an early defensive mistake and a dubious penalty gave North Cyprus a two goal head start against Zanzibar before the Africans pull a goal back, but the game finishes 3-1.

The semi-final line-up was practically decided that night after Tibet's defeat, leaving Greenland needing to beat Zanzibar to claim a semi-final spot, but Jens Tang Olesen is to be disappointed again. Zanzibar edge an exciting, eventful game 4-2, leaving Kreutzmann time to revise for his exams. In the semi-finals, North Cyprus confidently eliminate the hosts 2-0 and Zanzibar beat Joe Nunez's Gibraltar team by the same score.

The final is a re-match for Northern Cyprus and Zanzibar and 4,122 fans turn up, while others watch the game live on satellite TV - coverage that it later turns out was paid for by the organizers. The match descends into an unruly game with a Zanzibar player shown the red card in the sixty-eighth minute. Neither team takes the initiative and the match grinds out to a 0-0 draw before Northern Cyprus romp home 4-1 on penalties; Coskun Ulusoy slamming home the winner to send the first ever Wild Cup back to Lefkosa.

For Cengiz Uzun, the tournament is another successful piece of lobbying. He says: "Yes, it was a bit wild, but we won and that was great for us because the TV in Turkey and also Euronews mentioned us. Even Greek Cypriot TV is coming north for an interview. Things are getting better for us."

\*\*\*\*\*\*\*\*\*\*\*

Jean Luc Kit and his sidekick David Aranda attend the final to find that, while FIFI does not exist, Teutonic efficiency has delivered something in months that they have not been able to do in nearly a decade. The NF Board wanted to host a first world cup for nations that do not exist, but St Pauli have beaten them to it, rustling up enough sponsorship to cover a 140,000 bill to get five teams to travel to Hamburg and put them up in a five-star hotel. For Northern Cyprus and the NF Board, this sets a benchmark that the Viva World Cup will struggle to match. At the FIFI final, Kit and Uzun meet and seeds of discord are sown that are to undermine the plans of the NF Board and their putative hosts.

Unaware of what is going on between the NF Board and Northern Cyprus, the organisers of the Wild Cup are keen to stage another. Frahm adds: "There were hard tacklings (sic) at the final, but at least all teams were happy that they take part in the tournament. It was a great end, all the teams on the field. Because of the sponsors and the money, we could only have six teams, but maybe we can do this again in two years time with more players."

Another Wild Cup in the German cities of Mainz or Essen is actually mooted for 2007, but Frahm leaves St Pauli, sponsorship falls short and plans for another tournament are deferred for a year. The DfB's assertion that the Wild Cup could only be a one-off will not be tested just yet.

# CHAPTER FOURTEEN

# Africans Out In The Cold: Zanzibar

*"We cannot play in a league by ferry, that is a very unfortunate reason. That is not a reason at all."*
**Abdulghang Himin Msoma, chairman of Zanzibar National Sports Council**

## 30 May 2007, Hamburg, Germany

IN A PARK NEAR the Hotel Intercontinental, two national teams warm up on opposite sides for the Wild Cup, both sharing the same public space before they face each other later that day in St Pauli's Millerntor stadium. Northern Cyprus have a game under their belt, but Zanzibar's debut will be that day. The Zanzibaris look at odds with the setting, unsure of Hamburg's drizzle and cold. Standing with the team are the Zanzibar Football Association's delegates, led by Abdulghang Himin Msoma, standing erect and proud watching his team as it nears the final leg of its European tour.

Msoma is chairman of the National Sports Council in Zanzibar and a frustrated man, frustrated with FIFA's reason for ditching Zanzibar's bid to join world football's growing membership. "We cannot play in a league by ferry, that is a very unfortunate reason," sighs Msoma, reflecting on FIFA's justification for snubbing the ZFA's membership application [discussed in Chapter One]. "That is not a reason at all; it depends on the purchasing power of the people. That is why we have two leagues in Zanzibar: one in Zanzibar and one on the other main island of Pemba."

At the end of each season, the top four clubs from the two islands' 16-team amateur leagues meet in a super-eight series to decide a champion. Attendances for the finals at the Mao Tse Tung stadium, built, as the name suggests, with funding from China, can reach 6,000. Not so long ago, crowds were between 15,000 and 20,000, but that was before satellite TV reached Zanzibar. "People are seduced by this into watching Manchester United," says Msoma, shaking his head gently.

133

# OUTCASTS: The Lands That FIFA Forgot

Msoma watches Zanzibar and Northern Cyprus jog around the park, circumspectly avoiding each other, but pleased his team are getting a chance in the Wild Cup to play an international tournament outside Africa. Without that exposure and a chance to show the world that they really can play international football, Msoma knows the game in Zanzibar will struggle to survive. That is why he and the rest of his team are in Germany: To keep Zanzibar football alive.

Warming up with the national side is goalkeeper Salum Ali Salum, who plays for KMK in the ZFA Premier League and has 34 games under his belt for his national side. The statuesque Salum has managed to amass all those caps because, unlike some of the places that FIFA have decided to ignore, Zanzibar has a regular international outlet.

Along with the French island of Reunion, Zanzibar is an associate member of CAF, but unlike the French territory, the ZFA are also members of a subsidiary confederation, the Council of East & Central Africa Football Associations (CECAFA). This is partly funded to the tune of US$25,000 a year by CAF and holds an annual tournament with the likes of Zimbabwe, Malawi and Zanzibar's masters in Tanzania. Zanzibar has hosted the CECAFA Cup twice - in 1976 and 1990 - and won the event in 1995; beating Uganda 1-0 in a triumph that would fuel the impetus for that FIFA application.

***********

Football was introduced to Zanzibar during periods of colonial occupation by Great Britain and before that Germany, which had run the sultanate of Zanzibar up until 1896 before losing power to the British. The big spur for Zanzibar football came during the 1920s, when an influx of Arabs from Oman led to the creation of the ZFA in 1926 and the setting up of a league. Coaches were regularly imported from Europe. One club side, Malindi, even brought over a Hungarian coach.

In the early 1960s, Zanzibar gained independence along with the East African republic of Tanganyika and the pair joined together to form the United Republic of Tanzania. After the creation of the nation, the Omani Arabs left Zanzibar and the ZFA lost power under a centralised communist government. The Tanzanian Football Federation joined FIFA in 1964, but funding from that membership went solely to Dar es Salaam and little impact was felt in Zanzibar's capital of Stonetown.

In 1992, communism collapsed in Tanzania and, as part of a wider political settlement, Zanzibar has semi-autonomy under its own president and parliament. With a looser union, the ZFA regained some control. As Tanzania moved from communism to capitalism, the union has proved durable with little real drive for independence under Zanzibar's President Amani Karume, who was elected for a second term in 2005. Hassan Moyo, a retired Zanzibar politician, said: "The people of Zanzibar have all the rights of the union, they can travel freely and can do business. Zanzibaris recognise the value of this and so have always supported the union."

Zanzibaris have started to exert their own identity more strongly, though, and in 2004, Zanzibar adopted its own flag. With the purse strings still held by Dar es Salaam, there was little investment in Zanzibar football. The introduction of satellite TV began hitting crowds, but, in their hearts, Zanzibaris remain in love with the game. Msoma explains: "To us, football is second only to religion."

There are more than 640 clubs on Zanzibar and Pemba, but the ongoing problems over lack of funding from Tanzania were fuelling dissatisfaction. Neither the Tanzanian federation nor CAF were awash with cash, but the newly emboldened ZFA could see that FIFA certainly appeared to be. Securing membership of the game's governing body could provide impetus for that. Although relations between the Zanzibar and Tanzanian football authorities were not always great, FIFA membership would be a solution that could help everyone. The ZFA split with the Tanzanian federation in August 2002 and was welcomed by CAF, with Tanzania's blessing, as a member two years later. Tanzania and CAF both backed Zanzibar's bid to join FIFA, but that was to backfire spectacularly. By March 2005, Zanzibar had been snubbed by FIFA because their players could get the ferry and play in Tanzania, the country they recognise. To make matters worse, the ZFA had also been arbitrarily booted out of CAF.

This would have meant exclusion for Zanzibar's clubs from CAF club competitions. The ZFA initially rejoined the Tanzanian federation, while at the same time lobbying furiously for re-admission to CAF. The ZFA dashed off to meetings in Cairo twice, and eventually managed to secure re-entry, but only as an associate. Msoma explains: "We are permanent guests of CAF and have the same status as Reunion to play in their competitions, but not to vote. We hope that FIFA will understand and we will try and try again. We are using these simple chances [like the Wild Cup] to enhance our case."

Neither Reunion nor Zanzibar's side can play in qualifiers for the World Cup or African Nations Cup, but Zanzibari club teams regained entry to the African Champions League and the Confederation Cup, CAF's version of the UEFA Cup. Zanzibar's champions Police crashed out to Al Hilal of Sudan in the 2006/07 Champions League, while Mundu also went out at the first stage to Zimbabwe's Mwana Africa in the Confederation Cup. Reunion, CAF's other associate member, also put teams forward for both events, only for Saint-Pierroise to withdraw from the 2006/07 Champions League, although in the Confederations Cup Saint-Pauloise played but went out.

# OUTCASTS: The Lands That FIFA Forgot

The ZFA's original bid for FIFA admission had been led by phlegmatic Vice President Farouk Karim. He met with Jérôme Champagne, FIFA's deputy General Secretary and Blatter's main henchman, and was told that FIFA had no problems with Zanzibar playing internationals, but, according to their newly cleaned-up statutes, the ZFA could never be a member.

Zanzibar has not been shunned by FIFA, but patted on the head and told, like an over-ambitious small boy, not to be silly. Then, in March 2006, Zanzibar is 'recognised' by FIFA. The evidence is there in an article on FIFA's website about Zanzibari coach Suleiman Jabir as part of the world body's involvement with the SOS Children's Villages charity. Jabir coached Sharp Boys FC from a rural region of Zanzibar to the super eight stage in the 2003/04 season and also spent a brief period, according to FIFA, as a coach at Aston Villa. The FIFA article goes on at length about how Jabir is now an assistant coach to the Zanzibar 'national side' - a national side that FIFA does not recognize. Then how Jabir is helping to prepare a 'sports policy for his country'. There it is on FIFA's own website, an admission that should allow the ZFA into the world game, but nothing has changed - Zanzibar will stay out in the cold.

\*\*\*\*\*\*\*\*\*\*\*

The Wild Cup could be as good as it gets, but there is no sign of Farouk Karim with the Zanzibar delegation in Hamburg. Msoma does not explain where Farouk is, other than waving his hand and saying: "I think he has been delayed." As the rest of the ZFA delegation either do not speak English or defer to Msoma, there are no more details to be sniffed out. Perhaps having toured Germany with Zanzibar the previous year, Karim did not want to return, but his contribution to the FIFA bid will not be forgotten though as he is the star of a German film about the whole episode.

'The Dream of Zanzibar' was the idea of Alisan Saltik, a German TV director, who had made other documentaries on the island for German TV. He teamed up with Priamos Films and their producer, Stephan Ottenbruch, and ended up becoming a coach to the team. In Hamburg, Saltik keeps a low profile working with the team and keeping out of Abdulghang Himin Msoma's way. Ottenbruch enthusiastically joins in with the warm-up in the park despite difficulties communicating with the players, most of whom speak Arabic, but little English. Ottenbruch says: "Zanzibaris are a little bit like the Brazilians and they play with such fun and they cannot understand why they lose. It's football by the heart not football by tactics like German football. The film was Alisan's idea. He saw how they were fascinated with football and I was looking for a project also to do with football for before the World Cup.

Zanzibar has a problem as it does not get any money from Tanzania and they cannot invest in their youth. FIFA have no idea about Tanzania and Zanzibar, its history and its current affairs and problems."

Ottenbruch and Saltik's film aimed to address that, not just documenting the ultimately failed FIFA bid, but also providing an outlet for the Zanzibar team. Before the Wild Cup, Zanzibar came over to play some games against celebrity XIs and regional sides. To give the project prominence and help bring in sponsors like sports giants Adidas and Puma, supermarket chain Lidl and carmaker SEAT, who would all later come on board, Priamos recruited German comedian Oliver Pocher as a 'coach'.

The Wild Cup came at the right time for Priamos as 'The Dream of Zanzibar' was premiered in Berlin just a few months before Priamos and Saltik had planned to bring the Zanzibar team over for a tour anyway. The Wild Cup would be a dramatic conclusion to that. Unfortunately, the big club teams that the film-makers hoped to line-up as opposition for Zanzibar, such as Hertha Berlin and Fortuna Düsseldorf, did not materialise. There was a fixture with SV Waldhof Mannheim 07, but that was about as high profile as the warm up games for the Wild Cup got. Lower league sides such as SC Rot-Weiß Oberhausen were hardly Bundesliga giants, but at least Zanzibar were in Germany, playing games and being funded.

That in itself was surely the realisation of Msoma's dream. One that contact with the NF Board seems unlikely to provide. The ZFA initially agreed to be an NF Board member, but then backed out. For Jean Luc Kit and Christian Michelis, this was a blow and the NF Board's aspirations in Africa appeared to have dried up. The Wild Cup also presented opportunities for the leaders of the Zanzibar delegation, such as the dry-humoured Msoma, to make contacts that would prove useful for the challenge ahead in finding Zanzibar more opponents.

# CHAPTER FIFTEEN

# Tibet & The Kaos Pilot

*"What is a country? Recognition by a fellow country? What does it give you? Just a passport to travel and international recognition."*
**Karma Samdup, Tibetan footballer**

## 30 May 2007, Millerntor Stadium, Hamburg, Germany

AS TIBET KICKED OFF their first match in the Wild Cup, Christian Stadil swept into the stands of the Millerntor Stadium with a TV crew in tow. The owner of Hummel, who had been bought the sportswear chain for a pittance by his father after the business ran into financial problems, is in Hamburg to start negotiations over a shirt sponsorship deal with the Tibetans.

Some stories have suggested that the shaven-headed Stadil, a Buddhist, was behind the creation of the Tibet team. Certainly Tibet has been good for business. In the first five years since Hummel agreed to provide shirts for Tibet to take on Greenland in Copenhagen in 2001, the sportswear chain has sold 10,000 pieces of kit, either national team shirts or other sportswear bearing the Tibetan National Football Association (TNFA) logo. For supporters of Tibet's faltering campaign for independence, the Tibet football shirt is a powerful symbol.

But the media-hungry Stadil is not the man that helped create the TNFA. That man, another Dane, is also there in the Millerntor Stadium, watching quietly and with a wry smile as the TV crew try to keep up with Stadil, as he watches Tibet's game against the St Pauli side prowling the touchline. Michael Nybrandt is too modest to take all the acclaim for setting up the TNFA, but the team had been his dream - literally. After a cycling trip to Tibet in 1997, Nybrandt went to sleep one night and dreamt that Tibet had a national side.

Briefly a player with FC Copenhagen, he retired early due to injury and enrolled at the Kaos Pilots, an experimental and sometimes controversial business school in Denmark that was partially funded by the state until 2003. Born out of the Frontrunners movement in Aarhus, the Kaos Pilots provided a very different type of business qualification for young people. Before the subsidy cuts, 191 people had passed through the three-year Kaos Pilots course including former editor of UK style magazine ID Terry Jones and Body Shop founder Anita Roddick.

The Kaos Pilots have since been hit by a lack of funding, but continue to operate to the six core values that Nybrandt studied, which, according to their manifesto, are: "working with authentic projects, being streetwise: We should always think about young people - be aware of what's going on out there - at street level."

The Kaos Pilots also encourage their students to take risks, but seek balance and create a harmony between "body and soul, form and content and between economic, human and time resources." The final core value of the Kaos Pilots is compassion, to have "empathy and social responsibility."

Adhering to these values, each student had to come up with a graduation project. Nybrandt, who had built up football schools in Bosnia working for the Danish authorities, decided that his final project was going to be to realise that dream of a Tibetan national team. He recalls: "The Kaos Pilots is a modern project management school that teaches you to adapt to all sorts of project management. Not the theoretical, but with real customers. The idea about the Tibetan national team came before I went to the school. I said I wanted to coach the Tibetan team as a sort of joke. The principal said 'what if you were going to do that, how would you do it?' I got in contact with a Tibetan who is now in San Francisco and that led to the idea of a game and so I got in contact with Kalsang [Dhondup]."

***********

Tibetans were introduced to football by the occupying British forces in the days of the Raj. In 1904, Britain set up a mission in Lhasa due to concerns about a Russian invasion and the game soon vied with horse racing as the nation's favourite sport. In 1912, Tibet declared independence, but a national football team had not got off the ground by the time that China annexed the country in 1949. The Tibetan's' spiritual leader, the Dalai Lama, fled the country in 1959 after a Chinese crackdown and set up the Tibetan parliament in exile at Dharamshala in northern India. Joining him there was a small child called Kalsang Dhondup, who would grow up to love football and share Nybrandt's dream.

The first real spur for Tibetan football came not in Tibet itself, but from Dharamshala and the setting up in 1982 of a tournament for the exiled Tibetan Diaspora. Named after the Dalai Lama's mother Dickey Tsering - known to Tibetans as Gyalyum Chemo or the Great Mother - the first event included eight teams from settlements in northern India and refugee camps in the south. Inaugurating the event, Samdhong Ripoche, the Tibetan Prime Minister-in-exile, said: "Sports have become a means for achieving political gains and establishing friendly ties. For the exiled Tibetans, sports would be a medium to establish international relations, make political declarations and to exhibit the skills and aspirations of the Tibetan people."

In 1999, and spurred by Tibetan interest in football, Dhondup decided to take the idea one step further. He put together a squad and raised funding for a brief tour to Europe. The Tibetans ventured to Italy and played three low key warm-up games against club sides before an exhibition game against the rock group Dinamo in Bologna in a tour organised by Italian trade unions. By 2001, Dhondup was in touch with Nybrandt and the idea of another tour and a game against Greenland, still sore at being shunned by UEFA and FIFA, was dreamt up.

Nybrandt helped organise a coach, Jens Espensen, who went out to Dharamshala to conduct trials and put together a squad. The Tibetans played two friendlies in Nepal before the Greenland game, but visas were not forthcoming for all the team and some players had to miss out on a real trip of a lifetime. The heart-rendering impact this had on those that missed out was chronicled in a film about Nybrandt and Dhondup's attempts to organise the Tibet versus Greenland game. Partly funded by Danish TV channel TV2, 'The Forbidden Team' was directed by Rasmus Dinesen and Arnold Kroigaard, premiered in Greenland in 2003, was seen the same year by the Dalai Lama in Copenhagen and went on to win the best feature award at the 2004 Krasnogorksi Film Festival in Moscow.

Explaining how the film was the made, the two directors, slightly at odds with Nybrandt's version of events, said: "It all started on a bicycle ride in Tibet. Michael Nybrandt had a dream one night that he should be the coach for the Tibetan national team. The dream haunted him for a while until he found out that he had to react to the dream. He sent an e-mail to Tibet's government-in-exile in India. They forwarded the mail to Karma Ngodup, who is the main character in the film. Karma replied to Michael, and they met sometime in the year 2000. We met the team for the first time in January 2001. It was totally Michael's decision to play Greenland; for him it just sounded right, and Greenland accepted immediately to play the friendly game.

"For us the issues created all the intensity. It meant everything for Tibet to play that game - to hear their national anthem, to see all the Tibetan flags at the arena and feel the national identity that comes from playing for your country in a national kit. The game itself was really touching; it was really like a very big quest for peace and love and harmony. Everybody, and we are talking around 5,000 people, was smiling big-time the whole day.

"I guess for every country it means something playing for your national team, but it is shown in very different ways. This could also be a discussion about hooliganism. I think a lot of thugs need identification, and they feel welcome in groups that want to fight for their national side - but it is still identity, just in a more violent way. It means something not to feel lonely; it means something to have your own country; it means something to win the World Cup."

In 'The Forbidden Team', Nybrandt was content to take a back seat to Dhondup, but the amount of work he put in to make the game happen should not be underestimated. He did not want a repeat of the Tibetans' game against the rock band, but a proper 'international'. Greenland were keen, but the game was nearly derailed on a number of occasions right up to the kick off.

Airport workers in Greenland went on strike. This was not connected to the game, but meant that the Greenlanders also had to draft in late replacements. The Chinese embassy insisted no national flags were flown - even though the game was in Denmark not China - after an exchange of letters between Greenlandic Prime Minister Jonathan Motzfeldt and China's ambassador in Denmark, Wang Qiliang.

Motzfeltdt wrote on 17 May to try and pacify the Chinese, but also stood up for the Greenlandic Sporting Association. In his letter, Motzfeldt said: "Let me assure you that the Greenland Home Rule government has no part in this private sporting event. Within the framework of the Danish constitution it is neither possible nor advisable for my government to intervene."

Wang Canfren, a chargés d'affaires at the Chinese embassy, was more strident in his reply, saying: "As you know, there is only one China in the world and Tibet is part of it. More than 160 countries in the world including the Kingdom of Denmark recognize this principle. It is a splittist act that the Dalai Lama Group should brazenly send a football team in the name of so-called 'Tibetan national team' in unbridled propaganda for this event. This has fully demonstrated their ulterior motive to seek 'Tibetan independence' with the disguise of sports, split the motherland, and thus to cause troubles for Sino-Danish relations as well as Sino-Greenlandic relations.

"I would like to express my sincere hope that Mr Premier [Motzfeldt] will take the overall situation of Sino-Danish and Sino-Greenlandic relationship into account, exert your influence, and remind the Greenlandic Sporting Association not to be used by the Dalai Lama Group, and furthermore take concrete measures to guarantee that no signs concerning 'Tibet state' or 'Tibet independence' would appear during the football match."

According to Nybrandt that kind of behaviour would not permitted regardless of this diktat. "This wasn't allowed anyway as no flags can be raised of countries that are not recognised by Denmark," says Nybrandt. He also had to find a council-run stadium. If the game was in a club arena, the club would have been fined by FIFA. Booking the Vanlose Stadium early for a mere 500 DK (about £46), kept the entry cost down to 100 DK (just over £9).

That generated a good gate and decent amount of receipts, hence the trip to Freiburg for a second international with Christian Michelis' recently formed Monaco national team; and the foundations of the NF Board were laid.

***********

A few months after the game with Greenland, Tibetan football briefly returned to the news, but not because of any matches. That year, FIFA was forced into a humiliating apology to the Chinese government after referring to Tibet as a 'neighbouring country' to China. The Chinese newspaper, People's Daily, said: "The misinformation, spreading worldwide through the Internet, drew the ire of the Chinese people. Many domestic websites are awash with complaints from indignant readers and surfers who sent missives to FIFA seeking an explanation."

Defending the climb-down, FIFA said: "We simply made an editorial error. We are a sporting association, not a political one. Our correction was not a reflection of political views or a particular position, but an acceptance of a situation."

That is an opinion not shared among the Tibetans. "I can understand that FIFA was in a difficult position over the wording on its website as China has a particularly intimidating approach to organisations and governments that challenge its position in Tibet," says Karma Samdup. "But as far as Tibetans are concerned, it is not correct to say that Tibet is part of China and FIFA should be aware of that too. To accept Beijing's position without taking into account that of the Tibetan people would also be in breach of FIFA's non-political stance."

After the Greenland match, finding a Tibetan international - in Europe at least - is not easy. The Revolution bar in the Wiltshire market town of Swindon might seem an incongruous place to find a Tibetan international. That is where Samdup is having some lunch during a break from work at financial giant Zurich. Articulate and intelligent, Samdup explains his history; the not unusual history of the exiled Tibetan. He moved to the UK aged nine with his parents, who had been living in India and secured a UK passport. Today, he is one of around 400 Tibetans living in the UK.

Samdup lives in London and played in park matches, usually up-front, with other Tibetan friends before he answered the call-up for the Greenland game. As players dropped out after being denied visas, the TNFA started looking for replacements. The largest Tibetan community in Europe is in Switzerland and a handful of players play in Swiss leagues, but supposedly fearing retaliation from FIFA, only a couple of less experienced players travelled to Denmark.

Samdup and two friends had no such concerns and helped swell the Tibet squad. One of his friends did not make the cut and the other failed to get off the substitutes bench. For Samdup, playing was an experience he would not forget and one that made him feel even more Tibetan. He says: "What is a country? Recognition by a fellow country? What does it give you? Just a passport to travel and international recognition."

After the Greenland game, Tibet went on to play Monaco, but Samdup returned to London. The Tibetan still fancies the chance of playing for his country again. He says: "I'd like to get the Chinese all upset again like we did last time. I like the idea of the Chinese embassy having to pick themselves up and deal with it again."

That combative approach explains why Samdup was played in midfield against Greenland, because he had some bite. He adds: "The older guys from India don't go in for tackles so hard. I think it comes down to their temperament. I think I got picked because I play in an English way and tackle."

There is a history of the Tibetans' passive approach to life through their spiritual beliefs causing problems at football. Lobsang Tenzin, the Dalai Lama's septuagenarian gardener in Dharamshala, recalls one game being disrupted by Buddhist monks that feared the "Buddha's head" was being kicked.

Another older Tibetan, Thupten Choephel, who played in Lhasa against the Chinese and later managed the exiled team, recalls wishing ill-will on his then opponents. He said: "When the proper way doesn't come, one will try to hurt the good players of your opponents. Such intentions are anti-sports spirit. The game should be played with a spirit of good sportsmanship."

***********

The idea of a Tibetan team comprised purely of people who do not even live there playing international football might seem absurd, but FIFA themselves have set a precedent. In 1994, in a blatantly political act for a non-political organisation, FIFA admitted Palestine as a guest. The Palestine Football Association was formed in 1928, when Palestine was ruled under a British mandate. The national side even played in the qualifiers for the 1934 World Cup finals, but the PFA was superseded by the creation of the state of Israel after the Second World War until FIFA's intervention.

Due to the security concerns there, the side is mostly made of exiled players from as far apart as Chile, the United States, Lebanon and Kuwait and can neither play nor train at home. Matches are generally played in Qatar, but the side has plugged on. Like the Tibetans, a film was even made about their ultimately failed attempt to qualify for the 2006 World Cup finals. Maya Sanbar, co-director of 'World Cup Inshallah', says: "The football team is an analogy for the Palestinian state. We think the film has a positive message at the end, but we are not here to glorify Palestine. Only in sport is there such a place as Palestine."

The Palestinians are certainly not recognised as a state at the UN, where they are cautiously referred to as the Palestinian Authority. Tibet, perhaps due to China's place on the UN security council, cannot even manage that tentative recognition, but some visitors to Dharamshala consider the entire Tibetan community there to be little more than an artifice. Mario Rodrigues, editor of Indian sports magazine All Sports, says: "I have been to Dharamshala and it appears to me that the whole Tibetan movement there is being kept alive by western funds."

The cash-strapped TNFA managed to raise US$2,000 (about £1,000) from seven Tibetan associations in the US to help contribute to the Wild Cup trip. Although expenses were covered by the organisers, the TNFA still pays players at its training camps a fee of about four lakh rupees a day to attend. The only regular income is the deal with Hummel. After the Greenland game, Nybrandt took a break after three years helping the TNFA. The Marseille schoolteacher Thierry Marcade tried to help the Tibetans out. In 2003, a Tibetan under-13 team visited Monaco for a game against a school in the principality watched by Prince Albert before playing a number of other games across southern France. The full men's team still found matches hard to come by. Dhondup tried to organise a trip to France in 2003 only to be denied visas again, so the team returned to Denmark for the Aarhus Asian Festival to play an all-star team sponsored by Stadil's Hummel organisation.

In October 2005, a trip to Muret in France to take on the Occitànians was set up then had to be cancelled at the last minute due to lack of visas. Dhondup explained: "For this we had one month (sic) intensive training. Unfortunately at the last moment the French embassy here in India denied visas to the team and we are forced to cancel all programs (sic)."

Michael Nybrandt had tried to help the Tibetans with their 2003 visit only for the team to insist on stopping over in France. Having taken so much trouble to get the team into Denmark last time, he realised that this was going to cause problems. The resulting lack of visas was no surprise to the Kaos Pilot, who had an amicable parting of ways with the Tibetans, but still retained his enthusiasm for their country. In 2004, Nybrandt tried to re-enter Tibet while travelling in Nepal, but was, perhaps unsurprisingly, denied a visa by the Chinese.

After being involved with the genesis of the NF Board and then dropping out of view, Nybrandt resurfaced in London for the NF Board meeting, then drifted away from a movement he helped inspire. At least part of the reason that Nybrandt became detached was what he felt were a 'lack of shared values' in the NF Board and the admittance of bogus teams like Scaland and its adopted side based in Aalborg.

"That undermines the case of places like Greenland. So maybe this street could be a national team?" asks Nybrandt rhetorically, gesturing out onto the street outside of the Irish bar in downtown Copenhagen that he sits in, patiently answering questions.

The web-based community of the NF Board have slowly began to realise this and Mark Cruickshank removes Sealand from his Roon Ba website in April 2006 after a brief discussion on the forum. In a post on the Roon Ba discussion board, Cruickshank says: "I have received a few e-mails regarding Sealand recently, some in favour of my decision to remove them from the Non-FIFA rankings, with some (the minority) against. I am strongly in favour of the NF Board's policy of 'football for everyone', but I do not believe, for example, that my pub team or the local Christian Association's football team should be allowed to apply for membership. I deliberately mention these two teams, as this is how I believe Sealand should be treated. The 'country' was artificially created, not for any ethnic or cultural reasons, but purely for publicity. The people are English. The football team representing Sealand are all Danish citizens. Sealand do issue passports, yes, but this is just because they are exploiting a loophole in international law. None of the holders of this passport will think of themselves as Sealanders, even although they may say they do. Sealand is no more real than Lilleputia or Narnia. How can we take the capturing of an abandoned platform in the North Sea as a serious attempt at building a nation? If I declare my house an independent state, and invite people to live here so we can form a football team, does that make me eligible to apply for membership? International law may be indecisive on the status of Sealand, but common sense is not."

Is that a first sign of the NF Board's web community fracturing?

\*\*\*\*\*\*\*\*\*\*

After his writing trip to Cuba for four months, Nybrandt had agreed with Jean Luc Kit and the NF Board to project manage the Viva World Cup. As the only person with real experience in such a potentially problematic task, he suggested that the event in North Cyprus should only feature eight teams. He knew from personal experience that a single match was hard enough to organize in the face of FIFA and other institutional pressure. The NF Board eventually took this on board, but Kit and Michelis had bigger ambitions and then went ahead with an NF Board meeting in Geneva in January 2006 without telling Nybrandt. Again, Nybrandt lost touch.

# OUTCASTS: The Lands That FIFA Forgot

Thierry Marcade has visited Dharamshala 10 times and succeeded in bringing junior Tibetan football teams and also cross country athletes to France and Monaco. Like so many NF Board members, Marcade is not easy to track down, but he is in the stand at the match between Occitània and North Cyprus in Vendargues outside Montpellier. He says: "I will go to Dharamshala in June. If we can get sponsorship, the Viva World Cup is possible. That will be our focus."

That turns out not to be the case as the Tibetans are invited to the Wild Cup a year beforehand and Christian Stadil has a chance to start negotiations over a new shirt deal. For Michael Nybrandt, the relatively short train ride from Copenhagen to Hamburg also presents an opportunity to catch up with some of his friends that he helped turn into international footballers.

**********

In the lounge of the Intercontinental Hotel again, Gibraltarian players lounge about as one of the Tibetan players, Pablo Lobsang, appears. He is selling scarves for the Tibetan cause, but that is not all he has on offer. He reveals a handful of Tibetan national team shirts. Not the ones that Dhondup's squad are wearing at the Wild Cup, but older versions from the original encounter that he played in. These shirts would be enough to send a shiver down Stadil's spine. The Tibetans have been to Bangkok and got fakes produced of their own; national shirts to help raise some cash. Imagine Frank Lampard selling fake England shirts in Nuremberg hotels later that summer to fund the England trip to the World Cup.

After the Aarhus trip, the Tibetans were unable to play outside of India, but Hummel continued to produce shirts in the distinctive colours of the Tibetan flags through the Free Tibet campaign or trendy UK outlets such as Microzine in London and Liverpool. After five years, the contract was up for renegotiation and the Buddhist Stadil wanted to start negotiations with Dhondup and the TNFA in person. The Tibetans were helped by having a strong squad, including the most accomplished Tibet player, Dorjee Dsawa. Prior to the Wild Cup in Cyprus, Dsawa had spent the previous dozen years as a professional in the Swiss leagues with top clubs St Gallen, Neuchatel Xamax and FC Zurich, a brief spell at AC Bellinzona in Italy, and then back to Switzerland with FC Schaffhausen.

After the Greenland game, a story had circulated that Dsawa, a tall defender who was born in Switzerland but whose parents were from Dharamshala, had not played for fear of retribution from FIFA. He discounts this, saying: "Now we have holidays and I can play. I didn't have the time before. My contract is finished at the end of June. I want a new contract or to play for another team. My manager said it is not a problem playing here."

Also with Dsawa in Hamburg is his brother, who is a defensive midfielder at Fortuna, a Swiss Third Division side from St Gallen. Apart from the lone US-based Tibetan, the rest of the squad comes from India and Nepal, including Sonam Richem from Pokhara FC and Lobsang Norbu, more commonly known as Lobo, who scored the opening goal against Greenland in 2001.

The squad is the best that Dhondup believes he has assembled, but Tibetan players do not always find getting a game in India easy. Michael Nybrandt suggests: "In India, football is much more of a rich person's sport and sometimes parents pay for their children to get a place on a team."

For the Tibetans living around Dharamshala, there is not a great deal of money going around and this is hardly an option. The increasing interest in the game in India does not help either. Englishman Stephen Constantine coached the Nepal national team from 1999 to 2002 and then the Indian side from 2002 until 2005. Before Dhondup's squad left to play Greenland, Constantine let the players train with his Nepal side. Now coaching the Malawi national side in Africa, Constantine says: "I have not heard of people buying their sons places and thereby excluding the Tibetans [but] there is a huge interest in Indian football and a lot of very good players. I don't think a Tibetan who was good enough and eligible to play would be excluded."

In Hamburg, Dhondup's side fall too easily to St Pauli and are eventually eliminated without scoring a goal; not providing a great start for negotiations. Stadil and Dhondup have some preliminary discussions with Nybrandt present before the Hummel boss leaves, although not before asking his fellow Dane, rather presumptuously, to get the Tibetan team to sign a new national jersey for him. With that, Stadil sweeps out of the stadium, TV crew following dutifully behind.

For Nybrandt, being present at those early negotiations and hearing the deal being offered to the Tibetans by Hummel, incites him into action. After the Wild Cup and their elimination, Dhondup and the Tibetan team disperse again. Nybrandt returns to Copenhagen and is drawn into representing the TNFA to try and get them the best possible deal. Concerned that Hummel are only offering royalties on kit with the TNFA logo instead of the entire Tibet football range, he spends the next few months thrashing out a deal. Hummel are not in a shoe-in. The Tibet brand is established now and Nybrant is contacted by a number of other interested parties, including an agent for a fashion brand from Italy.

Finally, in February 2007, a contract arrives and is signed off. Nybrandt feels vindicated at getting involved again. He says: "I have to admit it's interesting that we have reached a level where we attract offers from various companies. When I compared the offers there was no doubt that Hummel was our first priority. The contract is a long-term extension of the current partnership between the two parties. In terms of finance, it is my belief that it's the best contract a non-FIFA team ever achieved and it will secure a sustainable development of Tibetan football in the following years. I hope it will inspire other non-FIFA teams and initiate a period that will make the associations more sustainable and able to develop their football culture. The non-FIFA teams have been going through a turbulent period the last five to six years. I think it's time to move to the next level."

What that level is remains to be seen. The Dalai Lama won the Nobel Peace prize in 1989, despite stopping calling for Tibetan independence back in 1988. China is believed to be considering allowing Tibet's ageing spiritual leader to return to his homeland in order to limit unrest caused by his eventual death.

As Hong Kong and Macau remain FIFA members despite giving up their colonial status, could Tibet be accommodated in a similar arrangement? Only with China's acquiescence. But given its enthusiasm for developing the world's game in the economic powerhouse that is modern-day China, FIFA would surely bend its own rules just as it did for Palestine. But doing that could also fuel Tibetan nationalism and the likelihood remains that Palestine will play a 'home' international match before the Tibetans.

# CHAPTER SIXTEEN

# The Viva World Cup

*"I don't want to think about FIFA anymore. I have realized we have too much mention of FIFA in our constitution and we must change that."*
**Christian Michelis, NF Board President**

## 30 September 2006, The Hague, Netherlands

IN THE MERCURE Hotel in the Dutch capital, the NF Board have materialised again from the ether of the Internet. After nearly a decade of dreams, this will be the year for the Viva World Cup.

Up on the walls sit plans for the draw and lined up at the end of the table sit the NF Board executive: Jean Luc Kit, Christian Michelis, David Aranda and George Wuethrich. But all is not well. A bellwether for the occasion is Kit's usually buoyant quiff, now flattened down on his head and Brylcreemed back. Like Kit's quiff, the NF Board has wilted. The big contingent that swelled the London meeting just over a year ago has dispersed. There is no-one from the Channel Islands, Gibraltar or Somaliland, no Kurds or Scalanders, not even the likes of Mark Cruickshank or Steven Parsons. Has the NF Board failed to turn their Web-based dream into a reality?

On one side of the room is Pèire Costa of Occitània, sitting by the representatives of the Roma, who have pitched up this time in the snappily dressed form of Franky 'Junior' Reinnhardt and Franky 'Zac' Renard. On Costa's other flank is a middle-aged man representing Monaco. Like the Roma, he only speaks French, as does Florent Costa from the town council of Hyères in Occitan southern France, which is now hosting the first Viva World Cup. The event looks like being a fairly Gallic affair, although on the opposite side of the room to this Gallic bloc is Leif Isak Nilut and Hakan Kuorak, both in traditional Sami dress. A few chairs further along sits one of the South Lower Saxony Skins, empty chairs all around him. Apart from a female representative of the UNPO, which is based in the Hague, that is it.

A sign suggests that Giorgio Rosa of Western Sahara should be there. Another suggests a representative of the Free State of Rijeka called Slobodan Milosevic is turning up too. This must surely be a bad joke, but if so, no-one at the the NF Board has got it. Where have all those football nomads from the

Star Wars 'bar scene' fifteen months ago in London gone? No-one is saying, but not much has developed since for the NF Board.

The Chagos did manage a game in April 2006. They did not travel the world. They played a game against a group of ex-pats from Mauritius in Epsom. And lost 6-1.

That sums up the NF Board since that first glorious flowering in London in 2005, when the idea of a 16-team world cup for the national teams that do not exist had looked, on the attendance then, realistic. The event that Jean Luc Kit wants to stage in 2006 has been whittled down to six teams. Occitània, Monaco and the Sami will take part along with the Roma. Two sides have been picked up from the association with the UNPO, Southern Cameroon and West Papua, now full NF Board members although neither has made it to The Hague so far.

The main problem for the NF Board has been a damaging row with Northern Cyprus that escalated after the Wild Cup in Hamburg. Both sides' version of events differ. The NF Board cite a change in direction at the KTFF since the heart attack of Taner Yolcu, who was their first contact. Since then, the nationalist Northern Cypriot leader Denktash was replaced by Mehmet Ali Talat. The presentation by Talat of the winning trophy at the Formula One grand prix in Istanbul to Felipe Massa appears to encapsulate the problem for the NF Board. Talat was widely condemned as an unsuitable, too political a choice to present the trophy and the Turkish organizers were fined a thumping £2.7 million. For the NF Board, this was simply more evidence that sport, for the Northern Cypriots, was a political tool. The NF Board felt they had simply been used by the KTFF for the vast contracts, many admittedly speculative, drawn up by Kit.

Christian Michelis explains: "The new [KTFF] board promised in November 2005 to respect the agreements [about the VWC] even though it had not seen the documents the former executive had seen, but the new government expressed restrictions concerning the participation of some teams."

In contrast, Uzun and the KTFF insist that the NF Board asked for 2,000 euros for the rights to host the tournament plus another 100 euros per team participating and exclusive broadcast rights outside Northern Cyprus. Even if Uzun is right, that is hardly a large sum, but this led to relations breaking down between the pair. The NF Board certainly did not want to start barring teams; that was the reason for its creation in the first place. When the NF Board did not meet a KTFF deadline of 15 June to supply more info, relations were severed. The Viva World Cup needed a new home.

In response, NF Board Communique number ten - sent out by email, obviously - accused the Northern Cypriot government of being "greedy of international acknowledgement at every cost, even and above all acting by betraying the simpler and better known way."

\*\*\*\*\*\*\*\*\*\*\*

Months have since passed by, but in The Hague, Jean Luc-Kit is still so upset and angry that he does not trust his English enough to discuss the subject. He leaves this to Georges Wuethrich, who does have better English. One reason for ditching Northern Cyprus, says Wuethrich, was a constantly changing situation, such as accommodation costs, which got progressively more expensive and reached 60 euros per person.

He says: "After Jean Luc and David Aranda went to Hamburg, they said they would send all the details to the KTFF when they got back, but when they got home they received an ultimatum about how many teams would be participating, but we were still waiting on what the cost of hotels would be. We never had a definite project and it became very hard to find a sponsor. Then they made another ultimatum: they had no money but wanted us to organize everything for nothing. So then it was over. A few days later, we find out they have loads of money and were organizing everything themselves. They had used the NF Board to make news politically and taken our ideas. When we have this situation, we have to find something else."

And so the NF Board, with Costa's contact help, secured Hyères as a venue. Uzun and the KTFF, meanwhile, went ahead and started organizing their own event, which would cover expenses for the teams attending. This was a major bit of foul play as far as the NF Board were concerned, hence the dour mood in The Hague. Christian Michelis had just read 'Foul!', the expose of FIFA practices by investigative journalist Andrew Jennings and was in a downbeat mood. He said: "I don't want to think about FIFA anymore. I have realized we have too much mention of FIFA in our constitution and we must change that."

The afternoon does brighten late on when Michael Ayong, the organizing secretary of the Southern Cameroon National Council, a Rotterdam-based organization representing the part of the African state seeking independence, finally appears. Briefly a trainee at Ajax Amsterdam before an injury ended his football dreams, he works in the mortgage department of a Dutch bank. Small but enthusiastic for the NF Board's dream, Ayong wants to bring players over from Africa to play, not just use Dutch ex-pats. A couple of his cohorts bolster the Southern Cameroon team later on and, although West Papua never turn up, suddenly the long-held dream of Jean Luc Kit and Christian Michelis might kick off after all.

# OUTCASTS: The Lands That FIFA Forgot

Although the KTFF are offering expenses, this does not mean a lot to the Sami Football Association. Nilut and Kuorak remained committed to the NF Board after having come in for some flak back home for the games against Northern Cyprus. Nilut cryptically explains: "It was very noisy in Northern Cyprus when we were there and, when we got home, critical sounds. The press were very hard on this as a political issue and they used sport as politics."

Pèire Costa's Occitània needed to raise 6,000 euros to play, but the trip to Hyères is going to cost the Sami ten times that amount to get the squad together and hire a coach. Having already visited Northern Cyprus before and caused consternation back home, the split with Cengiz Uzun's organisation was a relief for Nilut and Kuorak. Sitting by Kuorak in The Hague and looking more than a little dejected, Nilut adds: "The Sápmi parliament was very sceptical to finance another trip to Northern Cyprus because of the special situation on the island. We couldn't send in the [grant] papers to the Sami parliament until very late as I didn't know where it [the Viva World Cup] would be held and I couldn't tell a lie. When the news broke that the NF Board were going to move the event, everyone understood indirectly why."

But for the NF Board, the situation worsens after the team disassemble in The Hague and are beamed back up into the Internet. The Roma team simply vanishes. Then West Papua disappear into the Web. Hardly a surprise as their team was based in Holland yet could not make a weekend meeting in The Hague. West Papua eventually resurface only to pull out weeks before the big kick-off citing political pressure. The western part of the island of New Guinea, West Papua was a former Dutch colony and is now part of Indonesia. Many of the team come from the Netherlands and organiser Maybe Ireeuw blamed the Dutch, saying: "We regret that the struggle we have as West Papua people not only politically but in sports has made us come to this conclusion [to pull out]. The cowardly Dutch government is to blame for not taking a stand in the case of the West Papua issue; they hide themselves and also cover up their mistakes. Sponsors would not be willing to help because of this delicate issue."

And then there was three. Southern Cameroon were supposed to be fielding a team mainly from Belgium and the Netherlands. Players like Bisong Eyong, who, on the thought of donning the blue and white strip of Southern Cameroon, said: "It is extraordinary to be playing for my country. I am very happy. I am sending a signal to the world that Southern Cameroon is here. I feel very proud to be standing up for my country." But just before kick off, Southern Cameroon vanish back into the Web too. Later, Michael Ayong explains: "We had financial problems. Players were refused visas from home."

Some watchers at the tournament, such as Ante Jovna Gaup, a Sami journalist who attended all the matches, are more sceptical and suspect that Southern Cameroon's withdrawal was merely a stunt to gain publicity. Gaup said: "Six hours beforehand they are still coming. I think you know if your team is not going to turn up for a tournament just six hours before."

Particularly as many of the Southern Cameroon side were coming not from Africa but the Netherlands. But, with the VWC about to kick-off, Southern Cameroon stay in - on paper at least - with the three remaining teams all receiving a 3-0 walkover against Ayong's non-existent team. Somehow that is fitting. A world cup for national teams that does not exist includes a team that is not even there.

## Perruc Stadium, Hyères, southern France

Monaco vs Southern Cameroon should be the first game in the Viva World Cup, but, not only are there no fans, there are no teams. With Ayong's team out of the series, Occitània kick off the VWC against the Sami. Leif Isak Nilut kept the promise he made at the NF Board meeting in London by bringing the strongest possible squad of Sami players for the Viva World Cup, including half a dozen professionals.

Steffen Nystrom of Champions League regulars Rosenborg is in a squad that also includes Tom Hogli and Olaf Rastad, two former Norwegian Under-21 players playing professionally at top club side Bodo Glimt. Another Norway U-21 player, FK Haugesund's Jonas Johansen, was also in the squad along with Erick Sandvarn, who had just been voted top defender in the Finnish top flight, where he plays for Åland-based team IFK Marichamn.

Nilut had also been out and recruited Ivar Morten Normark on a short-term contract to coach Sápmi just for the Viva World Cup. A full-time coach in Norway for 11 years, including posts at Aalesund and three seasons at top flight side Tromso, he lost this last job and had been working as a TV pundit before being approached by the Sami. Nilut said: "[Normark] knows the team leaders, the assistant trainer [Odd Karl Stangnes] and most of the players, this makes things less complicated for us."

Though not a tribal member, Normark is a big believer in the project. He explains: "The tournament is a great idea, the important thing is that people play football and represent themselves." Normark has also taken four Sami players from his old side Tromso in Thomas Braaten, Hans Norby, Jo Nymo Matland and Vegard Braaten.

Kicking off at 3.30 on a Monday afternoon, the attendance could be described as sparse as best. With the Scandinavian season over, the Sápmi arrived in southern France early, but the Occitan players had played league matches that weekend and found themselves 4-0 down by the time of 'the lemons', as Costa described half-time. The Sami's superior fitness showed. Although Occitània tried to muster some attacks, these were easily mopped up by Jonas Johansen's defence. By the end of the 90 minutes, Nadeva Robinson, the Occitan's female trainer, saw another three goals hit the back of her side's net to complete a 7-0 victory. The following day was a crunch for the Occitan side. One match left and without a result against Monaco, they would be out.

Robinson had to send out a team of amateurs to play their third match in four days. Lacking energy, Occitània started defensively and this gave hope to Monaco, whose best players were only from the eighth league in France. A defensive mistake handed Monaco the lead after 20 minutes and then Occitan player Cristol Mouysset got himself sent off. Patrick Léglise equalized in the second half, but Monaco regained the lead on 53 minutes and then scored a third on 59 minutes. Sebastian Rojas pulled a goal back for Occitània with a header on 72 minutes, but Monaco held on. Occitània were out, but Costa does not mind. He says: "Our goal is to create a tool for cultural promotion. A player wanted to join the team without speaking Occitan. I sent him away to be educated. I achieved the objective."

The elimination of Costa's side led to the strange situation of Monaco playing a meaningless game against the Sami that would prove to be a pre-run of the final. Unfortunately, the fixture schedule may well have eliminated the second best team. In a bad-tempered game Monaco leaked 14 goals against Sápmi on 23 November. That was hardly a good advert for the Viva World Cup and not all the teams are happy with the organization, which Ante Jovna Gaup described as "catastrophic". The day before the final, Jean Luc Kit admits: "I don't even know how [the teams] are going to pay for accommodations."

But for Kit, Michelis and the rest of the NF Board, they believe they have achieved something. Georges Wuethrich says: "We believe sport can go beyond politics. Kosovo and Chechnya can play but that doesn't mean it needs to be political. We want to show the positive side of nations, but it doesn't mean we are standing behind claims for independence or autonomy. It is simply a way for an identity to be recognized through sport."

Sadly, for the NF Board, the first final will not be one to remember. Sore at their 14-0 pasting in the previous game, the Monégasque came out fighting and suffered two red cards. Against a side with six professionals and international players, this was too much for a fragile side with such a shallow pool of resources as Monaco. The Monegasque do manage to score once but Normark's side run in an embarrassing 21 goals to lift the Viva World Cup. During the game, the Monaco team are enraged at what they feel are increasingly patronizing celebrations among the Sami team - something they later deny - and some of the Nordic side are even spat on.

"I think the tournament is a fantastic idea, but [there is] a long way to go before we call it a real football tournament," says Sami right-back Leif Arne Brekke. "The organization was far from good and the teams were clearly on different levels. But when you think of the very first World Cup in 1930 you will see that they had the same problems. It's not easy to arrange a tournament, but I hope this tournament will grow bigger in the years to come."

For Jean Luc Kit, the score does not matter. He says: "Since the beginning we wanted to create a world cup for non-FIFA members simply for the pleasure of playing football. It is fantastic to see a team play internationally for the first time. There is a lot of emotion."

**********

Back home in Tromso, working again as a TV pundit and keeping fit down at the gym in the dark winter nights, Ivar Morten Normark still believes in the Viva World Cup, still believes that the concept has a future. He says: "The whole idea was great, but they [the NF Board] lack the knowledge of organising tournaments, hopefully they will be better in two years.

"To me, the NF Board did a lazy job because there were no fields to train on or fields that kids played on. It seems that they did everything but prepare for the tournament because the accommodation, the food and the people were great. It seemed to me that it was so important to them that they just got the tournament going.

The standard of the other teams was not so good. That is a challenge for the NF Board too, to find better teams or states. I don't care so much for the politics [the row with Northern Cyprus], but I think that the idea is great. Of course I would do it again if I was asked."

After the dust literally settles in Hyères, the Sami and the South Lower Saxony Skins express an interest in hosting a second Viva World Cup in 2008, but can it ever happen?

Southern Cameroon and the Roma do eventually manage to get sides together the following year as the NF Board change their membership qualifications. Provisional members must play a proper match in their first six months of membership to become a full member. So, on June 9, Southern Cameroon take on a mainly French Roma side in Paris in a friendly, Ayong's African exiles going down 3-1 to Reinnhardt's side in front of 200-odd fans but could either manage to send teams to a tournament overseas?

The first VWC took nine years to realize and, though the NF Board claims to have 21 members on its website - now a more professional looking site organized by Mexican City-based enthusiast Oswaldo Ugarte - how many really have teams? How many will ever be more than a concept in the copious files of Jean Luc Kit and the NF Board? Aware of this and in an attempt to bridge this gap between ideas and reality, in the summer of 2007 the NF Board changed their statutes.

In another communiqué released across the ether, Jean Luc Kit said: "For the sake of our image and the credibility of our NGO, we are proposing to change our statutes in response to certain criticisms.

"We would like to quieten down this criticism by proposing that would-be member FAs play at least one match during their period as a provisional member. Therefore, it is to be wished that in three to six months time all our member FAs can have played at least one match - three months being reasonable time for the organisation of such matches. We opened our doors to FAs that nobody took seriously. To these FAs now, it is up to you to show that we had every reason to believe in you."

The NF Board have had to grasp the thorny nettle of reality but they are not the only football body to have imaginary teams down as members; that malaise also appears to have blighted FIFA's confederations too.

# CHAPTER SEVENTEEN

# The Football Missionaries Of North Mariana

*"We prepare the best we can to represent the Marianas with dignity and pride. It is a tall task as our team is made up of guys 13 to 48, who are more adept at Ultimate Frisbee, triathlons and pub crawls than the football pitch, but here's to the world of futtie."*
**Vince Stravino, North Mariana midfielder**

## 16 November 2006, Papeete, Tahiti

The Oceania Football Confederation did not have a great deal to celebrate in the run-up to its fortieth birthday celebrations in the French colony of Papeete, Tahiti. The OFC had to hang its collective head in shame after its President Charlie Dempsey controversially decided to abstain in a crucial FIFA vote over who would host the 2006 World Cup finals. The whole world, it seemed, wanted football's biggest event to be awarded to the rainbow nation of Nelson Mandela instead of the only other bidders, Germany. Dempsey, at 79 and coming to the end of his tenure, was under such extreme pressure from all sides that he hid in his room, failed to carry out his confederation's wishes to vote for a first African hosting of a World Cup and the South Africans had to wait another four years for the World Cup to be theirs.

Then there was Australia quitting for the Asian confederation in 2005, but the OFC's fortieth birthday celebrations did give cause for celebrations. With Dempsey, now retired but still honorary President, in attendance, the OFC partied in style at the Radisson Hotel in the Tahitian capital of Papeete and welcomed in four new associate members in Palau, Tuvalu, the Federated States of Micronesia and Niue Island.

FIFA supremo Sepp Blatter was unable to attend. He was at the dentists. So he sent his side-kick Jack Warner, who found many similarities between the OFC and his own fiefdom on the other side of the world. Warner told the massed ranks of OFC's 11 full members: "CONCACAF and OFC share many challenges; we have long distances to travel; we have the expenses of this

157

travel and there are some people who think we are merely specks of dust in an ocean. But we are much more than that; we have overcome these great challenges in our own right."

Does that suggest that to survive the OFC needs to hoover up as many non-countries as possible and turn them into full FIFA members in order to provide another bloc of votes to keep Blatter in power? If that's the plan, no-one has told the football missionaries of North Mariana. According to the OFC's own website, North Marianas are already an associate member of the OFC, but the North Mariana Islands Football Association (NMIFA) know nothing about that and were not even invited to Papeete to hear Warner's speech.

"We wrote correspondence to Oceania numerous times and never got any response," explains NMIFA general secretary Peter Coleman. "When I organised [the league in North Mariana], there had been many years without any formally organised football on the island; therefore, [I am] not sure where Oceania gets their information about any association our commonwealth may have had in the past with their organization.

"My understanding is that in order to be a member of any FIFA-related group, an association must fulfil several conditions precedent and subsequent to admission. [I am] not sure how this could have occurred here as there was not an active football association here. I started this league. I, as an attorney, drafted all our incorporating documents, articles, byelaws, etc. Our league is new and not a continuation of any defunct league that may have been associated with Oceania in the past."

Coleman had arrived on North Mariana, which is three quarters of the way from Hawaii to the Philippines and perhaps best known for being the scene of some savage battles in World War Two between American and Japanese troops, a couple of years earlier in his role as a US attorney. A keen football fan, he went to live on Saipan, the largest of the chain of 14 islands, with his family. Like many fathers before him, Coleman went to try and find somewhere for his teenage soccer-loving son to get a game. And so began an incredible adventure for Coleman that saw him not only help found a junior league, but a national FA and eventually - as one does - a proper national team.

\*\*\*\*\*\*\*\*\*\*\*

North Mariana has a total population of a little over 82,000 and has been colonized four times, latterly by Japan and then the United States. The people of the North Marianas had decided against going for independence back in the 1970s, choosing instead to forge closer links with the US. A political union with the US came into force in 1976. Although a local government exists,

# The Football Missionaries Of North Mariana

North Mariana is part of the United Nations trust territory of the Pacific, which is administered by the US. Inhabitants enjoy US citizenship while having control over internal affairs. The inhabitants of North Mariana are all US citizens by birth, although the islands have many contract workers from the Philippines, Thailand, China and other parts of Asia.

So the head of state, for now at least, is US President George Bush. "[North Mariana] is a US Commonwealth [but] has greater autonomy than any other US affiliated place in the world," says Peter Coleman. "We are US citizens and as such have US passports. Most US laws apply, but we have our own taxation system and are exempt from US taxes. We have our own wage law. Finally, we conduct our own immigration. As a result of the last item, we can allow visitors into the Commonwealth of North Mariana Islands more readily than the US mainland or other affiliated places can. Thus, many people here are not US citizens. Despite this fact, in order to represent our islands one must hold a US passport."

When Coleman arrived on Saipan, he found an island dominated by US sports such as baseball and American football. Despite supposedly being part of the OFC, there were not even any junior leagues in Saipan for Coleman's children to play in. North Mariana had fielded national teams in the past, notably at the Micronesia Games in Palau in 1998, but the impetus had been lost by the time Coleman arrived. He struggled to find anyone who could even recall football being played on an organised basis.

All Coleman wanted was a league for his children to play in, so he decided to set one up himself. He started out by placing adverts in local newspapers the Saipan Tribune and the Marianas Variety to see if he could drum up some interest among adults to start a youth league. Several months later, Coleman was contacted by a local businessman called Jerry Tan, who had been living in another US administered Pacific territory, Guam. Tan was friendly with the President of the Guam Football Association, Richard Lai, and the pair joined forces with Coleman to help create a new North Mariana Islands Football Association (NMIFA).

This new league and association saw Tan elected as President with a local physician David Khorram agreeing to be Vice President, while banker Vicki Izuka became Treasurer and Coleman the General Secretary. As US sports monopolised the few sports fields suitable for a match, this new team had problems finding a field on an island that is just 20km long and 9.5km wide. Coleman and his new team eventually secured the use of Saipan's American Memorial Field, which was the scene of those World War Two battles. Having found a pitch, they drummed up support for goals, nets and balls and found some adults willing to be coaches and held a try-out - and were met with surprising results.

Coleman adds: "We had originally anticipated 150 players, but instead found ourselves with more than 300. This presented some logistical problems and we soon realized that we had an obvious shortage of adult volunteers. Needless to say our first season was wrought with new trials and we muddled through. Our good friends in Guam, the GFA, were always quick to assist, whether it be through additional equipment, donations or through time and effort."

In Guam between 2001 and 2006, the number of players playing football rocketed from a mere 500 to more than 2,000. With experience of starting afresh, Guam sent coaches to Saipan and held clinics. Interest snowballed and many women and girls wanted to play too, so Coleman's wife Patricia, a local teacher Brenda Schultz and an Argentinian living on Saipan, Marcos Alonso, pitched in to set up a women's league. Alonso and Schultz later joined the NMIFA board.

The big breakthrough for North Mariana came not from Oceania, though, but from the East Asian Football Federation (EAFF). The EAFF is a subsidiary grouping of the AFC that was set up in May 2002 prior to that year's World Cup in Japan and South Korea. The EAFF features China, Taiwan, Hong Kong, Macau, Japan, South Korea, North Korea, Mongolia and Guam. An EAFF representative team led by General Secretary Takeo Okada visited North Mariana in January 2006. An application was then made by the Marianas to join FIFA with EAFF backing, but rejected.

Although North Mariana sends other sporting representatives to Oceania-orientated events, such as the 2007 South Pacific Games in Samoa, the NMIFA decided to stick with the EAFF despite that rebuff. As a result, North Mariana were invited to send a team to the EAFF Under-14 competition in Beijing. At the start of that season, Coleman had simply been trying to set up a local league and now he had an invite to an international tournament on his hands. The EAFF was offering to cover expenses for airline tickets, accommodation and meals, so 'yes' was the only answer.

Supervised by coach Jahangir Hossain, a team of the best boys from North Mariana's year-old league travelled to Beijing to play against the best U-14 players from places like South Korea, whose senior side made the semi-final of the 2002 World Cup. Football was in its infancy in Saipan and the 18-boy North Mariana squad, which did not include any of Coleman's children, was made up of players that grew up playing other sports. Many had only recently taken up the world's most popular game; players like Cooper Graf, a keen swimmer who left his goggles at home and took up one of the two spots in the squad for a goalkeeper. Before leaving, Graf said: "I've been there [Beijing] already, but I'm still excited. I can't wait to see what the competition is like so that we can learn from it, but I am also going to enjoy and have fun with these guys."

# The Football Missionaries Of North Mariana

Also in the squad was Calvin Yang, who was a regular on the Saipan tennis courts before getting the football bug. He had not been to Beijing before and was even more excited than Graf. The midfielder said: "Man, we're just going to have a lot of fun and I'm happy I can get to experience this."

The team set off in July 2006 and in a missive to the local Saipan Tribune newspaper after he landed, Coleman said: "Most of the other teams arrived [and] most are taller than players in our squad and have been in these types of competition before. Nevertheless, our team is excited and looking good out on the pitch."

That height and experience was to tell. The games were played in halves of 15 minutes each way, which was probably just as well as a tight schedule included as many as three games on one day. North Mariana went down 0-5 to North Korea in their first game, then played South Korea and suffered a 0-16 hiding, which was followed by an 0-11 tonking from China - all on the same day. Not impressive, but North Mariana received a 'green card' for good behaviour after each match as they refused to resort to foul play despite the hammerings and bowed to each of their opponents after the final whistle.

The next day saw a more respectable 0-5 defeat at the hands of Mongolia, which was followed by a 0-12 pasting by Japan before the team leaked another five goals without reply to Macau. A day later, the team suffered a 0-7 defeat by Hong Kong and a 0-13 thrashing by Taiwan before finally getting a well-deserved rest. That, unfortunately, did little good as Guam beat them 12-0 in their final match, but Coleman was unbowed.

He says: "While we were little competition for the other EAFF member nations, the spirit of the sport was evident in our youth players and the experiences and memories garnered from that trip will most definitely have long lasting effects for those involved."

After just one season, Coleman and the rest of the NIMFA had not only created a league with 400 youth players aged four to 17, but a four-team women's league and an eight-team men's league and had played in international competition.

"Our league is made up 100 per cent of volunteers," says Coleman. "We have grown at an amazing rate. We do not have the luxury of corporate sponsors, although local companies have stepped up and sponsored individual teams. We are making mistakes and we are having fun. We consider ourselves work in progress and experience growing pains all of the time. In the end we are having fun, the kids are getting physically fit, the sport has been introduced to many and it is taking off."

Not bad for a group of parents who just wanted to provide their kids with a game.

# OUTCASTS: The Lands That FIFA Forgot

All this was achieved with lots of help from their neighbours the Guam FA, but not a jot from the game's guardians, FIFA. The EAFF were keen to help, though, and on 17 December 2006 at their nineteenth executive committee meeting, North Mariana were admitted as a provisional member. That meant no voting rights, but every other right enjoyed by the EAFF's other nine members, including fielding a full men's national team. NMIFA had no intention of letting the 120 male players or the 60 or so women players on Saipan sit about, unable to represent their little commonwealth, to hold on to a sense of identity about what it means to come from North Mariana.

***********

After the first season, some board members left and other new ones joined, including Vince Stravino. He took charge as the league organiser with responsibility for creating a division for teams from the outer islands in the North Mariana chain and bolster the pool of players. A member of Sam's Army, the US football supporters club that is modelled on Scotland's Tartan Army and attends most US games and has parties afterwards, away from the game Stravino is a physician for the US government.

He explains: "My involvement with soccer, er football, is essentially as a diehard US fan, but that somehow got translated here as a person worthy of being on the Federation board and organizing the men's league. Now, due to lack of viable players, I have dragged my body out of comfortable middle-age and am doing my best impression of a field player. I trained as a wrestler through college and my field experience is limited to recreational co-ed leagues."

Like Stravino, the rest of the North Mariana national team - affectionately nicknamed the Blue Ayuyus after the word in the local Chamorro dialect for the Coconut Crab, the world's largest crab and a local delicacy in the Western Pacific - must all be US passport holders due to the chain's political affiliation to the US. With this proviso, trials were set up early in 2007 to recruit a national team for a two-legged game with Guam that would be a qualifier for the East Asian Cup. If Guam had not been so helpful to the NMIFA, they would have had a more direct route straight to the finals, so the games are a risk for North Mariana's neighbours.

North Mariana recruited a coach from the US mainland in Ziggy Kortyoski, who is an assistant coach at Wright State University's Raiders soccer team in the national NCAA league Division One. Trials were held and a squad selected. Kortyoski institutes a punishing training regime, including a 5.30am beach run and conditioning at the American Memorial Park. Full of enthusiasm for the forthcoming encounter, Stravino joins in the runs and says:

# The Football Missionaries Of North Mariana

"We prepare the best we can to represent the Marianas with dignity and pride. It is a tall task as our team is made up of guys 13 to 48 who are more adept at Ultimate Frisbee, triathlons and pub crawls than the football pitch, but here's to the world of footy."

The big Ultimate Frisbee man is Tyce Mister, a teacher from Marianas High School, who is down to start in midfield. His sporting resumé includes beach volleyball, scuba diving, adventure racing, triathlons and cliff jumping, but he only took up soccer relatively recently. "I am amazed with coach Ziggy's bag of tricks," says Mister. "He has such an incredible repertoire of drills, games and conditioning exercises to get us in better shape and to understanding the intricacies of the game."

After the two-match series with Guam, Mister will journey to Samoa in the summer and represent North Mariana in volleyball in the South Pacific Games along with another of the soccer squad, Mark McDonald. North Mariana's team also includes kite-boarding dentist Mike Hall and Wesley Matthew, a lawyer from Papago, who is more at home on a long-board surfing the waves than playing international football, but will play in midfield. Like Matthew, Pete Houk, a marine biologist from Navy Hill and veteran soccer player, really took to the intensive training under Kortyoski. Houk says: "He is the best coach I have ever trained under, albeit a bit harsh at times. I trained in Guam when they were getting their national team started six years ago and the intensity and direction Ziggy brings to the field is unmatched. I also trained under several coaches during school and none have had the ability to engage the entire team in Ziggy's manner."

In the run-up to the Guam tie, North Mariana submitted a 25-man roster, but players were to drop out, some being unable to cope with Kortyoski's daily training regime. Even Houk admitted to waking up in pain every day leading up to the first game. One potential player, a 48 year-old midfielder, broke his leg. Another promising player had to drop out after the NMIFA found out he had played for Guam as an Under-19 player and was therefore ineligible under EAFF criteria.

**\*\*\*\*\*\*\*\*\*\*\***

The Blue Ayuyus met Guam in the first leg of the qualifiers in Saipan on 25 March at the Oleai Sports Complex in front of a crowd of 750 fans. An aggressive opening from both sides followed, but the home team soon conceded a goal. Guam's Alan Jamison took a quick free-kick and slotted the ball to the right of North Mariana keeper Ross Benjamin Wood as his defenders prepared a wall to his left. The home side fought back, battling hard for possession, and forced Guam keeper Brett Maluwelmeng into some saves, but Wood was consistently the busier keeper.

# OUTCASTS: The Lands That FIFA Forgot

A half-time pep talk from Kortyoski sent North Mariana out in an aggressive mood. Mark McDonald won possession and nudged the ball past Maluwelmeng in the 57th minute to level the scores. That is North Mariana's first international goal. Eight minutes later Guam regained the lead when Zachary J Pangelinan caught Wood unawares, only for McDonald to level the scores in the 75th minute. Could North Mariana hold out for another 15 minutes and land an amazing draw in their debut match? Football, unfortunately, rarely pans out like that and three minutes later Pangelinan scores what proves to be the winner.

A keen Mick Jagger fan, Stravino initially had no intention of trying out for the team, but after the first game said: "We were really in the match, surprisingly. We had them 2-2 at the 75th minute. Maybe we got greedy for a win at home and should have bunkered a bit, but that is hindsight. It will be hard work in Guam on the return. They are much more talented and speedy. I am sure they will make adjustments to counter our minimal skills and approach. We were outshot 13-4. Both our goals came off dead balls. Our big advantage is size, as we towered over the Guam players.

"Having a coach in place really helped organize and condition us. We still had to field three players who had never been in a real match of any kind before...and one of those was our keeper. He played nicely, but did let in two very soft goals that dribbled through his hands and legs. No substitute for experience."

Despite losing, many of the crowd hung around after the game to revel in their own national team. "It was great to see them sticking around after the match," Kortyoski told the Saipan Tribune. "It was incredible, it's good for the island."

\*\*\*\*\*\*\*\*\*\*\*

On 1 April, North Mariana took to the field in Guam with a 14 year-old and a 48 year-old in the same team to play the second leg under floodlights. The 14 year-old Blue Ayuyu is Lucas Knecht, who went on the trip to Beijing and only celebrated his fourteenth birthday two days before the second leg. For Coleman's dream team, the chance of recovering that deficit and advancing to another qualifier against either Hong Kong or Macau looks faint.

Guam come straight at North Mariana and land an early goal, followed by a penalty after a North Mariana player brings down a Guam attacker from behind. For North Mariana, a slide rule pass splits Guam's defence and one of their attackers is clear on goal from thirty yards only to get brought down from behind. The visitors expect a red card, but there is only a yellow and a free kick, which the Guam keeper claws out of the top corner. Then a long range shot just before half-time goes through the North Mariana keeper's hands to send the visitors in three goals down. In the break, Kortyoski tears into his team, makes a few positional changes and North Mariana come out attacking, but this lets Guam in at the back. By the 60-minute mark, North Mariana are seven goals down. North Mariana miss another good chance with a header narrowly missing, but Guam land two more goals and canter out 9-0 winners.

After the game, Stravino says: "I would like to blame the floodlights, but that would be stretching it. It was still sunlight til about half-time. We pretty much just got smoked by an angry, younger, fresher squad, who made us look old, slow and foolish when we left our defensive bunker. Our coach had decided to have us try to push forward in hopes of gaining a two goal victory. It backfired as we left large gaps for their speedy guys to fill and receive passes. In the end, we just had a few too many injuries and no replacements for a turnaround game. Plus, the decision to approach the match and try to get a two goal victory on the road was ambitious under the best of circumstances. Ah, live and learn. They played well and we played poorly. We just didn't muster the intensity we were able to in front of our home crowd. For what it's worth, our atmosphere and crowd size was far better than what Guam presented."

With that Stravino retires from international football, hoping that the youth programmes put in place by the NMIFA will bring through more players for subsequent contests.

Stravino adds: "I think our federation has learned a great deal about the need for a true technical director to run the program. We just won't progress with soccer videos and soccer moms trying to introduce the skills basic players need. Having the volunteer coach from the US for these matches really was essential to any success. He kicked our ass for two months and had us believing we could actually compete."

North Mariana's ladies team also played in Guam and were drawing 0-0 until just before half-time against a team that has a number of international victories to their name - only for the debutants to then shed seven goals without reply in the second half.

After the game, Jerry Tan admitted that North Mariana are a baby compared to Guam, who move on to another qualifier. The winner of that two-legged game then goes to take on Mongolia, North Korea and Taiwan in a round-robin series. The top side joins heavyweights China, Japan and South Korea at the EAFF finals in the Chinese city of Chongqing in 2008. Kortyoski heads back to Wright State University, but at least North Mariana have made their international bow.

# OUTCASTS: The Lands That FIFA Forgot

For Peter Coleman, Jerry Tan, Vince Stravino and the other football missionaries there, this Guam series is just the start of something even bigger. Coleman reveals: "We have made an application to the AFC. Due to the proximity of the member nations and a greater ability to travel to those locations [such as direct flights to those countries], we decided to focus our attention in this area. Our local government has been in vocal support for our league and measures are underway to secure a sight for the future home of the NIMFA. We would like to develop proper pitches for our players and to eventually host international tournaments."

Having started out just trying to find a game for his kids, Peter Coleman created a national team of players all with the passports of a potentially rival country, one that has become part of the FIFA umbrella within two seasons - a state of affairs that would baffle the people of Greenland.

# CHAPTER EIGHTEEN

# The World Cup That Didn't Exist

*"It would be funny to send Jesper Gronkjaer a shirt to see if he wanted to play for us as he could still be playing at 40."*
**Niklas Kreutzmann, Greenland**

## 20 November 2006,
## Girne, The Turkish Republic of Northern Cyprus

THE GREENLAND TEAM amble out of the hotel, Niklas Kreutzmann in their midst, on their way to the side's opening match in the ELF Cup. Kreutzmann waves hello, then shouts that he has been made team captain and points with a smile to the armband over his tracksuit - a St Pauli skull and crossbones. "I bought it in Hamburg," he says with a smile, then, almost as an afterthought before he boards the bus adds: "I passed all my exams and we got promoted!"

Eighteen months after Taner Yolcu let slip that Northern Cyprus would be hosting a World Cup for nations that do not exist, the event is underway, but not with the NF Board in charge. With connections severed, Uzun had to find as many teams as he could to play in the ELF - Equality, Liberty, Fraternity - Cup. He may have lost the help of the NF Board, but he had something they did not have: money. Each of the teams invited to the TRNC will have their travel expenses and accommodation paid. And, like the Wild Cup, their matches will go out live on TV via satellite station Turksat.

Greenland said 'yes' to Uzun's invite, while Zanzibar, now receiving support from the Egyptian FA, sent their under-20 team. In charge of the young Zanzibaris is Badre-el-din Abdulaziz, a former Egypt international and right-back with top club Zamalek. Kalsang Dhondup's Tibet took up the opportunity to strut their stuff in their new Hummel kit. Gibraltar were invited, but, with UEFA yet to make a decision on their admission, Joe Nunez did not want to provide their congress with a reason to say 'no'. Edmund Rugova is in Kosovo's hot seat and has an eye on UEFA membership too, so Kosovo decided to stay at home as well. Turkey's amateur team were invited, but changed their mind for fear of offending FIFA.

# OUTCASTS: The Lands That FIFA Forgot

Uzun tried to get the Vatican team involved, but that proved politically impossible, although an emissary from the Holy See did attend the event. In addition to being a school teacher, Uzun is also doing a masters thesis on international terrorism. This helped him garner political contacts overseas in places such as Kyrgyzstan. The TRNC has a sort of unofficial embassy there that sees hundreds of Kyrgyz come to Northern Cyprus to work in the tourism industry. Kyrgyzstan had sent a team of veterans and youth players over before to play Northern Cyprus and agreed to send a side again. So did Tajikistan, although neither specified whether this would be their full national side.

That left one slot to fill, but even with the offer of covering team's expenses that space was proving difficult to fill. So Uzun decided to invite a FIFA member that could surely not afford to say 'no'. International opportunities are rare for the national side that represents the turbulent state of Afghanistan. Uzun got in touch, but forgot about the NF Board, whose web community were monitoring the gestation of the ELF Cup. The Afghan FA eagerly agreed to a chance to play in an 'international' tournament against sides that would be a good match for their embattled national side. Then Jean Luc Kit took it upon himself to write to FIFA and let them know what was going on. FIFA got on the case and told the Afghans not to go.

"I had a friend who knows an Afghan MP," explains a frustrated Uzun. "He put me in touch with their FA and they even called up two players from Iran. And then there was the interference from Mr Kit."

As a last minute replacement, Uzun recruited a side from Gaugazia, a UNPO member and autonomous region within Moldova. Gaugazia, population 156,000, is the only place where Turkish Christians are a majority, which appealed to Uzun as it helped show the world that the TRNC was not full of Islamic fanatics, but a cosmopolitan place worthy of recognition.

FIFA and the NF Board were stumped and the bulky Gaugazians wobbled off the plane in Northern Cyprus after a long journey from Comrat via Chisinau and Istanbul to Northern Cyprus. Some of their players wobble due to tiredness, one or two also enjoyed the in-flight hospitality.

Uzun is relieved that the event is finally underway, although he has not completely forgiven the NF Board. "The NF Board is nothing," he rages quietly. "They have nothing, no office, no secretary, so how can they ask me for money?"

Perhaps the request was to help provide an office, so they had something? But none of this matters to the Crimean players lining up against Tibet for their ELF group match in Uzun's home city of Güzelyurt, where his school children have the afternoon off lessons. Wearing Northern Cyprus t-shirts, they are running around collecting loose balls and generally boosting the crowd.

# The World Cup That Didn't Exist

The 7,000 capacity military stadium at Güzelyurt is one of four hosting ELF games. The others are at the 28,000 capacity Atatürk Stadium in Turkish Nicosia built by Ahmet Esenyel's father, a 1,000 capacity athletics stadium in Girne and the 7,000 capacity Dr. Fazil Küçük Stadium in Magusa City.

In Güzelyurt, Uzun's schoolchildren see a turgid first half broken only by Arsen Ablyametov's 41st minute penalty for Crimea. In the only stand, a group of West Bromwich Albion fans do their best to get excited, while a Southampton fan in a Tibet t-shirt also tries to get animated, but the real entertainment is provided by the Crimean coach. Like a tiger on a leash, he prowls up and down the touchline roaring commands. Down the touchline, the worried Kalsang Dhondup is Tibetan serenity in comparison. Getting visas for some of his squad has again been a problem. Like his team, Dhondup is simply happy to be there. The game drags out, neither team looking like scoring and the final scoreline finishes 1-0 to the Crimea.

A second game promises more, with Northern Cyprus up against Tajikistan. This is not the full Tajikistan team, but a team of second team or international futsal players led by the moustachioed, lugubrious Khusravbek Murodov. The Tajikistan squad includes some players from clubs such as Vakhsh and Khima in the 16-team Tajik Premier League, but the senior players are getting ready for the forthcoming Asian Cup.

In the Northern Cypriots' first group game - a 5-0 demolition of the Crimeans - there was a march past of TRNC soldiers. In Güzelyurt, a few soldiers linger about, but Uzun's schoolchildren are the bigger boost to the paltry crowd. Uzun is not concerned as this second group match is on a Monday.

"What is missing here is professional organisers," he says wearily. "I had to face nearly every problem by myself as I am the only English-speaking person in the FA. I had to get all the advertising, the programmes, even the press passes. But I need to motivate our team. We need to pay internationals. We started to play more internationals because of me. All the players keep fit and want to look after themselves and play for the national team, that is very good."

As the Tajiks had put three goals without reply past Tibet, the game should be close. On 12 minutes, the visitors take an early lead through Daler Aknazarov, but Northern Cyprus equalize half an hour later through Dervis Kolcu. In the second half, Northern Cyprus make a rash of substitutions, bring on Ahmet Esenyel, now out of retirement, and the course of the game is changed. Kolcu grabs another, then Kemal Uçaner scores, followed by Çoskun Ulusoy, before Uçaner makes the score 5-1. Uzun can relax, his side comfortably through. For Murodov's Tajik side, the tournament continues to get worse. A goal by Crimean Halil Hayredinov in the 87th minute sends his side to a 2-1 defeat in their final game in Magusa City and out of the tournament. Exhausted by three matches in three days, the Tibetans are thrashed 10-0 by the hosts.

***********

In the other group, there is just a chance that captain Niklas Kreutzmann, Jens Tang Olesen and the Greenlanders might finally make some progress in a competition at the third time of asking in the last 18 months. The small Greenlanders beat the chunky Gaugazians 2-0 in Girne, Kristian Sandgreen scoring after 33 minutes and Kreutzmann ramming home a second half penalty. Suleiman Kassim Suleiman's ninth minute goal for the young Zanzibar side clinched a 1-0 against Kyrgyzstan in the other game.

In the second round of matches in Magusa City, Kyrgyzstan thrash Gaugazia 6-2 and Olesen's Greenlanders clinch a late draw against the skilful Zanzibar side when Pelle Mortensen, who is at Danish side Odense, equalizes after 78 minutes. For Greenland it is game on: avoid defeat in their final match against Kyrgyzstan and they are in the semi-finals.

The final matches see all four sides return to the pretty tourist town of Girne - Kyrenia to the Greek Cypriots - where a handful of the Kygrz students studying in Northern Cyprus are in the stands. They are virtually alone apart from a couple of UK groundspotters - as the Kyrgz trot out to face Greenland on a sunny day, the pitch perfect. Like Tajikistan, the Kygrz side is not the full national team. The thin squad of 13 players is made up mostly of international futsal players and boosted by the presence of charismatic goalkeeper Hamrakulov Shakir, a former XI-a-side international who has fallen foul of the latest coach. Their party is led by the equally fascinating Kiyalbeck Diykanov, a Kyrgrz politician - though by his own admission an unelected one - in his early thirties, who on the trip rents a Mercedes to drive some of his players around the TRNC.

A keen Chelsea fan with excellent English, Diykanov gives himself a game against Greenland, acquitting himself reasonably well. In the first 20 minutes, the Kygrz miss two good chances. Greenland respond positively, but Kassava Heeb is too easily boxed into the corners by the Kyrgz defenders. Then disaster. The Greenland keeper Anders Cortesen of N48 Ilulissat concedes a soft goal: 1-0 to Kyrgyzstan. If the score stays that way, Kreutzmann's side are out.

In the second half, they press hard, Mortensen the hardest working player on the entire pitch, but too often isolated up front. Olesen shouts instructions, but is unlikely to be making the same suggestions as his opposite number, Djetylaev Nurtazin. The Kygrz coach exhorts his side with offers of girls and massages if they hold their lead. Djetylaev Nurtazin clearly thinks no-one else

170

can understand Russian, unaware that an Israeli cameraman can comprehend every word.

Time is running out for the Greenlanders, but Kreutzmann lives up to his role as captain. Winning the ball in his own defence, twice he drives through the Kygrz ranks with no concern for his latest injury, a heavily strapped hand. In the dying moments, Kreutzmann sends a long cross raking across the ground into the Kyrgyz box, but Mortensen is heavily marked and can't quite reach. The ball shoots just past the post. Olesen's head is in his hands. Moments later the referee blows his whistle.

Kreutzmann slumps in the dug-out, foiled again, but there are no recriminations. Olesen congratulates his team on outplaying Kyrgyzstan. As the phlegmatic Olesen likes to say: that is how it will be. Greenland are out unless the Gaugazians, who look very much like a pub team not to be messed with, can upset Zanzibar.

Greenland's team shower and all sit together in the stands, talking, laughing and watching the game, unconvinced that Gaugazia can do them any favours. The eastern Europeans' physical game does secure their first point, but the 1-1 draw is no good to Greenland: they are out, again.

\*\*\*\*\*\*\*\*\*\*\*

The end of the group games sees Uzun chaperoning the party leaders, such as Kalsang Dhondup, Diykanov, Murodov, Olesen and the Greenlandic FA president Lars Lundblad, on trips for a chat with TRNC Prime Minister Ferdi Sabit Soyer and a chance to be spoken at by Mehmet Ali Talat.

The Greenlanders and Tibet had wanted to play a game against each other, but exhaustion was taking its toll and the official meetings for Olesen and Dhondup clogged up the schedule. Instead, the players get to experience Northern Cyprus, for some a chance to see somewhere that without football they would not know existed.

Jens Tang Olesen says: "To come here, this is such a big thing for the players as they like to travel, but some don't have the money to do anything more than get the boat to the next town."

For the Greenlanders that defeat to Kyrgyzstan could be their last international for some time. The following year, the Island Games will be in the Greek island of Rhodes, but for the first time there will be no Greenlandic male team. Again the problem is money. To send a squad to Rhodes would cost around 30,000 euros. If the Greenlandic FA drop their sponsor Coca-Cola in favour of the umbrella confederation's main sponsor Faxe Kondi and switched kit supplier to Nike, they would raise a total of around 8,500 euros. They would also lose two sponsors and still need to find another 21,500 euros.

Even if they could find the cash, that would only cover the men's side and the Greenland women's team would be left at home. To the likes of the phenomenally fair-minded Olesen and the Greenland FA, unable due to the island's autonomy to take any money from Denmark and abandoned by FIFA, there is no real choice. Kreutzmann's team will miss the next Island Games. Olesen explains: "It is in the way of money, so we will just send a women's team to Rhodes."

There is a long-term plan to lay an artificial turf pitch in Greenland and host a small tournament, but everything in the Arctic island costs twice the price compared to Denmark. Money, again, the problem.

At the two semi-finals in the Atatürk Stadium, Greenland's players all congregate in the side of the stadium kissed by the sun enjoying the late afternoon rays, sitting and talking, everyone together. Some of the Tibetans come to join them. No-one knows when the next tour for either side will be, when Niklas Kreutzmann will get the chance to be Greenland's captain again. In the ramshackle tea-room in the bowels of the stadium, Kreutzmann confides that he gets 200 euros a month from Aarhus Fremand and trains five times a week, but one player at big city rivals Aarhus gets paid more than the entire squad at Aarhus Fremand. Despite this, Kreutzmann is confident they are far enough clear of the drop to avoid relegation and remain in the same league. Of Greenland's future he is less sure. "It would be funny to send Jesper Gronkjaer a shirt to see if he wanted to play for us as he could still be playing for us at 40," says Kreutzmann without a hint of jealousy, as he and Olesen wander back to the rest of their squad and the warmth of the late afternoon sun.

The presence of the Greenland squad provides a fillip for Cengiz Uzun, who has also persuaded most of the other players to be there. The four eliminated squads provide the majority of the attendance. A big Friday night club game involving top side Çetinkaya might draw a crowd of 2,000 to the Atatürk stadium. For the ELF final, Uzun and the KTFF are expecting between 6,000 and 8,000 people to turn up. To help boost the crowd, everyone that buys a 20 Turkish Lira ticket goes into a raffle to win a new car, but the back-to-back semi-finals draw pitiful attendances.

Near the dug-outs, on the opposite side of the stadium to the Greenland and Tibetan players, sits the remainder of the competing teams, Khusravbek Murodov among them. "We could not have brought our full team. They would have eaten North Cyprus, but we cannot because of FIFA," says the magnificently chilled out Murodov, shrugging his shoulders as he indicates the Northern Cyprus squad warming up for their semi-final against Zanzibar.

Before that match, Kyrgyzstan had been surprisingly beaten by a more energized Crimea side. Crimea took the lead through a spectacular scissors kick, but Kyrgyzstan scored a late equalizer to send the game into extra time, during which the Crimeans scored two quick goals. Kyrgyzstan pulled one back and Crimea had a player sent off after two yellow cards, but hung on for the win.

Despite their victory, the Crimeans will not be speaking to anyone according to a blond female minder accompanying the squad. "Why do you want to know if anyone speaks English? For what purpose do you want to do this? No-one in the team speaks English," she says humourlessly. Her claim is strange as their keeper, Yakubov Nariman, exchanged pleasantries with a cameraman in English. But the minder, who refused to give her name, will not budge. No-one from the team will speak to the press - in any language.

As Zanzibar warm up for the second semi-final, German filmmaker Alisan Saltik cuts an isolated figure, standing alone and helping the keeper practice. In the stands, members of the Zanzibar party, particularly sports administration executive Ally Saleh, are not best pleased with Saltik. The officials feel that Saltik has not kept his promises with regards to training equipment from Puma and Adidas that he had promised for the Africans. A rift has developed between the two sides that looks irreparable. Saleh says: "I told Alisan that this trip does not help because it is only once a year. What we need is a big club having an academy in Zanzibar and coming over every year, like Manchester United. We have reached a place where we are stuck and can't go anywhere. We have a strong history of conflict with Tanzania. We are trying to channel our ideas through the TFF as FIFA want that all our projects go through them. We have a good relationship with the TFF on the surface, but underneath there is self-interest."

In the game, the young Zanzibaris are swept aside by the muscular Northern Cypriot hosts. Unable to make any impression on the home defence, Zanzibar are two down at half-time through goals from Ertaç Taskiran. The same player doubles that tally in the second half and a Coskun Ulusoy strike finishes off a 5-0 win. To the pleasure of Uzun and the KTFF officials, their side are in the final. Whether anyone else in the TRNC has noticed is debatable.

**\*\*\*\*\*\*\*\*\*\***

Two days later, on 25 November, the Atatürk Stadium hosts what should be the biggest game in Northern Cyprus football history. The match is previewed in the newspapers, but the 50 people watching a league match in Girne outnumber the crowd in the Atatürk Stadium watching the third place match between Zanzibar and Kyrgyzstan.

What should be a meaningless game produces some of the biggest drama of the ELF Cup, with the effervescent Kiyalbeck Diykanov, the Kyrgz goalkeeper, at its heart. Zanzibar go two goals up playing good, fluid football, but the Kyrgyz come back to equalise in the dying minutes. There is no extra time, straight to penalties and Diykanov is in his element. Constantly moving, up and down, he saves the third Zanzibar penalty only for one of his players to hit the post, as does the next Kyrgyz penalty. The Zanzibar keeper makes a save, but Suleiman Ali steps up for the final penalty and sends the ball over the bar, out-psyched by Diykanov. Kyrgyzstan triumph 9-8 and Diykanov's ecstatic reaction shows that the win means as much to him as Greenland's elimination meant to Kreutzmann.

The result also clearly meant something to Suleiman Ali, who has to be carried from the pitch crying uncontrollably. The post-match Zanzibar dressing room is filmed by the Israeli camera crew for a proposed TV series called 'Loca Room' about what happens in team changing rooms after the final whistle. The result here is absorbing. Coach Badre-el-din Abdulaziz is clearly disgusted. All completely terrified of their coach, the young Zanzibaris mutely follow his orders and remove their shoes and pray - for an alarming, riveting 20 minutes. This episode of the 'Loca Room' should make a gripping piece of TV.

In the final, the Crimea's improved run comes to an end. Their squad has some good players, including 17 year-old Rizvan Ablitarov, a professional in the Ukraine at Dnepr Dnepropetrovsk. Others have contracts in their native Ukraine, like CSKA Moscow's Fakhri Dzhelyalov, but most do not travel for fear of jeopardising their career. The Crimea are better than their first game against Northern Cyprus, but not good enough in a game watched by fewer than 1,000 people. That estimate includes police, officials and visiting teams. If Northern Cyprus cannot even attract a four figure crowd at six o'clock in the evening on a Saturday night, what future is there for the team?

"It will take a little time for the people to learn to love their national team," says Cengiz Uzun, as always eternally optimistic. "The people here complain about the embargoes and should come and support their national team, but they are not used to this, they would rather watch the big league matches from Turkey.

"We have peaceful feelings towards our neighbours, so why should FIFA put bans on our players? These are questions for the Greeks. If we can play internationals, we think that in a couple of years we can reach the same level as the Greek Cypriots. If we are able to play internationals, we can transfer players abroad and this will motivate the players that remain at home and will create a circle."

# The World Cup That Didn't Exist

His side has the Crimea running around in circles immediately. Hamis Çakir scores in the first minute. The female lineswoman, like all the ELF Cup officials a local, tentatively starts to raise her flag as he races through, then changes her mind. The visitors fail to respond, go in 1-0 down and fall further behind straight after the re-start to a goal from Hasan Sapsizoslu. It's effectively game over already. Ertaç Taskiran runs in a third on 55 minutes and although Irfan Ametov, a professional at Estonian champions Flora Tallin, shows some good touches, he goes to ground far too easily. Marlen Ablyatifov of Crimean side Krymgeofizika grabs a goal, but it is too late and Northern Cyprus run out easy 3-1 winners

The team celebrate wildly on the pitch as Queen's We Are The Champions predictably plays on the PA. In a 28,000 stadium barely occupied, the scene verges on eerie and the number of paying customers is best illustrated by the referee winning the car in the raffle. It makes you wonder if anyone bought a ticket for the ELF Cup?

The tournament cost around £135,000 and half of this was covered by the KTFF. Was it worth it? With the trophy added to the Peace Cup and the Wild Cup and the team unbeaten in 14 games, Northern Cyprus are looking for bigger opposition. Captain Hüseyin Amcaoglu says: "Now I think I want to play against San Marino, Malta or Luxembourg, but not Germany." A laudable and realistic ambition, but not one that FIFA will allow him to realize.

At the Atatürk Stadium, what crowd there is melts away into the TRNC and the teams return to Girne for a celebration dinner. For all the teams at the ELF Cup that are forgotten by FIFA, the question is 'where next?' For Zanzibar, there is a return to their African island, but Alisan Saltik is certainly not welcomed there by some members of the ZFA, such as Ally Saleh.

The pair's dispute rumbles on long after the ELF is finished. Zanzibar are invited to Germany, but do not go and at one point Saltik is rumoured to have left to coach Somalia. Zanzibar's president, Amani Karume, and Ali Ferej Tamin eventually becoming involved in the row over the role of the German film director in the Zanzibar team. "The problem was because of money," says Saltik from Germany. "Ali Juma Shamhuna is the new Sport Minister. Before it was Mr Haruna, and there was no problems because he also was involved in our film. But now Kombo Hassan [a ZFA official], Mr Salleh (sic) and Mr Shamunha are interested in cash-money, not sport and not Promotion. They don't know how difficult is it to finance a non-profit film in Europe and how expensive is an invitation to Germany. My reaction was to stop to talk with Mr Saleh, Mr Kombo and Shamunha, because they ask me to make together business, and I told them I am a filmmaker not a businessman. They are free to contact with business people in Germany, but not with me. Then they become angry, and then they refuse me to be team manager, but [ZFA President] Tamim call me and said to me, I am still the manager of Zanzibar."

Ally Saleh sees it differently, saying: "It is not true that the Minister and Alisan have settled. In fact, the Minister wrote to him that he should not at all involve himself with the Zanzibar team. Also he refused [an] Alisan call to get me and one delegate, Kombo Hassan, to be sacked from sports administration here in Zanzibar. He wrote a very destructive letter on my character and the Minister refused to agree with him, saying he knew me, Ally Saleh, better than Alisan knew me. He has to be involved in nothing as far as Zanzibar football matters is concerned. I think the ZFA still like him, but since the minister Ali Juma Shamhuna has said 'no', then it will remain 'no'."

Saltik's long-term role in Zanzibar football, despite publicizing their plight, seems in jeopardy, but for the KTFF and Cengiz Uzun, the Zanzibaris prove good contacts in their quest to establish the notion of Northern Cyprus as a state. In March 2007, the Northern Cyprus team, along with Cengiz Uzun, visit Tanzania and Zanzibar on a short tour and prove a big draw. The Tanzanian national team originally agree to take on Northern Cyprus then back out, but matches against two club sides attract crowds of 20,000. Northern Cyprus beat Tanzanian league champions Simba FC with two goals from Yasin Kansu and then draw 2-2 with cup winners, Yanga. After those games, Northern Cyprus spend five days in Zanzibar and take on their hosts' national side in a night match in front of a 6,000 crowd, but lost 2-1 despite taking the lead on 27 minutes through Hüseyin Amcaoslu.

For the well-travelled Uzun and the rest of the Northern Cypriot team, the trip was one of a lifetime. Uzun explains: "The spectators were amazing. The trip was very long and tiring, but it was so interesting that we will never forget. Africa was amazing, but the people are poor and need help. I will arrange a campaign for the schoolchildren for Zanzibar and juniors of Tanzania [for] shoes and schoolbags. I will be happy to succeed [in] this."

\*\*\*\*\*\*\*\*\*\*\*

A few months earlier, Uzun and the NF Board had made up, sending Christmas and New Year messages across the web. Everyone back together and still involved; but as far away from official recognition on the football pitch and FIFA membership as ever.

Then, in July 2007, English league side Luton Town visit Northern Cyprus for a training camp and a friendly is arranged with Çetinkaya at the Atatürk Stadium. The Greek Cypriots predictably cry foul and the match is cancelled, but FIFA and UEFA respond by asking the KTFF and their Greek Cypriot counterparts to Switzerland for talks on September 20. Progess.

# CHAPTER NINETEEN

# Football As Religion:
# The Vatican

*"The Vatican could, in future, field a team that plays at the top level with Roma, Inter Milan, Genoa and Sampdoria. We can recruit lads from the seminaries. I remember that in the World Cup of 1990 there were 42 players among the teams who made it to the finals who came from Salesian [Catholic] training centres all over the world. If we just take the Brazilian students from our Pontifical universities we could have a magnificent squad."*
**Cardinal Tarcisio Bertone, Vatican Secretary of State**

## 24 February 2007, Rome, Italy

TWO TEAMS OF PRIESTS from the seminaries of Pontifical Gregorian and Mater Ecclesiae are respectfully silent as a Cardinal Pio Laghi warns them they are "in sight of St Peter's, so behave". With that team talk over, the Brazilians of Pontifical Gregorian and the Latino, African and Asian side of Mater Ecclesiae - 'Mother of the Church College' in English - kick off the Clericus Cup in a small arena overlooking the Vatican. Played on artificial turf, the first game is viewed by a few hundred spectators, plus TV crews from Latin America and Germany. The Clericus Cup features 16 teams and over 200 clergymen from more than 50 countries, ranging from Papua New Guinea to Brazil and Rwanda.

That first fixture sees Mater Ecclesiae, featuring a goalkeeper called Jesus, score first with a penalty and romp home 6-0. The final is months away with many more matches before two sides are found to see who wins the odd little Clericus Cup trophy, but the early matches meet with approval of the clergymen playing. "I expect [the cup] to create a friendly relationship among the players and the teams," says Emil Martin from the Pontifical Urban College team. "I hope each one can learn to win, but also to lose because everybody needs to know how to lose."

The Clericus Cup was launched after a traumatic period in Italian football following the Azurri's World Cup triumph in Germany in 2006. Prior to that glory, a corruption enquiry had led to punishments for a number of leading clubs, including the relegation of Serie A giants Juventus. Then there was the continuing serious hooliganism at a number of matches that included the death of Inspector Filippo Raciti in Sicily just three weeks before the Clericus Cup kicked off.

Organised by the Italian Sporting Centre, which promotes Christian activity through sport, and with the Vatican's blessing, the Clericus Cup was trying to promote a different type of football. The matches in the tournament, a sort of mini-Catholic world cup for seminaries around Rome, are only 30 minutes each way. There is a blue card for indiscipline and offenders are sent to a sin-bin to reflect on any indiscretion on the pitch. There is a red card too, reserved for taking the Lord's name in vain and, unlike in the professional Italian leagues, no matches are played on a Sunday. Could the Clericus Cup save football's Italian soul or is the event about something else?

***********

The late Pope John Paul II was famously a former goalkeeper in his native Poland and the idea for the Clericus Cup comes from deep inside the Vatican itself, Cardinal Tarcisio Bertone, the Secretary of State at the Vatican and an ardent Juve fan. With its short matches aimed at encouraging older clergy into playing and its blue cards, the Clericus Cup could easily be dismissed as a religious stunt, but there is a more serious side to an event greeted as an "intelligent initiative" by the Italian Olympic Committee president, Gianni Petrucci.

Just two months before the Clericus Cup, Cardinal Bertone surprised Italians, UEFA and probably many Catholics with his suggestions that the Vatican could have a team in Serie A. He said: "The Vatican could, in future, field a team that plays at the top level with Roma, Inter Milan, Genoa and Sampdoria. We can recruit lads from the seminaries. I remember that in the World Cup of 1990 there were 42 players among the teams who made it to the finals who came from Salesian [Catholic] training centres all over the world. If we just take the Brazilian students from our Pontifical universities we could have a magnificent squad. Stadiums are modern temples, frequented by thousands of youths. I once carried out a Stations of the Cross in the Ferraris stadium [in Genoa].

"I don't exclude the possibility that in the future the Vatican could field a football team of the greatest value, at the level of the most famous professional clubs."

Bertone, the equivalent of Prime Minister in the Vatican, outlined his ideas as he was being awarded an honorary citizenship of Alassio near

Genoa. The idea provoked international media coverage, with Giovanni Trapattoni, a former manager of the Italian national team and then manager of FC Salzburg in Austria, being tipped as a coach for the Vatican side.

The suggestions even drew a response from UEFA, which knew that under its own rules the Vatican, as a member of the UN, could hardly be refused membership. Shortly after Bertone outlined his ideas, William Galliard, UEFA's chief spokesman, said: "We already have states of 30,000 citizens like San Marino, Liechtenstein and Andorra. If the Vatican wants to become a member of UEFA all it has to do is apply. If it meets the requirements it will be accepted."

That the Vatican is only 0.2 square miles in area and does not have a pitch (the Clericus Cup was played just outside the Holy See) did not seem to perturb anyone. It does help to have friends in high places. Then, the following day, Bertone was to swiftly retract his wishful thinking, saying: "It was fantasy fun to spread some cheer and maybe fill half a page of the newspapers."

Bertone's idea was not a complete Yuletide gag, though, which he made clear after Christmas to UEFA's own website, saying: "Trappatoni has not signed any contract and I think that no coach will sign a contract with Vatican clubs because it will still take quite some time. The idea reported by the newspapers is unfeasible. I've more important things to do than managing a Vatican football team."

Was Bertone joking or misinterpreted? Certainly about fielding a Serie A team, but perhaps not about the Vatican actually having a representative side, as the Clericus Cup featured just that, with a side taken from the Swiss Guards, the mini-army of Catholics drawn from Switzerland.

Only 800-odd people live and work in the micro-state of the Vatican, including the Swiss Guard, papal councillors and museum guards, who are Italian citizens. The Swiss Guard take Vatican citizenship, but they are a tiny force and finding time to field a team is not easy.

The Vatican side that played Monaco in 2002 was drawn from the Swiss Guard, but like many things in the Vatican, the team is shrouded in mystery - even the result of that game remains a subject of debate with the Roon Ba putting it at 0-0, but Vatican insiders insisting it was 1-1. There was another 'international' against San Marino, which also reputedly was a draw, though the exact result remains unclear. Apparently, this game was part of a mini-tournament played on an amateur level that was won by Siena, who beat the Vatican in the final. There was also another game that was more widely publicised in 2006, when the Vatican side thrashed Swiss non-league club SV Vollmond 5-1.

The team has been organized in the past by Sergio Valci, but he does not like to be drawn on the subject of the Vatican international side, which the organisers of the Wild Cup, the Viva World Cup and the ELF Cup all tried without success to invite to their tournaments. What is less widely known is that someone involved with the Vatican side was invited and did attend the ELF Cup to make contact. Nothing further has come of it yet, but seeds have been sown.

The Vatican team are a popular choice of opponent that only rarely play games and then only against uncontroversial opposition because of what a fixture against the Holy See means: a form of recognition that politicians cannot or will not provide. In an era when politics means less and less, particularly in more industrialized countries, when fewer and fewer people turn out to vote, sport crystalizes the notion of a nation perhaps more than anything else. The higher echelons of the Holy See realize that and are not about to confirm this form of nation status on just about anyone, much to FIFA and UEFA's relief, so games for the Vatican side are likely to remain occasional affairs. Certainly the Northern Cypriots would view such a match as a major stepping stone to recognition as a nation in both political and football circles.

The Clericus Cup's attempt to produce a different sort of football does not entirely work out. The long-anticipated final is contested on 27 May between the Pontifical Lateran University and a side from Redemptoris Mater College, led by a Costa Rican striker, but the sides are mostly made up of Italians. The Redemptoris XI even includes one player who was formerly on the youth team at Serie A side Chievo Verona. Redemptoris, coached by Simone Bondi, won the trophy due to a dubious spot-kick that caused uproar among the Pontifical Lateran University side. The Lateran side insisted that the Costa Rican striker had dived and a host of blue cards were handed out to their players for hectoring the referee. Afterwards, Lateran's university rector, Bishop Rino Fisichella, said of his team: "These are children of our time."

If and when the Vatican do manage to get another 'international' match arranged, do not expect saintly football.

# CHAPTER TWENTY

# Tribal Football: The Sápmi

*"It's not a land at all, actually. Samiland is a theoretical conception.
It has no borders, therefore it can stretch."*
**Harald Gaski, professor of Sami literature at the University of Tromso**

## 8 July 2007, Karasjok, Norway

THE WIND PICKED up the sand lying around the two grass pitches at the home of Nordlys IL in Karasjok, the Norwegian capital of Sápmi, and blew particles into the faces of the fans and players. The sun was shining, but any warmth was being taken away by the wind and a few dozen fans left before the Sami Cup final kicked off in the later afternoon, Guovdageainnu Luntta II lining up against Stil.

A couple of hours earlier, the broad, cheery Leif Isak Nilut had strode across the pitches at Nordlys, resplendent in leather trousers and his traditional Sami jacket. The President of the Sami FA, the SSL, had arrived. His Vice-President, Hakan Kuorak, had been there for hours, though, strolling around in defence for the sole Swedish entrants in the Sami Cup, Storlule Sameforening.

Reindeer herding and lasso throwing are traditional Sami sports, but since the first cup was held in 1978, the tribe have taken football to their hearts. The Sami Cup is the largest of more than a dozen football competitions held over the Nordic summer for Sami players. Since first being staged, the Sami Cup has alternated around Sápmi, traversing the borders of Norway, Sweden and Finland. For the first time a team of Russians has travelled the five hour journey from near Murmansk on the Kola pensinula to take part.

The Sami tribe are seemingly re-united by football. Nilut is pleased, his ambition that bit closer to being met. "Our aim is to join FIFA," said Nilut the night before, smoking a cigarette outside the Hotel Rika Annekset in his normal clothes, his previously long hair all shorn.

The ambitions for the SSL of Nilut, who was a volleyball player in his youth rather than a footballer, and Kuorak are growing. Jens Tang Olesen invited the Sami to come to Copenhagen for a friendly in two months to play his Greenland side and possibly Northern Cyprus. Nilut declined. "After Occitania, we need to

181

play the strongest teams possible," he explains. "I have been to Torshavn and met with the Faroes FA. We have good relations and our aim for this season will be a game with their national team, but these things take time."

Nilut's experience in Sami affairs landed him the job, with Kuorak brought in for his football knowledge. Finding a tournament for the Sami side to play in was a necessary vindication for the tribe's football devotee's decision to leave their umbrella sports organization in 2003 and set up the SSL. For the first time, there was no Swedish Sami or Norwegian Sami, just one tribal team representing the common people regardless of borders.

After Nilut's performance at the 2005 NF Board meeting in London, discovering that he works out of the National Sami theatre in Norway is not a surprise. That heartfelt yoik in the Royal National Hotel two years ago is, according to the locals, a regular occurrence for Nilut. After winning the VWC, he yoiked and he will, undoubtedly, yoik again. "He's a showman," says one local with a smile.

Like the Occitànians, the Sami are asserting their identity through a variety of means from football to the arts and yoiking. One of Europe's oldest forms of music, singers do not perform a yoik, but yoik about a subject, like Sami football, invoking a feeling such as joy or sadness. The Sami language has many different dialects and a singer yoiks in the dialect they were brought up with. A musical movement has grown in recent years pioneered by yoikers such as Sara Marielle Gaup and Lawra Somby and leading to offshoots such as heavy yoik.

Nilut had yoiked to the baffled assembled NF Board over what it meant to be a Sami and what it meant to be a Sami in a different context - on the football field.

A sort of throat singing crossed with Guns'N'Roses, one of the leading exponents of the art of yoik, Intrique, are playing as part of a three-day music festival held in Karasjok to coincide with the Sami Cup. One can almost imagine this method of expressing one's support for a team catching on in football culture in a wider context. It is guttural, tribal, and perhaps as naked an expression of affiliation to a team or country as English fans singing one of their more infamous chants. Mind you, in this world where elements of culture can be appropriated by audiences across the globe in an instant, it is possible to imagine Wembley resound to an 'English' yoik, while the Sami adapt the terrace chant in support of their national team, adapting it to their own very particular situation by singing, "He's here, He's there, He's every fucking where; Santa Claus!"

***********

# Tribal Football: The Sápmi

The idea of a national team based on a disparate tribe sounds unworkable. NF Board contacts with a group supposedly representing a football body for the Maasai tribe in Africa seem to have gone nowhere, but there are examples of tribal-based national sides in other sports. The New Zealand Maori are a fixture in rugby union. The team is a form of development side for the New Zealand Rugby Football Union and a plum fixture for touring sides, although the Maori do not compete in world cups.

One tribal side that does compete in a world championship is the Iroquois Nationals. The sport of lacrosse was developed in the Iroquois confederacy of around half a dozen tribes in North America and, to recognise this, the Iroquois were admitted to the Australian-based International Lacrosse Federation in 1990. No-one still involved with the ILF wants to recall how a tribe came to join countries such as Australia, Canada, the Czech Republic, Japan, Sweden and the United States and take a place at the Lacrosse World Cup. President Peter Hobbs would only say: "The Iroquois people were the inventors of lacrosse and have a very strong national identity which crosses over national borders between USA and Canada [although] they are generally located around the area of the Great Lakes."

At the 1999 world championship, the Iroquois finished third - ahead of England and hosts Australia - then managed fourth place at both the 2002 championships in Perth, Australia, and London, Ontario. Iroquois players also play professionally in North America, which provided an example for Kuorak and Nilut and the Sami team.

The term Sami refers to the people themselves and Sápmi to their land, which is more commonly known as Lapland to outsiders, though none of the various Sami from Sweden, Norway, Finland and the Kola peninsular in Russia accept that name or refer to themselves as Laps.

Inger Marie G. Eira, a Sami academic doing a thesis on the affect of global warming on reindeer herding, explains: "We don't like the term Lapland because it is derogatory. People come here looking for Laps, but there are not any Laps only Sami. It's the same in Greenland if you talk about Eskimo. They are Inuit."

The Sami are reclaiming their original name and their language. Three Norwegian newspapers funded by the state write solely in Sami, of which there are 10 dialects. But the Sami are not, so far, reclaiming their territory. Harald Gaski, professor of Sami literature at the University of Tromso, says: "It's not a land at all, actually. Samiland is a theoretical conception. It has no borders, therefore it can stretch."

In fact a Lapland border was drawn up in 1751 and technically still exists, but as the Sami do not recognise that term, they cannot recognise that border. Sometimes referred to as the gypsies of the north, the Sami are a Christian indigenous tribe that has been suppressed in all four countries, particularly in Sweden, where about 20,000 of the 70,000 Sami live. The majority live in Norway - about 40,000 of the tribe - with another 6,000 in Finland. Over the centuries, their language was discouraged, land appropriated by states they did not recognize and their medicine men were even flogged at one point.

This continued into the twentieth century and between 1920 and 1939 Sami were forcibly removed from parts of northern Sweden and relocated in the south. The introduction of national parks across Scandinavia took its toll on the traditional Sami activity of reindeer herding. Legalisation of small game hunting in Sami areas was another problem and by the 1970s, a campaign of civil disobedience had started that led to hunger strikes and a bridge being blown up at Alta in Norway. Concerned that the Sami could launch a bid for independence, the Norwegian secret service started monitoring Sami activists, but the political mood towards the tribe changed. In 1973, Finland set up the first Sami parliament and four years later, the Swedish government officially recognized the Sami as their country's indigenous people. A Sápmi flag was adopted in 1986 and three years later, a Sápmi parliament was set up in Norway in Karasjok, followed by another in Sweden in 1993. In 1998, the Swedish government formally apologised to the Sami for the state's oppression.

Today the Sami in Norway, Sweden and Finland co-operate in a larger parliamentary Council, a sort of forum that also includes representatives of the 2,000 Russian Sami in the Kola Peninsula. The forum and the parliaments are part of the Sami assuming more responsibility for their own affairs, including language, education and reindeer husbandry, which employs around 10,000 Sami. It is a similar style of devolution that has marked the modern Labour era in the UK.

Before the appearance of the NF Board on message boards and internet forums, Nilut and Kuorak's passion, Sápmi football, had no outlet. The national team had played ad hoc internationals since making its debut in a 4-2 away defeat to Åland in 1985. The team managed a game against the old East German side in 1987 and proved handy opponents over a handful of games for Estonia prior to the Baltic states' breakaway from Russia and entry into UEFA. The Sápmi side does not include players from Russian's Kola peninsula, but the very idea of a national team drawn from a tribe covering three countries was too much for FIFA to cope with and an application from the Sami to join in the mid-1990s was predictably rejected.

After that disappointment, the Sápmi team suffered and the annual Sami tournament was the only focus left. Football then was part of a larger Sami Athletics Association and that, for Nilut and Kuorak, contributed to the problem of the dissipation of the game that they both loved.

# Tribal Football: The Sápmi

Kuorak explains: "You wonder why the Sami football was set up separately? It was because the Sami Athletic Association could have people who only mind about skiing and all the money that the association gets goes into skiing. Some other year it comes to people who mind about other sports, such as reindeer running and athletics."

Nilut and Kuorak broke away from the athletics association to set up the SSL and attended the founding meeting of the NF Board in Brussels on 12 December 2003 as they started a search for more wide-spread opponents. Nilut explains: "In October 2003, that was our first general meeting. What we achieved in [the first two years] was to put together a national league and we have had a training camp for the girls' national team. Before, the organisation was not working. We decided to join the NF Board because it represents indigenous people and organisations that cannot ever be recognised by FIFA."

The new Sami Football Association crucially retained the support of the Sápmi parliaments, who were asked to help out with a chronic shortage of funds.

***********

Unlike some of the other nascent national teams banging on FIFA's door, Nilut and Kuorak knew they had a decent pool of players to draw from. Probably the most famous Sami player in the UK is Blackburn Rovers' winger Morten Gamst Pedersen. Pedersen grew up in Vadso, a town of just 6,000 people in the far north east of Norway on the same latitude as Alaska, Greenland and Siberia. His father Ernst is a director at Bodo Glimt, a northern Norwegian side recently relegated to the country's second tier, but Pedersen signed for First Division side Tromso. He was then picked up by Blackburn and now has celebrity status in Norway, advertising hair products and even spending one summer in a boy-band called The Players that had a big hit across Scandinavia in 2006 with a single called 'This is for Real'. Unfortunately for Nilut and Kuorak, although Pedersen has often been to and played in Sami Cup competitions in the past, he has shown little interest in the Sápmi team; probably because he is a regular in the Norwegian national side.

"Morten Gamst will play when he has retired from the Norway team," says Nilut confidently. "None of the football federations here have a problem with us because we always have our papers in order and insurance."

Other Sami playing professionally in Scandinavia have shown more interest in the team. Nilut and Kuorak also knew there existed the foundations of a team in the Sami Cup and that there was plenty of passion to represent their people among the Sami. Players like Leif Arne Brekke, a right back with Åmot in the Norwegian Second Division, who plays in the same position for the Sami team.

# OUTCASTS: The Lands That FIFA Forgot

In Karasjok, Brekke is playing for Johkahtte Searat. He gets on the score sheet, but, after three days of qualifying matches among the 15 teams, which are comprised of friends or relatives or associations like the Karasjok Reindeer Herders' Association, Brekke's side do not make the semi-finals. The local reindeer herders do, but are edged out by Guovdageainnu Luntta II to set up a final with the 2005 winners, Stil.

Brekke says: "I'm proud to be here and play for the Sami team because it's important to both my people and my family. The interest for football is huge in my family, so it means a lot to me to be a member of the team. For the Sami team it will always be a question of money. We have good players and trainers, but need more money to develop ourselves. Sometimes it goes three to four years between matches because our football association can't afford to send us anywhere, and that is our main problem today."

After that NF Board meeting in Brussels, Northern Cyprus were obvious initial opponents and Nilut and Kuorak persuaded the KTFF to send a team to Tromso in July 2004. That fixture was the first organised by the Sami Football Association and the cost of staging the game - about 30,000 Norwegian Krone (£2,500) - was covered by the Norwegian government. Perhaps predictably, the Greek Cypriots objected, insisting that by supporting the game, the Norwegian government was promoting separatism, but the game went ahead.

When Northern Cyprus invited Nilut's Sápmi side for a re-match in the Peace Cup in 2005, the burly Sami had to go to the Norwegian parliament and beg for funds. The plan was to take a 22 man squad for what was initially expected to be a four way tournament with the hosts, Kosovo and Monaco before the Monégasque got cold feet and pulled out. The Norwegian parliament agreed to stump up 100,000 Norwegian Krone (£8,400) and the Sami Football Association matched that amount, but Nilut was still short by 50,000 (£4,200) Norwegian Krone. He was relying on funding from the Ministry of Local Government & Regional Development, but that ran into problems. To compromise, the squad was cut to 18 players and the Sami team went ahead, perhaps glad that the Monégasque could not make it, thus shortening their stay and financial commitments.

The NF Board's announcement that the first Viva World Cup would be in Northern Cyprus caused some consternation in Sápmi and the expense and political consternation caused by the Sami team's trip out for the Peace Cup did little to soothe that situation. Nilut, Kuorak and the Sami Football Association faced another difficult decision. To justify their new association's existence, to feel like Sami on a football field, in the traditional red, blue and yellow colours of their tribe, they needed a tournament to play in. The problem was that, if that tournament was going to be in Northern Cyprus, their chances of getting the cash to fund the trip out of any of the three Sápmi parliaments was - due to Greek Cypriot pressure - going to be virtually non-existent.

Six months after returning from southern France, Nilut reckons the trip ended up costing something like 320,000 Norwegian Krone (about £27,000). For now, the Sami are lying low, waiting for their next chance to play again. Nilut knows that to go back for more money he needs better opponents than the VWC provided - hence the attempt to play the Faroes.

**********

In Karasjok, Stil romp to victory. The Stil side is made up mostly of players from Bossekop, who were leading their regional third tier before the mid-season break. After withstanding some early pressure, Stil take the lead as Karstin Pettersen lobs the Guovdageainnu goalkeeper from his own half and score a second through captain Morten Jagervand. The game is virtually lost for Guovdageainnu when they have a player sent off before half-time.

Guovdageainnu tried to take the game to Stil after the break, but let in three more goals with a fine strike from Jagervand - the game's best player - followed by goals from Ermin Bectesevic and Oyvind Veseth Olsen. The Guovdageainnu goalkeeper then came charging out of his area to make a clumsy clearance and was also sent off. Lasse Person converted the penalty and his brother Per Erland Person scored a seventh and final goal, also from the spot, on the final whistle.

The sendings off were an exception to an otherwise well-behaved tournament. The Sami, it seems, do not generally like hurting each other, but the two red cards were indicative of how the tournament is becoming more professional.

"Not all these are Sami," adds Inger Marie G. Eira, who has two sons and a daughter playing in the Sami Cup. Not only is there a men's tournament, but also a competition for women and boys - albeit relegated to the sole artificial turf in Karasjok.

The Sami Cup is at a crucial point in its development. Teams are taking it more seriously, bringing in ringers and not all the smaller Sami villages are entering teams as they once did. A rival tournament - not strictly for the Sami - was also set up a few years ago. The Verdde Cup is named after the term that refers to the annual summer exchange between Sami reindeer herders and the people who lived by the sea shore. The herders would trade reindeer pelts and meat for fish and that was known as Verdde. Local Sami journalist Ante Jovna Gaup explains: "The important thing at that tournament is the meeting and the friendship, but it's only right that the Sami get more professional if they want to join FIFA."

# OUTCASTS: The Lands That FIFA Forgot

For the SSL to achieve its ultimate goal - FIFA membership - it faces the price of acceptance at the high table of world football: something it seems has to be lost if football is going to be used to keep alive the idea of a single Sami identity.

***********

As the world's most popular team sport, football keeps alive the idea of a national identity undefined by political borders better than most. The notion of Englishness and Scottishness, for example, has been kept alive by sport as much as anything else since the Act of the Union in 1707. In places where identity is slowly starting to mean less and less, in an age of globalization where satellite TV is watering down local sports in favour of global brands, some peoples are trying to keep alive an identity that is being lost through football.

As the game's supposed guardian, FIFA can - and has - conferred a notion of nationhood through membership on places that are anything but. Other sports are able to be more flexible than FIFA because they are not as popular as football, not as high profile, not as meaningful in a global and political sense. But if FIFA is really running football for the good of the game, as Sepp Blatter's slogan declares, what was good for football about stopping the Afghanistan team from playing in the ELF Cup? What is good for football about leaving Greenland's football association so impoverished that they cannot field a team every two years to represent its 5,000 footballers? What is good for football in having the Monaco national team effectively barred from playing in their own country by the presence of a club side?

FIFA cannot admit every place or organization that is using football as a promotional means, and nor should they, but if FIFA chooses to continue to ignore places that cannot, for whatever reasons, help themselves, how is that for the good of the game?

# RESULTS

This results section is mostly taken from the archive of the Roon Ba website and features results of places covered in chapter order. Results are only included in the Roon Ba where teams have played against another territory's full national XI and not B or under-21 teams. The Roon Ba contains many more results and forthcoming fixtures of other non-FIFA teams and full FIFA members, women's football and international futsal. The site can be accessed at http://www.roonba.co.nr.

## ISLAND GAMES FOOTBALL 2005

### GROUP ONE

|              | P | W | D | L | F  | A  | PTS | +/- |
|--------------|---|---|---|---|----|----|-----|-----|
| Shetlands    | 4 | 3 | 1 | 0 | 8  | 1  | 10  | 7   |
| Isle of Man  | 4 | 2 | 1 | 1 | 12 | 3  | 7   | 9   |
| Saarema      | 4 | 1 | 2 | 1 | 5  | 5  | 5   | 0   |
| Aland        | 4 | 1 | 0 | 3 | 4  | 7  | 3   | -3  |
| Falklands    | 4 | 1 | 0 | 3 | 3  | 16 | 3   | -13 |

### GROUP TWO

|               | P | W | D | L | F  | A  | PTS | +/- |
|---------------|---|---|---|---|----|----|-----|-----|
| Guernsey      | 4 | 4 | 0 | 0 | 14 | 1  | 12  | 13  |
| Western Isles | 4 | 1 | 2 | 1 | 10 | 10 | 5   | 0   |
| Yns Mon       | 4 | 1 | 2 | 1 | 2  | 3  | 5   | -1  |
| Greenland     | 4 | 1 | 2 | 1 | 6  | 11 | 5   | -5  |
| Orkney        | 4 | 0 | 0 | 4 | 5  | 12 | 0   | -7  |

### PLAY-OFFS

| | | | |
|---|---|---|---|
| **Final**   | Shetlands      | Guernsey    | 2-0 |
| **Bronze**  | Western isles  | Isle of Man | 4-0 |
| **5th-6th** | Saarema        | Yns Mon     | 2-3 |
| **7th-8th** | Aland          | Greenland   | 3-2 |
| **9th-10th**| Falkland Isles | Orkney      | 0-2 |

**Source: IGA**

## UNPO CUP 2005

| | | | |
|---|---|---|---|
| **Semi-final** | Chechnya | Southern Cameroon | 2-2 |
| | (Chechnya on penalties) | | |
| **Semi-final** | South Moluccas | West Papua | 1-1 |
| | (South Moluccas won on penalties) | | |
| **Final** | Chechnya | South Moluccas | 1-3 |

**Source: UNPO**

## WILD CUP 2006

**GROUP A**

| | P | W | D | L | F | A | PTS | +/- |
|---|---|---|---|---|---|---|---|---|
| St Pauli | 2 | 1 | 1 | 0 | 8 | 1 | 4 | 7 |
| Gibraltar | 2 | 1 | 1 | 0 | 6 | 1 | 4 | 5 |
| Tibet | 2 | 0 | 0 | 2 | 0 | 12 | 0 | -12 |

**GROUP B**

| | P | W | D | L | F | A | PTS | +/- |
|---|---|---|---|---|---|---|---|---|
| North Cyprus | 2 | 2 | 0 | 0 | 4 | 1 | 6 | 3 |
| Zanzibar | 2 | 1 | 0 | 1 | 5 | 5 | 3 | 0 |
| Greenland | 2 | 0 | 0 | 2 | 2 | 5 | 0 | -3 |

| | | | |
|---|---|---|---|
| **SEMI FINALS** | North Cyprus | Gibraltar | 2-0 |
| | St Pauli | Zanzibar | 1-2 |
| **THIRD PLACE** | St Pauli | Gibraltar | 1-2 |
| **FINAL** | North Cyprus | Zanzibar | 0-0 |
| | (North Cyprus win 4-1 on penalties) | | |

## VIVA WORLD CUP

| | | | |
|---|---|---|---|
| **Group games** | Occitania | Sapmi | 0-7 |
| | Occitania | Monaco | 2-3 |
| | Sapmi | Monaco | 14-0 |
| **Final** | Sapmi | Monaco | 21-0 |

# ELC CUP

**GROUP A**

|  | P | W | D | L | F | A | PTS | +/- |
|---|---|---|---|---|---|---|---|---|
| Kyrgyzstan | 3 | 2 | 0 | 1 | 7 | 3 | 6 | 4 |
| Zanzibar | 3 | 1 | 2 | 0 | 3 | 2 | 5 | 1 |
| Greenland | 3 | 1 | 1 | 1 | 3 | 2 | 4 | 1 |
| Gagauzia | 3 | 0 | 0 | 3 | 3 | 9 | 0 | -6 |

**GROUP B**

|  | P | W | D | L | F | A | PTS | +/- |
|---|---|---|---|---|---|---|---|---|
| North Cyprus | 3 | 3 | 0 | 0 | 20 | 1 | 9 | 19 |
| Crimea | 3 | 2 | 0 | 1 | 3 | 6 | 6 | -3 |
| Tajikistan | 3 | 1 | 0 | 2 | 5 | 7 | 3 | -2 |
| Tibet | 3 | 0 | 0 | 3 | 0 | 14 | 0 | -14 |

| **SEMI FINALS** | Kyrgyzstan | Crimea | 2-3 |
|---|---|---|---|
|  | North Cyprus | Zanzibar | 5-0 |
| **THIRD PLACE** | Kyrgyzstan | Zanzibar | 2-2 |
|  | (Kyrgystan win 9-8 on penalties) | | |
| **FINAL** | North Cyprus | Crimea | 3-1 |

# ISLAND GAMES FOOTBALL 2007

**GROUP A**

|  | P | W | D | L | F | A | PTS | +/- |
|---|---|---|---|---|---|---|---|---|
| Gibraltar | 2 | 1 | 1 | 0 | 3 | 2 | 4 | 1 |
| Jersey | 2 | 1 | 1 | 0 | 2 | 1 | 4 | 1 |
| Menorca | 2 | 0 | 0 | 2 | 1 | 3 | 0 | -2 |

**GROUP B**

|  | P | W | D | L | F | A | PTS | +/- |
|---|---|---|---|---|---|---|---|---|
| Bermuda | 2 | 1 | 0 | 1 | 3 | 2 | 3 | 1 |
| Aland | 2 | 1 | 0 | 1 | 4 | 4 | 3 | 0 |
| Yns Mon | 2 | 1 | 0 | 1 | 4 | 5 | 3 | -1 |

**GROUP C**

|  | P | W | D | L | F | A | PTS | +/- |
|---|---|---|---|---|---|---|---|---|
| Rhodes | 2 | 2 | 0 | 0 | 5 | 1 | 6 | 4 |
| Froya | 2 | 1 | 0 | 1 | 4 | 5 | 3 | -1 |
| Saarema | 2 | 0 | 0 | 2 | 2 | 5 | 0 | -3 |

## GROUP D

| | P | W | D | L | F | A | PTS | +/- |
|---|---|---|---|---|---|---|---|---|
| Western Isles | 2 | 2 | 0 | 0 | 5 | 2 | 6 | 3 |
| Gotland | 2 | 0 | 0 | 2 | 2 | 5 | 0 | -3 |

## PLAY-OFFS

| | | | |
|---|---|---|---|
| **Final** | Gibraltar | Rhodes | 4-0 |
| **Bronze** | Bermuda | Western Isles | 0-1 |
| **5th-6th** | Jersey | Gotland | 1-0 |

Source: IGA

# INDIVIDUAL TEAM RESULTS BY CHAPTER ORDER

### THE MURATTI VASE

06-05-2007 • Guernsey 0-0 Jersey • in Guernsey •
After extra-time, Jersey won 3-2 on penalties
17-03-2007 • Alderney 0-4 Guernsey in Alderney
01-05-2006 • Jersey 3-2 Guernsey • in Jersey
15-05-2005 • Jersey 3-3 Guernsey • in Jersey
• After extra-time, Full-time 2-2, Guernsey won 3-2 on penalties
02-05-2005 • Guernsey 0-0 Jersey • in Guernsey
• After extra-time, Full-time 0-0
12-03-2005 • Alderney 1-2 Guernsey • in Alderney
03-05-2004 • Jersey 3-0 Guernsey • in Jersey
18-05-2003 • Jersey 1-0 Guernsey • in Jersey
05-05-2003 • Guernsey 3-3 Jersey • in Guernsey
• After extra-time, Full-time 1-1
22-03-2003 • Alderney 1-4 Guernsey • in Alderney
06-05-2002 • Jersey 2-1 Guernsey • in Jersey
07-05-2001 • Guernsey 4-1 Jersey • in Guernsey
24-03-2001 • Alderney 0-6 Guernsey • in Alderney
01-05-2000 • Jersey 1-0 Guernsey • in Jersey
03-05-1999 • Guernsey 2-0 Jersey • in Guernsey
• After extra-time, Full-time 0-0
27-03-1999 • Alderney 0-1 Guernsey • in Alderney
04-05-1998 • Jersey 2-0 Guernsey in Jersey
05-05-1997 • Guernsey 2-1 Jersey • in Guernsey

# Results

22-03-1997 • Alderney 0-6 Guernsey • in Alderney
19-05-1996 • Guernsey 0-1 Jersey • in Guernsey
06-05-1996 • Jersey 0-0 Guernsey • in Jersey
• After extra-time, Full-time 0-0
16-03-1996 • Alderney 0-2 Guernsey • in Alderney
30-04-1995 • Guernsey 1-2 Jersey • in Guernsey
02-05-1994 • Jersey 3-1 Guernsey • in Jersey
03-05-1993 • Guernsey 1-2 Jersey • in Guernsey
20-03-1993 • Alderney 0-10 Guernsey • in Alderney
04-05-1992 • Jersey 2-3 Guernsey • in Jersey
• After extra-time, Full-time 2-2
21-03-1992 • Guernsey 9-1 Alderney • in Guernsey
06-05-1991 • Guernsey 3-0 Jersey • in Guernsey
07-05-1990 • Jersey 2-1 Guernsey • in Jersey
31-03-1990 • Guernsey 4-0 Alderney • in Guernsey
01-05-1989 • Guernsey 0-4 Jersey • in Guernsey
02-05-1988 • Jersey 0-1 Guernsey • in Jersey
26-03-1988 • Alderney 1-5 Guernsey • in Alderney
01-05-1987 • Guernsey 3-4 Jersey • in Guernsey
• After extra-time, Full-time 3-3
09-05-1986 • Jersey 3-2 Guernsey • in Jersey
09-04-1986 • Guernsey 7-0 Alderney • in Guernsey
06-05-1985 • Guernsey 4-3 Jersey • in Guernsey
09-05-1984 • Jersey 6-2 Guernsey • in Jersey
• After extra-time, Full-time 2-2
31-03-1984 • Alderney 0-6 Guernsey • in Alderney
02-05-1983 • Guernsey 2-1 Jersey • in Guernsey
09-05-1982 • Jersey 2-1 Guernsey • in Jersey
24-03-1982 • Guernsey 5-1 Alderney • in Guernsey
04-05-1981 • Guernsey 1-4 Jersey • in Guernsey
09-05-1980 • Jersey 1-2 Guernsey • in Jersey
• After extra-time, Full-time 1-1
29-03-1980 • Alderney 0-5 Guernsey • in Alderney
09-05-1979 • Guernsey 5-0 Jersey • in Guernsey
09-05-1978 • Jersey 0-2 Guernsey • in Jersey
01-04-1978 • Guernsey 12-0 Alderney • in Guernsey
09-05-1977 • Guernsey 1-5 Jersey • in Guernsey
09-05-1976 • Jersey 3-1 Guernsey • in Jersey
20-03-1976 • Alderney 0-5 Guernsey • in Alderney
26-05-1975 • Jersey 2-3 Guernsey • in Jersey
• After extra-time, Full-time 2-2
09-05-1975 • Guernsey 2-2 Jersey • in Guernsey
• After extra-time, Full-time 2-2
09-05-1974 • Jersey 1-2 Guernsey • in Jersey
• After extra-time, Full-time 1-1

30-03-1974 • Guernsey 6-0 Alderney • in Guernsey
09-05-1973 • Guernsey 1-4 Jersey • in Guernsey
09-05-1972 • Jersey 0-3 Guernsey • in Jersey
• After extra-time, Full-time 0-0
03-04-1972 • Guernsey 5-0 Alderney • in Guernsey
15-05-1971 • Guernsey 0-1 Jersey • in Guernsey
09-05-1970 • Jersey 2-0 Guernsey • in Jersey
04-04-1970 • Guernsey 5-0 Alderney • in Guernsey
09-05-1969 • Guernsey 2-1 Jersey • in Guernsey
• After extra-time, Full-time 1-1
09-05-1968 • Jersey 2-1 Guernsey • in Jersey
30-03-1968 • Guernsey 2-0 Alderney • in Guernsey
09-05-1967 • Guernsey 1-3 Jersey • in Guernsey
• After extra-time, Full-time 1-1
09-05-1966 • Guernsey 3-1 Jersey • in Guernsey
05-05-1966 • Jersey 1-1 Guernsey • in Jersey
• After extra-time, Full-time 1-1
02-04-1966 • Guernsey 10-0 Alderney • in Guernsey
06-05-1965 • Guernsey 2-4 Jersey • in Guernsey
07-05-1964 • Jersey 1-0 Guernsey • in Jersey
11-04-1964 • Guernsey 3-0 Alderney • in Guernsey
02-05-1963 • Guernsey 1-4 Jersey • in Guernsey
03-05-1962 • Jersey 2-1 Guernsey • in Jersey
29-03-1962 • Guernsey 6-1 Alderney • in Guernsey
04-05-1961 • Guernsey 1-2 Jersey • in Guernsey
05-05-1960 • Jersey 5-1 Guernsey • in Jersey
31-03-1960 • Guernsey 5-1 Alderney • in Guernsey
30-04-1959 • Guernsey 2-3 Jersey • in Guernsey
01-05-1958 • Jersey 2-1 Guernsey • in Jersey
27-03-1958 • Guernsey 8-2 Alderney • in Guernsey
02-05-1957 • Guernsey 6-4 Jersey • in Guernsey
03-05-1956 • Jersey 2-1 Guernsey • in Jersey
22-03-1956 • Guernsey 4-0 Alderney • in Guernsey
30-05-1955 • Jersey 1-0 Guernsey • in Jersey
05-05-1955 • Guernsey 0-0 Jersey • in Guernsey
• After extra-time, Full-time 0-0
06-05-1954 • Jersey 3-5 Guernsey • in Jersey
01-04-1954 • Guernsey 2-1 Alderney • in Guernsey
30-04-1953 • Guernsey 0-2 Jersey • in Guernsey
01-05-1952 • Jersey 1-3 Guernsey • in Jersey
03-04-1952 • Guernsey 7-2 Alderney • in Guernsey
03-05-1951 • Guernsey 3-1 Jersey • in Guernsey
• After extra-time, Full-time 1-1
04-05-1950 • Jersey 0-2 Guernsey • in Jersey
30-03-1950 • Guernsey 3-1 Alderney • in Guernsey

# Results

05-05-1949 • Guernsey 1-2 Jersey • in Guernsey
06-05-1948 • Jersey 6-3 Guernsey • in Jersey
15-04-1948 • Guernsey 3-0 Alderney • in Guernsey
01-05-1947 • Guernsey 1-3 Jersey • in Guernsey
02-05-1946 • Guernsey 0-4 Jersey • (Peace Cup) in Guernsey
11-04-1946 • Jersey 7-0 Guernsey • (Peace Cup) in Jersey
04-05-1939 • Guernsey 0-1 Jersey • in Guernsey
05-05-1938 • Guernsey 3-1 Alderney • in Jersey
28-04-1938 • Guernsey 4-3 Jersey • in Guernsey
17-05-1937 • Guernsey 3-3 Jersey • in Guernsey
• After extra-time, Full-time 3-3
29-04-1937 • Jersey 2-2 Guernsey • in Jersey
• After extra-time, Full-time 2-2
15-04-1937 • Guernsey 4-1 Alderney • in Guernsey
07-05-1936 • Guernsey 2-1 Jersey • in Guernsey
09-05-1935 • Guernsey 5-0 Alderney • in Guernsey
11-04-1935 • Jersey 0-1 Guernsey • in Jersey
26-04-1934 • Jersey 0-1 Guernsey • in Jersey
12-04-1934 • Guernsey 3-0 Alderney • in Guernsey
04-05-1933 • Guernsey 4-1 Jersey • in Guernsey
• After extra-time, Full-time 1-1
01-05-1932 • Guernsey 4-2 Alderney • in Jersey
14-04-1932 • Guernsey 2-0 Jersey • in Guernsey
28-04-1931 • Guernsey 2-4 Jersey • in Guernsey
14-04-1931 • Guernsey 1-0 Alderney • in Jersey
01-05-1930 • Jersey 2-3 Guernsey • in Jersey
02-05-1929 • Guernsey 5-0 Alderney • in Guernsey
18-04-1929 • Jersey 1-7 Guernsey • in Jersey
03-05-1928 • Jersey 2-1 Guernsey • in Jersey
• After extra-time, Full-time 1-1
19-04-1928 • Guernsey 4-0 Alderney • in Guernsey
28-04-1927 • Guernsey 1-0 Jersey • in Guernsey
15-04-1926 • Guernsey 1-5 Jersey • in Guernscy
30-04-1925 • Guernsey 2-1 Jersey • in Guernsey
02-04-1925 • Guernsey 3-0 Alderney • in Jersey
01-05-1924 • Jersey 1-0 Guernsey • in Jersey
26-04-1923 • Guernsey 3-2 Alderney • in Guernsey
12-04-1923 • Jersey 0-1 Guernsey • in Jersey
27-04-1922 • Jersey 1-2 Guernsey • in Jersey
06-04-1922 • Guernsey 8-0 Alderney • in Guernsey
28-04-1921 • Guernsey 0-1 Jersey • in Guernsey
29-04-1920 • Alderney 1-0 Guernsey • in Jersey
15-04-1920 • Guernsey 1-0 Jersey • in Guernsey
21-04-1919 • Guernsey 2-0 Jersey • (Victory Cup) in Guernsey
23-04-1914 • Guernsey 2-1 Jersey • in Guernsey

02-04-1914 • Guernsey 4-0 Alderney • in Jersey
17-04-1913 • Jersey 2-4 Guernsey • in Jersey
25-04-1912 • Guernsey 4-0 Alderney in Guernsey
19-04-1912 • Jersey 2-5 Guernsey • in Jersey
18-04-1912 • Jersey 3-3 Guernsey • in Jersey
• After extra-time, Full-time 3-3
27-04-1911 • Jersey 4-1 Guernsey • in Jersey
20-04-1911 • Guernsey 2-1 Alderney • in Guernsey
21-04-1910 • Guernsey 2-3 Jersey • in Guernsey
25-03-1909 • Guernsey 2-0 Alderney • in Jersey
18-03-1909 • Guernsey 3-0 Jersey • in Guernsey
09-04-1908 • Guernsey 0-4 Jersey • in Guernsey
02-04-1908 • Guernsey 3-0 Alderney • in Jersey
04-04-1907 • Jersey 2-3 Guernsey • in Jersey
• After extra-time, Full-time 2-2
02-04-1906 • Guernsey 1-0 Alderney • in Guernsey
29-03-1906 • Jersey 1-2 Guernsey • in Jersey
27-04-1905 • Jersey 0-1 Guernsey • in Jersey
17-04-1905 • Guernsey 6-0 Alderney • in Guernsey

**GUERNSEY**
15-07-2005 • Shetland 2-0 Guernsey • Island Games in Shetland
14-07-2005 • Guernsey 3-0 Anglesey • Island Games in Shetland
13-07-2005 • Guernsey 6-0 Greenland • Island Games in Shetland
11-07-2005 • Guernsey 2-1 Western Isles • Island Games in Shetland
10-07-2005 • Guernsey 3-0 Orkney • Island Games in Shetland
04-07-2003 • Guernsey 3-1 Isle of Man • Island Games in Guernsey
03-07-2003 • Guernsey 3-1 Isle of Wight • Island Games in Guernsey
01-07-2003 • Guernsey 2-1 Rhodes • Island Games in Guernsey,
abandoned after 70 minutes
30-06-2003 • Guernsey 10-0 Orkney • Island Games in Guernsey
29-06-2003 • Guernsey 7-1 Alderney • Island Games in Guernsey
13-07-2001 • Anglesey 0-0 Guernsey • Island Games in Isle of Man,
Guernsey won 3-1 on penalties
12-07-2001 • Guernsey 3-2 Isle of Wight • Island Games in Isle of Man
10-07-2001 • Isle of Man 2-3 Guernsey • Island Games in Isle of Man
09-07-2001 • Guernsey 3-0 Falkland Islands • Island Games in Isle of Man
02-07-1999 • Guernsey 6-5 Shetland • Island Games in Gotland
01-07-1999 • Guernsey 4-2 Frøya • Island Games in Gotland
29-06-1999 • Anglesey 1-1 Guernsey • Island Games in Gotland
28-06-1999 • Guernsey 0-0 Rhodes • Island Games in Gotland
04-07-1997 • Isle of Wight 3-1 Guernsey • Island Games in Jersey
02-07-1997 • Jersey 4-0 Guernsey • Island Games in Jersey
01-07-1997 • Greenland 0-0 Guernsey • Island Games in Jersey
30-06-1997 • Guernsey 3-0 Frøya • Island Games in Jersey

# Results

29-06-1997 • Guernsey 2-1 Gibraltar • Island Games in Jersey
21-07-1995 • Guernsey 2-1 Anglesey • Island Games in Gibraltar
18-07-1995 • Guernsey 1-1 Isle of Wight • Island Games in Gibraltar
17-07-1995 • Jersey 1-0 Guernsey • Island Games in Gibraltar
16-07-1995 • Åland 2-2 Guernsey • Island Games in Gibraltar
28-06-1991 • Shetland 2-1 Guernsey • Island Games in Åland
26-06-1991 • Guernsey 1-1 Isle of Wight • Island Games in Åland
25-06-1991 • Åland 2-0 Guernsey • Island Games in Åland
24-06-1991 • Anglesey 1-0 Guernsey • Island Games in Åland

**JERSEY**
05-07-2007 • Jersey 1-0 Gotland • Island Games in Rhodes
04-07-2007 • Jersey 1-0 Åland• Island Games in Rhodes
01-07-2007 • Gibraltar 1-1 Jersey • Island Games in Rhodes
30-06-2007 • Jersey 1-0 Menorca • Island Games in Rhodes
04-07-2003 • Jersey 3-0 Isle of Wight • Island Games in Guernsey
03-07-2003 • Isle of Man 2-1 Jersey • Island Games in Guernsey
01-07-2003 • Gotland 0-0 Jersey • Island Games in Guernsey
30-06-2003 • Jersey 5-0 Shetland • Island Games in Guernsey
29-06-2003 • Jersey 5-1 Frøya • Island Games in Guernsey
13-07-2001 • Jersey 2-0 Isle of Wight • Island Games in Isle of Man
12-07-2001 • Anglesey 2-2 Jersey • Island Games in Isle of Man, Anglesey won 4-3 on penalties
10-07-2001 • Jersey 2-1 Gibraltar • Island Games in Isle of Man
08-07-2001 • Jersey 12-0 Orkney • Island Games in Isle of Man
02-07-1999 • Isle of Wight 2-0 Jersey • Island Games in Gotland
01-07-1999 • Isle of Man 1-0 Jersey • Island Games in Gotland
29-06-1999 • Jersey 5-1 Gibraltar • Island Games in Gotland
27-06-1999 • Jersey 1-0 Åland • Island Games in Gotland
04-07-1997 • Jersey 1-0 Anglesey • Island Games in Jersey
03-07-1997 • Jersey 3-2 Gibraltar • Island Games in Jersey
02-07-1997 • Jersey 4-0 Guernsey • Island Games in Jersey
30-06-1997 • Jersey 2-1 Greenland • Island Games in Jersey
29 06-1997 • Jersey 4-1 Frøya • Island Games in Jersey
21-07-1995 • Jersey 6-3 Greenland • Island Games in Gibraltar
20-07-1995 • Gibraltar 1-0 Jersey • Island Games in Gibraltar
18-07-1995 • Jersey 3-1 Åland • Island Games in Gibraltar
17-07-1995 • Jersey 1-0 Guernsey • Island Games in Gibraltar
16-07-1995 • Jersey 2-0 Isle of Wight • Island Games in Gibraltar
09-07-1993 • Jersey 5-1 Isle of Man • Island Games in Isle of Wight
06-07-1993 • Anglesey 2-2 Jersey • Island Games in Isle of Wight
05-07-1993 • Jersey 4-2 Greenland • Island Games in Isle of Wight
04-07-1993 • Jersey 2-1 Gibraltar • Island Games in Isle of Wight
28-06-1991 • Åland 0-2 Jersey • Island Games in Åland
26-06-1991 • Faroe Islands 5-3 Jersey • Island Games in Åland

25-06-1991 • Jersey 2-0 Shetland • Island Games in Åland
24-06-1991 • Jersey 4-3 Greenland • Island Games in Åland

## ALDERNEY
04-07-2003 • Alderney 1-0 Saaremaa • Island Games in Guernsey
03-07-2003 • Greenland 3-0 Alderney • Island Games in Guernsey
01-07-2003 • Orkney 3-1 Alderney • Island Games in Guernsey
30-06-2003 • Rhodes 5-1 Alderney • Island Games in Guernsey
29-06-2003 • Guernsey 7-1 Alderney • Island Games in Guernsey

## SARK
03-07-2003 • Frøya 15-0 Sark • Island Games • in Alderney
01-07-2003 • Greenland 16-0 Sark • Island Games • in Guernsey
30-06-2003 • Isle of Wight 20-0 Sark • Island Games • in Guernsey
29-06-2003 • Gibraltar 19-0 Sark • Island Games • in Guernsey

## GREENLAND
19-11-2006 • Greenland 2-0 Gagauzia • ELF Cup in Northern Cyprus
31-05-2006 • Zanzibar 4-2 Greenland • FIFI Wild Cup in Germany
15-07-2005 • Åland 3-2 Greenland • Island Games in Shetland
13-07-2005 • Guernsey 6-0 Greenland • Island Games in Shetland
12-07-2005 • Greenland 4-4 Western Isles • Island Games in Shetland
11-07-2005 • Greenland 2-1 Orkney • Island Games in Shetland
10-07-2005 • Anglesey 0-0 Greenland • Island Games in Shetland
04-07-2003 • Gotland 2-1 Greenland • Island Games in Guernsey,
after extra-time, Full-time 1-1
03-07-2003 • Greenland 3-0 Alderney • Island Games in Guernsey
01-07-2003 • Greenland 16-0 Sark • Island Games in Guernsey
30-06-2003 • Gibraltar 2-0 Greenland • Island Games in Guernsey
29-06-2003 • Greenland 2-1 Isle of Wight • Island Games in Guernsey
13-07-2001 • Greenland 2-0 Saaremaa • Island Games in Isle of Man
12-07-2001 • Greenland 4-0 Falkland Islands • Island Games in Isle of Man
09-07-2001 • Rhodes 2-0 Greenland • Island Games in Isle of Man
08-07-2001 • Greenland 0-0 Isle of Wight • Island Games in Isle of Man
04-07-2001 • Sápmi 5-1 Greenland • Friendly in Denmark
30-06-2001 • Greenland 4-1 Tibet • Friendly in Denmark
02-07-1999 • Gotland 7-2 Greenland • Island Games in Gotland
01-07-1999 • Rhodes 2-0 Greenland • Island Games in Gotland
29-06-1999 • Isle of Wight 7-2 Greenland • Island Games in Gotland
28-06-1999 • Greenland 3-1 Frøya • Island Games in Gotland
27-06-1999 • Greenland 4-1 Saaremaa • Island Games in Gotland
03-07-1997 • Frøya 2-1 Greenland • Island Games in Jersey
02-07-1997 • Gibraltar 5-1 Greenland • Island Games in Jersey
01-07-1997 • Greenland 0-0 Guernsey • Island Games in Jersey
30-06-1997 • Jersey 2-1 Greenland • Island Games in Jersey

# Results

21-07-1995 • Jersey 6-3 Greenland • Island Games in Gibraltar
20-07-1995 • Isle of Wight 2-1 Greenland • Island Games in Gibraltar
18-07-1995 • Greenland 4-0 Isle of Man • Island Games in Gibraltar
17-07-1995 • Anglesey 2-1 Greenland • Island Games in Gibraltar
16-07-1995 • Gibraltar 0-1 Greenland • Island Games in Gibraltar
09-07-1993 • Åland 2-1 Greenland • Island Games in Isle of Wight
06-07-1993 • Greenland 5-0 Gibraltar • Island Games in Isle of Wight
05-07-1993 • Jersey 4-2 Greenland • Island Games in Isle of Wight
04-07-1993 • Greenland 1-0 Anglesey • Island Games in Isle of Wight
28-06-1991 • Isle of Wight 3-1 Greenland • Island Games in Åland
26-06-1991 • Shetland 5-2 Greenland • Island Games in Åland
25-06-1991 • Faroe Islands 3-2 Greenland • Island Games in Åland
24-06-1991 • Jersey 4-3 Greenland • Island Games in Åland
12-07-1989 • Anglesey 1-0 Greenland • Island Games in Faroe Islands
11-07-1989 • Åland 3-0 Greenland • Island Games in Faroe Islands
09-07-1989 • Faroe Islands 3-0 Greenland • Island Games in Faroe Islands
06-07-1989 • Greenland 4-1 Shetland • Island Games in Faroe Islands
01-01-1986 • Åland 5-3 Greenland • Friendly in Åland
07-08-1984 • Faroe Islands 4-2 Greenland • Friendly in Faroe Islands
05-08-1984 • Faroe Islands 1-0 Greenland • Friendly in Faroe Islands
03-08-1984 • Iceland 1-0 Greenland • Friendly in Faroe Islands
03-07-1983 • Greenland 2-3 Faroe Islands • Friendly in Greenland
29-06-1983 • Greenland 0-0 Faroe Islands • Friendly in Greenland
03-07-1980 • Iceland 4-1 Greenland • Friendly in Iceland
02-07-1980 • Faroe Islands 6-0 Greenland • Friendly in Iceland

## THE FALKLAND ISLANDS
15-07-2005 • Orkney 2-0 Falkland Islands • Island Games in Shetland
14-07-2005 • Åland 2-1 Falkland Islands • Island Games in Shetland
13-07-2005 • Isle of Man 9-0 Falkland Islands • Island Games in Shetland
12-07-2005 • Falkland Islands 2-1 Saaremaa • Island Games in Shetland
10-07-2005 • Shetland 4-0 Falkland Islands • Island Games in Shetland
13-07-2001 • Falkland Islands 4-1 Orkney • Island Games in Isle of Man
12-07-2001 • Greenland 4-0 Falkland Islands • Island Games in Isle of Man
09-07-2001 • Guernsey 3-0 Falkland Islands • Island Games in Isle of Man
08-07-2001 • Isle of Man 9-0 Falkland Islands • Island Games in Isle of Man

## THE ISLE OF MAN
15-07-2005 • Western Isles 4-0 Isle of Man • Island Games in Shetland
14-07-2005 • Shetland 1-0 Isle of Man • Island Games in Shetland
13-07-2005 • Isle of Man 9-0 Falkland Islands • Island Games in Shetland
12-07-2005 • Isle of Man 1-0 Åland • Island Games in Shetland
11-07-2005 • Isle of Man 2-2 Saaremaa • Island Games in Shetland
23-05-2004 • Gibraltar 1-0 Isle of Man • Gibraltar Cup in Gibraltar
22-05-2004 • Isle of Man 5-1 Isle of Wight • Gibraltar Cup in Gibraltar

04-07-2003 • Guernsey 3-1 Isle of Man • Island Games in Guernsey
03-07-2003 • Isle of Man 2-1 Jersey • Island Games in Guernsey
01-07-2003 • Isle of Man 2-1 Anglesey • Island Games in Guernsey
30-06-2003 • Isle of Man 4-0 Saaremaa • Island Games in Guernsey
13-07-2001 • Isle of Man 2-2 Shetland • Island Games in Isle of Man,
Isle of Man won 3-2 on penalties
12-07-2001 • Isle of Man 1-3 Rhodes • Island Games in Isle of Man
10-07-2001 • Isle of Man 2-3 Guernsey • Island Games in Isle of Man
08-07-2001 • Isle of Man 9-0 Falkland Islands • Island Games in Isle of Man
02-07-1999 • Anglesey 1-0 Isle of Man • Island Games in Gotland
01-07-1999 • Isle of Man 1-0 Jersey • Island Games in Gotland
29-06-1999 • Gotland 4-4 Isle of Man • Island Games in Gotland
28-06-1999 • Isle of Man 13-0 Hitra • Island Games in Gotland
27-06-1999 • Isle of Man 2-1 Shetland • Island Games in Gotland
21-07-1995 • Åland 4-1 Isle of Man • Island Games in Gibraltar
18-07-1995 • Greenland 4-0 Isle of Man • Island Games in Gibraltar
17-07-1995 • Gibraltar 2-1 Isle of Man • Island Games in Gibraltar
16-07-1995 • Anglesey 2-0 Isle of Man • Island Games in Gibraltar
09-07-1993 • Jersey 5-1 Isle of Man • Island Games in Isle of Wight
06-07-1993 • Isle of Man 5-1 Shetland • Island Games in Isle of Wight
05-07-1993 • Isle of Man 2-0 Åland • Island Games in Isle of Wight
04-07-1993 • Isle of Wight 1-0 Isle of Man • Island Games in Isle of Wight

## GIBRALTAR
06-07-2007 • Rhodes 0-4 Gibraltar • Island Games in Rhodes
04-07-2007 • Gibraltar 2-0 Bermuda U-23 • Island Games in Rhodes
02-07-2007 • Gibraltar 2-1 Menorca • Island Games in Rhodes
01-07-2007 • Gibraltar 1-1 Jersey • Island Games in Rhodes
01-06-2006 • Northern Cyprus 2-0 Gibraltar • FIFI Wild Cup in Germany
31-05-2006 • Gibraltar 5-0 Tibet • FIFI Wild Cup in Germany
27-05-2005 • Gibraltar 4-0 Monaco • Gibraltar Cup in Gibraltar
23-05-2004 • Gibraltar 1-0 Isle of Man • Gibraltar Cup in Gibraltar
21-05-2004 • Gibraltar 2-0 Isle of Wight • Gibraltar Cup in Gibraltar
04-07-2003 • Anglesey 2-0 Gibraltar • Island Games in Guernsey
03-07-2003 • Gibraltar 7-1 Orkney • Island Games in Guernsey
01-07-2003 • Isle of Wight 2-1 Gibraltar • Island Games in Guernsey
30-06-2003 • Gibraltar 2-0 Greenland • Island Games in Guernsey
29-06-2003 • Gibraltar 19-0 Sark • Island Games in Guernsey
18-02-2002 • Gibraltar 2-2 Monaco • Friendly in France
13-07-2001 • Gibraltar 2-0 Rhodes • Island Games in Isle of Man
12-07-2001 • Gibraltar 2-0 Shetland • Island Games in Isle of Man
10-07-2001 • Jersey 2-1 Gibraltar • Island Games in Isle of Man
09-07-2001 • Gibraltar 2-0 Orkney • Island Games in Isle of Man
02-07-1999 • Gibraltar 5-1 Frøya • Island Games in Gotland
01-07-1999 • Shetland 3-2 Gibraltar • Island Games in Gotland

29-06-1999 • Jersey 5-1 Gibraltar • Island Games in Gotland
28-06-1999 • Åland 2-1 Gibraltar • Island Games in Gotland
04-07-1997 • Shetland 2-1 Gibraltar • Island Games in Jersey
03-07-1997 • Jersey 3-2 Gibraltar • Island Games in Jersey
02-07-1997 • Gibraltar 5-1 Greenland • Island Games in Jersey
01-07-1997 • Gibraltar 4-0 Frøya • Island Games in Jersey
29-06-1997 • Guernsey 2-1 Gibraltar • Island Games in Jersey
22-07-1995 • Gibraltar 0-1 Isle of Wight • Island Games in Gibraltar
20-07-1995 • Gibraltar 1-0 Jersey • Island Games in Gibraltar
18-07-1995 • Gibraltar 2-0 Anglesey • Island Games in Gibraltar
17-07-1995 • Gibraltar 2-1 Isle of Man • Island Games in Gibraltar
16-07-1995 • Gibraltar 0-1 Greenland • Island Games in Gibraltar
08-07-1993 • Shetland 1-0 Gibraltar • Island Games in Isle of Wight
06-07-1993 • Greenland 5-0 Gibraltar • Island Games in Isle of Wight
05-07-1993 • Anglesey 1-0 Gibraltar • Island Games in Isle of Wight
04-07-1993 • Jersey 2-1 Gibraltar • Island Games in Isle of Wight

**TURKISH REPUBLIC OF NORTHERN CYPRUS**
24-01-2007 • Zanzibar 2-1 Northern Cyprus • Friendly in Zanzibar
25-11-2006 • Northern Cyprus 3-1 Crimean Tatarstan
• ELF Cup in Northern Cyprus
21-11-2006 • Northern Cyprus 10-0 Tibet • ELF Cup in Northern Cyprus
19-11-2006 • Northern Cyprus 5-0 Crimean Tatarstan
• ELF Cup in Northern Cyprus
03-06-2006 • Northern Cyprus 0-0 Zanzibar
• FIFI Wild Cup in Germany, Northern Cyprus won 4-1 on penalties
15-04-2006 • Occitània 0-3 Northern Cyprus • Friendly in Occitània
04-11-2005 • Northern Cyprus 6-2 Sápmi • Peace Cup in Northern Cyprus
02-11-2005 • Northern Cyprus 1-0 Kosovo • Peace Cup in Northern Cyprus
28-07-2004 • Sápmi 1-1 Northern Cyprus • Friendly in Sápmi
03-10-1980 • Libya 1-1 Northern Cyprus • Friendly in Turkey
02-10-1980 • Northern Cyprus 2-1 Malaysia • Friendly in Turkey
30-09-1980 • Saudi Arabia 2-0 Northern Cyprus • Friendly in Turkey
28-09-1980 • Turkey 5-0 Northern Cyprus • Friendly in Turkey
05-01-1977 • Northern Cyprus 0-1 Turkey • Friendly in Northern Cyprus
01-01-1962 • Northern Cyprus 0-5 Turkey • Friendly in Northern Cyprus

**OCCITANIA**
21-11-2006 • Occitània 2-3 Monaco • VIVA World Cup in Occitània
20-11-2006 • Occitània 0-7 Sápmi • VIVA World Cup in Occitània
15-04-2006 • Occitània 0-3 Northern Cyprus • Friendly in Occitània
17-12-2005 • Monaco 2-1 Occitània • Friendly in France
03-09-2005 • Occitània 14-0 Chechnya • Friendly in Occitània
12-02-2005 • Occitània 0-0 Monaco • Friendly in Occitània

# OUTCASTS: The Lands That FIFA Forgot

**MONACO**
24-11-2006 • Sápmi 21-1 Monaco • VIVA World Cup in Occitània
23-11-2006 • Sápmi 14-0 Monaco • VIVA World Cup in Occitània
21-11-2006 • Occitània 2-3 Monaco • VIVA World Cup in Occitània
22-04-2006 • Kosovo 7-1 Monaco • Friendly in France
18-02-2006 • Monaco 13-1 Chechnya • Friendly in France
17-12-2005 • Monaco 2-1 Occitània • Friendly in France
27-05-2005 • Gibraltar 4-0 Monaco • Gibraltar Cup in Gibraltar
12-02-2005 • Occitania 0-0 Monaco • Friendly in Occitània
23-11-2002 • Monaco 0-0 Vatican City • Friendly in Italy
18-02-2002 • Gibraltar 2-2 Monaco • Friendly in France
14-07-2001 • Monaco 2-1 Tibet • Friendly in Germany

**KOSOVO**
15-06-2007 • Kosovo 1-0 Saudi Arabia • Friendly in Turkey
22-04-2006 • Kosovo 7-1 Monaco • Friendly in France
03-11-2005 • Kosovo 4-1 Sápmi • Peace Cup in Northern Cyprus
02-11-2005 • Northern Cyprus 1-0 Kosovo • Peace Cup in Northern Cyprus
06-09-2002 • Kosovo 0-1 Albania • Friendly in Kosovo
14-02-1993 • Albania 3-1 Kosovo • Friendly in Albania

**ZANZIBAR**
24-01-2007 • Zanzibar 2-1 Northern Cyprus • Friendly in Zanzibar
02-12-2006 • Zambia 4-0 Zanzibar • CECAFA Cup in Ethiopia
29-11-2006 • Burundi 0-0 Zanzibar • CECAFA Cup in Ethiopia
26-08-2006 • Tanzania 1-0 Zanzibar • Friendly in Tanzania
03-06-2006 • Northern Cyprus 0-0 Zanzibar • FIFI Wild Cup in Germany, Northern Cyprus won 4-1 on penalties
31-05-2006 • Zanzibar 4-2 Greenland • FIFI Wild Cup in Germany
01-04-2006 • Tanzania 2-2 Zanzibar • Friendly in Tanzania
10-12-2005 • Uganda 0-0 Zanzibar • CECAFA Cup in Rwanda, after extra-time, Full-time 0-0, Zanzibar won 5-4 on penalties
08-12-2005 • Ethiopia 4-0 Zanzibar • CECAFA Cup in Rwanda
02-12-2005 • Tanzania 1-1 Zanzibar • CECAFA Cup in Rwanda
30-11-2005 • Zanzibar 2-1 Burundi • CECAFA Cup in Rwanda
28-11-2005 • Zanzibar 3-0 Eritrea • CECAFA Cup in Rwanda
26-11-2005 • Rwanda 0-1 Zanzibar • CECAFA Cup in Rwanda
09-11-2005 • Zanzibar 0-1 Tanzania • Friendly in Zanzibar
06-11-2005 • Tanzania 1-0 Zanzibar • Friendly in Tanzania
19-12-2004 • Ethiopia 3-0 Zanzibar • CECAFA Cup in Ethiopia
17-12-2004 • Burundi 2-1 Zanzibar • CECAFA Cup in Ethiopia
13-12-2004 • Zanzibar 4-2 Tanzania • CECAFA Cup in Ethiopia
11-12-2004 • Rwanda 4-2 Zanzibar • CECAFA Cup in Ethiopia
02-12-2003 • Rwanda 2-2 Zanzibar • CECAFA Cup in Sudan
30-11-2003 • Sudan 4-0 Zanzibar • CECAFA Cup in Sudan

# Results

08-12-2002 • Uganda 2-0 Zanzibar • CECAFA Cup in Tanzania
05-12-2002 • Zanzibar 1-0 Somalia • CECAFA Cup in Tanzania
02-12-2002 • Ethiopia 0-0 Zanzibar • CECAFA Cup in Tanzania
30-11-2002 • Rwanda 1-0 Zanzibar • CECAFA Cup in Tanzania
02-09-2002 • Tanzania 1-1 Zanzibar • Friendly in Tanzania
13-12-2001 • Ethiopia 5-0 Zanzibar • CECAFA Cup in Rwanda
24-09-2000 • Zanzibar 0-1 Tanzania • Friendly in Zanzibar
29-07-1999 • Sudan 1-1 Zanzibar • CECAFA Cup in Rwanda
25-07-1999 • Ethiopia 2-0 Zanzibar • CECAFA Cup in Rwanda
13-06-1999 • Kenya 0-1 Zanzibar • Friendly in Kenya
24-11-1996 • Kenya 1-0 Zanzibar • CECAFA Cup in Sudan
22-11-1996 • Rwanda 1-1 Zanzibar • CECAFA Cup in Sudan
06-12-1995 • Ethiopia 1-1 Zanzibar • CECAFA Cup in Uganda,
after extra-time, Full-time 1-1, Zanzibar won on penalties
30-11-1995 • Uganda 0-1 Zanzibar • CECAFA Cup in Uganda
29-11-1995 • Zanzibar 2-1 Rwanda • CECAFA Cup in Uganda
27-11-1995 • Kenya 2-0 Zanzibar • CECAFA Cup in Uganda
24-11-1992 • Malawi 3-1 Zanzibar • CECAFA Cup in Tanzania
21-11-1992 • Zambia 8-0 Zanzibar • CECAFA Cup in Tanzania
18-11-1992 • Tanzania 0-1 Zanzibar • CECAFA Cup in Tanzania
15-11-1992 • Ethiopia 3-0 Zanzibar • CECAFA Cup in Tanzania
30-11-1991 • Kenya 3-2 Zanzibar • CECAFA Cup in Uganda
27-11-1991 • Zambia 3-2 Zanzibar • CECAFA Cup in Uganda
25-11-1991 • Malawi 1-0 Zanzibar • CECAFA Cup in Uganda
19-12-1990 • Zanzibar 1-2 Tanzania • CECAFA Cup in Zanzibar
17-12-1990 • Zanzibar 0-1 Sudan • CECAFA Cup in Zanzibar,
after extra-time, Full-time 0-0
14-12-1990 • Zanzibar 2-1 Malawi • CECAFA Cup in Zanzibar
12-12-1990 • Zanzibar 0-1 Zimbabwe • CECAFA Cup in Zanzibar
08-12-1990 • Zanzibar 0-0 Tanzania • CECAFA Cup in Zanzibar
06-12-1989 • Zambia 1-0 Zanzibar • CECAFA Cup in Kenya
02-12-1989 • Malawi 0-0 Zanzibar • CECAFA Cup in Kenya
12-11-1988 • Zanzibar 1-0 Tanzania • CECAFA Cup in Malawi
10-11-1988 • Malawi 1-0 Zanzibar • CECAFA Cup in Malawi
08-11-1988 • Kenya 2-0 Zanzibar • CECAFA Cup in Malawi
26-12-1987 • Uganda 2-0 Zanzibar • CECAFA Cup in Ethiopia
23-12-1987 • Zimbabwe 1-0 Zanzibar • CECAFA Cup in Ethiopia
19-12-1987 • Zanzibar 2-0 Tanzania • CECAFA Cup in Ethiopia
17-12-1987 • Ethiopia 0-0 Zanzibar • CECAFA Cup in Ethiopia
14-12-1987 • Kenya 0-0 Zanzibar • CECAFA Cup in Ethiopia
09-12-1984 • Malawi 1-0 Zanzibar • CECAFA Cup in Uganda
06-12-1984 • Kenya 1-0 Zanzibar • CECAFA Cup in Uganda
03-12-1984 • Somalia 2-1 Zanzibar • CECAFA Cup in Uganda
20-11-1983 • Malawi 3-1 Zanzibar • CECAFA Cup in Kenya
16-11-1983 • Zimbabwe 2-1 Zanzibar • CECAFA Cup in Kenya

# OUTCASTS: The Lands That FIFA Forgot

14-11-1983 • Somalia 1-1 Zanzibar • CECAFA Cup in Kenya
26-11-1982 • Zimbabwe 3-0 Zanzibar • CECAFA Cup in Uganda
24-11-1982 • Uganda 3-0 Zanzibar • CECAFA Cup in Uganda
21-11-1982 • Kenya 2-2 Zanzibar • CECAFA Cup in Uganda
18-11-1982 • Zanzibar 1-0 Sudan • CECAFA Cup in Uganda
20-11-1981 • Malawi 4-1 Zanzibar • CECAFA Cup in Tanzania
17-11-1981 • Kenya 2-1 Zanzibar • CECAFA Cup in Tanzania
15-11-1981 • Tanzania 1-0 Zanzibar • CECAFA Cup in Tanzania
22-11-1980 • Zanzibar 2-1 Kenya • CECAFA Cup in Sudan
19-11-1980 • Zambia 3-0 Zanzibar • CECAFA Cup in Sudan
16-11-1980 • Malawi 1-0 Zanzibar • CECAFA Cup in Sudan
16-11-1979 • Tanzania 2-1 Zanzibar • CECAFA Cup in Kenya
14-11-1979 • Kenya 2-0 Zanzibar • CECAFA Cup in Kenya
09-11-1979 • Sudan 1-1 Zanzibar • CECAFA Cup in Kenya
04-11-1979 • Malawi 4-0 Zanzibar • CECAFA Cup in Kenya
04-12-1977 • Uganda 1-0 Zanzibar • CECAFA Cup in Somalia
02-12-1977 • Kenya 3-0 Zanzibar • CECAFA Cup in Somalia
30-11-1977 • Somalia 1-0 Zanzibar • CECAFA Cup in Somalia
11-11-1976 • Zanzibar 1-0 Somalia • CECAFA Cup in Zanzibar
08-11-1976 • Zanzibar 0-1 Uganda • CECAFA Cup in Zanzibar
06-11-1976 • Zanzibar 0-3 Zambia • CECAFA Cup in Zanzibar
05-11-1975 • Tanzania 4-0 Zanzibar • CECAFA Cup in Zambia
03-11-1975 • Malawi 4-2 Zanzibar • CECAFA Cup in Zambia
03-11-1974 • Zanzibar 2-1 Somalia • CECAFA Cup in Tanzania
01-11-1974 • Uganda 2-1 Zanzibar • CECAFA Cup in Tanzania
25-09-1973 • Tanzania 1-0 Zanzibar • CECAFA Cup in Uganda
23-09-1973 • Kenya 2-0 Zanzibar • CECAFA Cup in Uganda
03-10-1970 • Zanzibar 3-2 Kenya • East African Friendship Cup in Zanzibar
30-09-1970 • Zanzibar 1-2 Tanzania • East African Friendship Cup in Zanzibar
26-09-1970 • Zanzibar 0-1 Uganda • East African Friendship Cup in Zanzibar
03-10-1969 • Tanzania 3-0 Zanzibar • East African Friendship Cup in Uganda
30-09-1969 • Uganda 7-0 Zanzibar • East African Friendship Cup in Uganda
28-09-1969 • Kenya 2-1 Zanzibar • East African Friendship Cup in Uganda
10-10-1967 • Zanzibar 3-0 Tanzania • CECAFA Cup in Kenya
06-10-1967 • Uganda 2-0 Zanzibar • CECAFA Cup in Kenya
04-10-1967 • Kenya 6-0 Zanzibar • CECAFA Cup in Kenya
01-10-1966 • Zanzibar 1-3 Kenya • Gossage Cup in Zanzibar
01-10-1966 • Zanzibar 0-4 Tanzania • Gossage Cup in Zanzibar
01-10-1966 • Zanzibar 0-0 Uganda • Gossage Cup in Zanzibar
01-10-1962 • Uganda 8-0 Zanzibar • Gossage Cup in Uganda
01-05-1961 • Kenya 10-0 Zanzibar • Gossage Cup in Kenya
01-05-1953 • Zanzibar 1-7 Kenya • Gossage Cup in Zanzibar
01-05-1952 • Kenya 6-0 Zanzibar • Gossage Cup in Uganda
01-05-1949 • Zanzibar 2-3 Kenya • Gossage Cup in Zanzibar

# Results

**TIBET**

21-11-2006 • Northern Cyprus 10-0 Tibet • ELF Cup in Northern Cyprus
20-11-2006 • Crimean Tatarstan 1-0 Tibet • ELF Cup Cup in Northern Cyprus
31-05-2006 • Gibraltar 5-0 Tibet • FIFI Wild Cup in Germany
10-10-2003 • Sikkim 2-1 Tibet • Friendly in Sikkim
14-07-2001 • Monaco 2-1 Tibet • Friendly in Germany
30-06-2001 • Greenland 4-1 Tibet • Friendly in Denmark
06-11-1972 • Nepal 4-0 Tibet • Friendly in China

**NORTH MARIANAS**

01-04-2007 • Guam 9-0 Northern Marianas
• East Asian Cup Pre-qualifier in Guam
25-03-2007 • Northern Marianas 2-3 Guam
• East Asian Cup Pre-qualifier in Northern Marianas
12-07-1999 • Micronesia 7-0 Northern Marianas
• Micronesia Cup in Micronesia
03-08-1998 • Northern Marianas 3-0 Guam • Micronesia Games in Palau
02-08-1998 • Palau 1-12 Northern Marianas • Micronesia Games in Palau
30-07-1998 • Guam 2-1 Northern Marianas • Micronesia Games in Palau
    07-1998 • Northern Marianas 13-0 Pohnpei • Micronesia Games in Palau
    07-1998 • Northern Marianas 8-0 Yap • Micronesia Games in Palau

**VATICAN CITY**

23-11-2002 • Monaco 0-0 Vatican City • Friendly in Italy

**THE SAPMI**

24-11-2006 • Sápmi 21-1 Monaco • VIVA World Cup in Occitània
23-11-2006 • Sápmi 14-0 Monaco • VIVA World Cup in Occitània
20-11-2006 • Occitània 0-7 Sápmi • VIVA World Cup in Occitània
04-11-2005 • Northern Cyprus 6-2 Sápmi • Peace Cup in Northern Cyprus
03-11-2005 • Kosova 4-1 Sápmi • Peace Cup in Northern Cyprus
28-07-2004 • Sápmi 1-1 Northern Cyprus • Friendly in Sápmi
04-07-2001 • Sápmi 5-1 Greenland • Friendly in Denmark
07-08-1998 • Sápmi 0-0 Estonia • Friendly in Sweden
01-07-1992 • Estonia 2-1 Sápmi • Friendly in Estonia
01-06-1991 • Sápmi 2-1 Estonia • Friendly in Sápmi
01-10-1990 • Estonia 2-0 Sápmi • Friendly in Estonia
01-07-1987 • Åland 1-0 Sápmi • Friendly in Åland
01-07-1986 • Sápmi 2-0 Åland • Friendly in Sápmi
01-07-1985 • Åland 4-2 Sápmi • Friendly in Åland

**Source: The Roon Ba - http://www.roonba.co.nr**

# APPENDICES

## APPENDIX 1. FIFA & UNITED NATIONS MEMBERSHIP

| Country | Confederation | FA formed | FIFA | UN |
|---|---|---|---|---|
| Afghanistan | AFC | 1933 | 1948 | 1946 |
| Albania | UEFA | 1930 | 1932 | 1955 |
| Algeria | CAF | 1962 | 1963 | 1962 |
| Andorra | UEFA | 1994 | 1996 | 1993 |
| American Samoa | OFC | 1984 | 1998 | N/a |
| Angola | CAF | 1979 | 1980 | 1976 |
| Anguilla | CONCACAF | 1990 | 1996 | N/a |
| Antigua & Barbuda | CONCACAF | 1928 | 1970 | 1981 |
| Argentina | CONMEBOL | 1893 | 1912 | 1945 |
| Armenia | UEFA | 1992 | 1992 | 1992 |
| Aruba | CONCACAF | 1932 | 1988 | N/a |
| Australia | AFC | 1961 | 1963 | 1945 |
| Austria | UEFA | 1904 | 1907 | 1955 |
| Azerbaijan | UEFA | 1992 | 1994 | 1992 |
| Bahamas | CONCACAF | 1967 | 1968 | 1973 |
| Bahrain | AFC | 1957 | 1966 | 1971 |
| Bangladesh | AFC | 1972 | 1972 | 1974 |
| Barbados | CONCACAF | 1910 | 1968 | 1966 |
| Belarus | UEFA | 1989 | 1992 | 1945 |
| Belgium | UEFA | 1895 | 1904 | 1945 |
| Belize | CONCACAF | 1980 | 1986 | 1981 |
| Benin | CAF | 1962 | 1962 | 1960 |
| Bermuda | CONCACAF | 1928 | 1962 | N/a |
| Bhutan | AFC | 1983 | 2000 | 1971 |
| Bolivia | CONMEBOL | 1925 | 1926 | 1945 |
| Bosnia & Herzegovina | UEFA | 1992 | 1996 | 1992 |
| Botswana | CAF | 1970 | 1976 | 1966 |
| Brazil | CONMEBOL | 1914 | 1923 | 1945 |
| British Virgin Islands | CONCACAF | 1974 | 1996 | N/a |
| Brunei | AFC | 1959 | 1969 | 1984 |
| Bulgaria | UEFA | 1923 | 1924 | 1955 |
| Burkina Faso | CAF | 1960 | 1964 | 1960 |
| Burundi | CAF | 1948 | 1972 | 1962 |
| Cambodia | AFC | 1933 | 1953 | 1955 |

| | | | | |
|---|---|---|---|---|
| Cameroon | CAF | 1959 | 1962 | 1960 |
| Canada | CONCACAF | 1912 | 1912 | 1945 |
| Cayman Islands | CONCACAF | 1966 | 1992 | N/a |
| Cape Verde | CAF | 1982 | 1986 | 1975 |
| Central African Rep. | CAF | 1961 | 1963 | 1960 |
| Chad | CAF | 1962 | 1988 | 1960 |
| Chile | CONMEBOL | 1895 | 1912 | 1945 |
| China | AFC | 1924 | 1931 | 1945 |
| Colombia | CONMEBOL | 1924 | 1936 | 1945 |
| Comoros | CAF | 1979 | 2005 | 1975 |
| Congo (Rep. of the) | CAF | 1962 | 1962 | 1960 |
| Costa Rica | CONCACAF | 1921 | 1927 | 1945 |
| Côte d'Ivoire | CAF | 1960 | 1960 | 1960 |
| Cook Islands | OFC | 1971 | 1994 | N/a |
| Croatia | UEFA | 1941 | 1992 | 1992 |
| Cuba | CONCACAF | 1924 | 1932 | 1945 |
| Cyprus | UEFA | 1934 | 1948 | 1960 |
| Czech Republic | UEFA | 1907 | 1994 | 1993 |
| Dem Rep of the Congo | CAF | 1919 | 1962 | 1960 |
| Denmark | UEFA | 1889 | 1904 | 1945 |
| Djibouti | CAF | 1979 | 1994 | 1977 |
| Dominica | CONCACAF | 1970 | 1994 | 1978 |
| Dominican Republic | CONCACAF | 1953 | 1958 | 1945 |
| East Timor | AFC | 2002 | 2005 | 2002 |
| Ecuador | CONMEBOL | 1925 | 1926 | 1945 |
| Egypt | CAF | 1921 | 1923 | 1945 |
| El Salvador | CONCACAF | 1935 | 1938 | 1945 |
| England | UEFA | 1863 | 1905 | N/a |
| Equatorial Guinea | CAF | 1960 | 1986 | 1968 |
| Eritrea | CAF | 1996 | 1998 | 1993 |
| Estonia | UEFA | 1921 | 1992 | 1991 |
| Ethiopia | CAF | 1943 | 1953 | 1945 |
| Faroe Islands | UEFA | 1979 | 1988 | N/a |
| Fiji | OFC | 1938 | 1963 | 1970 |
| Finland | UEFA | 1907 | 1908 | 1955 |
| France | UEFA | 1904 | 1919 | 1945 |
| French Guyana | CONCACAF | 1962 | N/a | N/a |
| Gabon | CAF | 1962 | 1963 | 1960 |
| Gambia | CAF | 1952 | 1966 | 1965 |
| Georgia | UEFA | 1990 | 1992 | 1992 |
| Germany | UEFA | 1900 | 1904 | 1973 |

| | | | | |
|---|---|---|---|---|
| Ghana | CAF | 1957 | 1958 | 1957 |
| Greece | UEFA | 1926 | 1927 | 1945 |
| Grenada | CONCACAF | 1924 | 1976 | 1974 |
| Guam | AFC | 1975 | 1976 | N/a |
| Guatemala | CONCACAF | 1919 | 1946 | 1945 |
| Guinea | CAF | 1960 | 1960 | 1958 |
| Guadeloupe | CONCACAF | 2000 | N/a | N/a |
| Guinea-Bissau | CAF | 1974 | 1986 | 1974 |
| Guyana | CONCACAF | 1902 | 1968 | 1966 |
| Haiti | CONCACAF | 1904 | 1933 | 1945 |
| Honduras | CONCACAF | 1951 | 1951 | 1945 |
| Hong Kong | AFC | 1914 | 1953 | N/a |
| Hungary | UEFA | 1901 | 1906 | 1955 |
| Iceland | UEFA | 1947 | 1947 | 1946 |
| India | AFC | 1937 | 1948 | 1945 |
| Indonesia | AFC | 1930 | 1952 | 1950 |
| Iran | AFC | 1920 | 1945 | 1945 |
| Iraq | AFC | 1948 | 1950 | 1945 |
| Ireland | UEFA | 1921 | 1923 | 1955 |
| Israel | UEFA | 1928 | 1948 | 1949 |
| Italy | UEFA | 1898 | 1905 | 1955 |
| Jamaica | CONCACAF | 1910 | 1962 | 1962 |
| Japan | AFC | 1921 | 1929 | 1956 |
| Jordan | AFC | 1949 | 1958 | 1955 |
| Kazakhstan | UEFA | 1914 | 1994 | 1992 |
| Kenya | CAF | 1960 | 1960 | 1963 |
| Kiribati | N/a | 1980 | N/a | 1999 |
| Kuwait | AFC | 1952 | 1962 | 1963 |
| Kyrgyzstan | AFC | 1992 | 1994 | 1992 |
| Laos | AFC | 1951 | 1952 | 1955 |
| Latvia | UEFA | 1921 | 1992 | 1991 |
| Lebanon | AFC | 1933 | 1935 | 1945 |
| Lesotho | CAF | 1932 | 1964 | 1966 |
| Liberia | CAF | 1936 | 1962 | 1945 |
| Libya | AFC | 1962 | 1963 | 1955 |
| Liechtenstein | UEFA | 1934 | 1974 | 1990 |
| Lithuania | UEFA | 1922 | 1992 | 1991 |
| Luxembourg | UEFA | 1908 | 1910 | 1945 |
| Macedonia | UEFA | 1908 | 1994 | 1993 |
| Madagascar | CAF | 1961 | 1962 | 1960 |
| Malawi | CAF | 1966 | 1967 | 1964 |

| | | | | |
|---|---|---|---|---|
| Malaysia | AFC | 1933 | 1956 | 1957 |
| Maldives | AFC | 1982 | 1986 | 1965 |
| Mali | CAF | 1960 | 1962 | 1960 |
| Malta | UEFA | 1900 | 1959 | 1964 |
| Marshall Islands | N/a | N/a | N/a | 1991 |
| Martinique | CONCACAF | N/a | N/a | N/a |
| Mauritania | 1961 | 1964 | N/a | 1961 |
| Mauritius | CAF | 1952 | 1962 | 1968 |
| Mexico | CONCACAF | 1927 | 1929 | 1945 |
| Micronesia | OFC | N/a | N/a | 1991 |
| Moldova | UEFA | 1990 | 1994 | 1992 |
| Monaco | 2000 | N/a | N/a | 1993 |
| Mongolia | AFC | 1959 | 1998 | 1961 |
| Montenegro | UEFA | 1931 | N/a | 2007 |
| Montserrat | CONCACAF | 1994 | 1996 | N/a |
| Morocco | CAF | 1955 | 1956 | 1956 |
| Mozambique | CAF | 1975 | 1980 | 1975 |
| Myanmar | AFC | 1947 | 1957 | 1948 |
| Namibia | CAF | 1990 | 1992 | 1990 |
| Nauru | N/a | N/a | N/a | 1999 |
| Nepal | AFC | 1951 | 1970 | 1955 |
| Netherlands | UEFA | 1889 | 1904 | 1945 |
| Netherlands Antilles | CONCACAF | 1921 | 1932 | 1945 |
| New Caledonia | OFC | ?? | 2006 | N/a |
| New Zealand | OFC | 1891 | 1948 | 1945 |
| Nicaragua | CONCACAF | 1931 | 1950 | 1945 |
| Niue | OFC | ?? | 2006 | N/a |
| Niger | CAF | 1967 | 1967 | 1960 |
| Nigeria | CAF | 1945 | 1959 | 1960 |
| North Korea | AFC | 1945 | 1958 | 1991 |
| Northern Ireland | UEFA | 1880 | 1911 | N/a |
| Norway | UEFA | 1902 | 1908 | 1945 |
| Oman | AFC | 1978 | 1980 | 1971 |
| Pakistan | AFC | 1948 | 1948 | 1947 |
| Palau | OFC | N/a | N/a | 1994 |
| Palestine | AFC | 1962 | 1998 | 1945 |
| Panama | CONCACAF | 1937 | 1938 | N/a |
| Papua New Guinea | OFF | 1962 | 1963 | 1975 |
| Paraguay | CONMEBOL | 1906 | 1921 | 1945 |
| Peru | CONMEBOL | 1922 | 1924 | 1945 |
| Philippines | AFC | 1907 | 1928 | 1945 |

| | | | | |
|---|---|---|---|---|
| Poland | UEFA | 1919 | 1923 | 1945 |
| Portugal | UEFA | 1914 | 1923 | 1955 |
| Puerto Rico | CONCACAF | 1940 | 1960 | N/a |
| Qatar | AFC | 1960 | 1970 | 1971 |
| Reunion | CAF | N/a | N/a | N/a |
| Romania | UEFA | 1909 | 1922 | 1955 |
| Russia | UEFA | 1912 | 1992 | 1945 |
| Rwanda | CAF | 1972 | 1976 | 1962 |
| Saint Kitts & Nevis | CONCACAF | 1932 | 1992 | 1983 |
| Saint Lucia | CONCACAF | 1979 | 1988 | 1979 |
| St Vincent & Grenad's | CONCACAF | 1979 | 1988 | 1980 |
| St Martin | CONCACAF | 1999 | N/a | N/a |
| Samoa | OFC | 1968 | 1986 | 1976 |
| San Marino | UEFA | 1931 | 1988 | 1992 |
| Sao Tome & Principe | CAF | 1975 | 1986 | 1975 |
| Saudi Arabia | AFC | 1959 | 1959 | 1945 |
| Scotland | UEFA | 1873 | 1910 | N/a |
| Senegal | CAF | 1960 | 1962 | 1960 |
| Serbia & Montenegro | UEFA | 1919 | 1919 | 2000 |
| Seychelles | CAF | 1979 | 1986 | 1976 |
| Sierra Leone | AFC | 1967 | 1967 | 1961 |
| Singapore | AFC | 1892 | 1952 | 1965 |
| Sint Maarten | CONCACAF | N/d | N/a | N/a |
| Slovakia | UEFA | 1993 | 1994 | 1993 |
| Slovenia | UEFA | 1920 | 1992 | 1992 |
| Solomon Islands | OFC | 1978 | 1988 | 1978 |
| Somalia | CAF | 1951 | 1960 | 1960 |
| South Africa | CAF | 1991 | 1992 | 1945 |
| South Korea | AFC | 1928 | 1948 | 1991 |
| Spain | UEFA | 1913 | 1904 | 1955 |
| Sri Lanka | AFC | 1939 | 1950 | 1955 |
| Sudan | CAF | 1936 | 1948 | 1956 |
| Suriname | CONCACAF | 1920 | 1929 | 1975 |
| Swaziland | CAF | 1968 | 1978 | 1968 |
| Sweden | UEFA | 1904 | 1904 | 1946 |
| Switzerland | UEFA | 1885 | 1904 | 2002 |
| Syria | AFC | 1936 | 1937 | 1945 |
| Tahiti | OFC | 1989 | 1990 | N/a |
| Tajikistan | AFC | 1936 | 1994 | 1992 |
| Tanzania | CAF | 1930 | 1964 | 1961 |
| Thailand | AFC | 1916 | 1925 | 1946 |

| | | | | |
|---|---|---|---|---|
| Togo | CAF | 1960 | 1962 | 1960 |
| Tonga | OFC | 1965 | 1994 | 1999 |
| Trinidad & Tobago | CONCACAF | 1908 | 1963 | 1962 |
| Tunisia | CAF | 1956 | 1960 | 1956 |
| Turkey | UEFA | 1923 | 1923 | 1945 |
| Turkmenistan | AFC | 1992 | 1994 | 1992 |
| Turks & Caicos | CONCACAF | 1996 | 1998 | N/a |
| Tuvalu | OFC | N/a | N/a | 2000 |
| Uganda | CAF | 1924 | 1959 | 1962 |
| Ukraine | UEFA | 1991 | 1992 | 1945 |
| United Arab Emirates | AFC | 1971 | 1972 | 1971 |
| United Kingdom | N/a | N/a | N/a | 1945 |
| USA | CONCACAF | 1913 | 1914 | 1945 |
| Uruguay | CONMEBOL | 1900 | 1923 | 1945 |
| Uzbekistan | AFC | 1946 | 1994 | 1992 |
| Vanuatu | OFC | 1934 | 1988 | 1981 |
| Venezuela | CONMEBOL | 1926 | 1952 | 1945 |
| Vietnam | AFC | 1962 | 1964 | 1977 |
| Wales | UEFA | 1876 | 1910 | N/a |
| Yemen | AFC | 1962 | 1980 | 1947 |
| Zambia | CAF | 1929 | 1964 | 1964 |
| Zanzibar | CAF | 1925 | N/a | N/a |
| Zimbabwe | CAF | 1965 | 1965 | 1980 |

**Source: FIFA/UN**

# Appendix 2. UNPO MEMBERSHIP

| Members | Year of Membership |
|---|---|
| Abkhazia | 1991 |
| Aboriginals of Australia | 1991 |
| Acheh | 1991 |
| Ahwazi | 2003 |
| Albanians in Macedonia | 1994 |
| Assyria | 1991 |
| Bashkortostan | 1996 |
| Batwa | 1993 |
| Bougainville | 1991 |
| Buffalo River Dene Nation | 2004 |
| Buryatia | 1996 |
| Cabinda | 1997 |
| Chechen Republic of Ichkeria | 1991 |

# OUTCASTS: The Lands That FIFA Forgot

| | |
|---|---|
| Chin | 2001 |
| Chittagong Hill Tracts | 1991 |
| Chuvash | 1993 |
| Circassia | 1994 |
| Cordillera | 1991 |
| Crimean Tatars | 1991 |
| East Turkestan | 1991 |
| Gagauzia | 1994 |
| Greek minority in Albania | 1991 |
| Hmong ChaoFa | 2007 |
| Hungarian minority in Romania | 1994 |
| Ingushetia | 1994 |
| Inkeri | 1993 |
| Inner Mongolia | 2007 |
| Iranian Kurdistan | 2007 |
| Iraqi Kurdistan | 1991 |
| Iraqi Turkoman | 1991 |
| Ka Lahui Hawai'i | 1993 |
| Karenni State | 1993 |
| Khmer Krom | 2001 |
| Komi | 1993 |
| Kosova | 1991 |
| Kumyk | 1997 |
| Lakota | 1994 |
| Maasai | 2004 |
| Maohi | 1994 |
| Mapuche | 1993 |
| Mari | 1991 |
| Mon | 1996 |
| Montagnards | 2003 |
| Nagalim | 1993 |
| Nahuas Del Alto Balsas | 2004 |
| Nuxalk | 1998 |
| Ogoni | 1993 |
| Oromo | 2004 |
| Rehoboth Basters | 2007 |
| Rusyn | 1998 |
| Sanjak | 1993 |
| Scania | 1993 |
| Shan | 1997 |
| Sindhi | 2002 |

| | |
|---|---|
| Somaliland | 2004 |
| Southern Azerbaijan | 2007 |
| Southern Camerooons | 2004 |
| South Moluccas | 1991 |
| Taiwan | 1991 |
| Talysh | 2005 |
| Tatarstan | 1991 |
| Tibet | 1991 |
| Tsimshian | 2007 |
| Tuva | 1996 |
| Udmurt | 1993 |
| Vhavenda | 2003 |
| West Balochistan | 2005 |
| West Papua | 1991 |
| Zanzibar | 1991 |

**Source: UNPO**

## Appendix 3. NF BOARD MEMBERSHIP

| Territory | Status |
|---|---|
| Chagos Islands | Full member |
| Greenland | Full member |
| Monaco | Full member |
| Rijcka | Full member |
| The Roma | Full member |
| Sapmi | Full member |
| Somaliland | Full member |
| South Moluccas | Full member |
| Southern cameroon | Full member |
| Tibet | Full member |
| Turkish Republic of Northern Cyprus | Full member |
| Chechnya | Provisional member |
| Easter Island | Provisional member |
| Kiribati | Provisional member |
| Maasai | Provisional member |
| Western Sahara | Provisional member |
| Zanzibar | Provisional member |
| Republic of Saugeais | Associated member |
| Sealand | Associated member |
| South Lower Saxony | Associated member |

## Appendix 4. ISLAND GAMES ASSOCIATION MEMBERS

Aland (FIN)              Alderney (UK)
Bermuda (UK)             Cayman Islands (UK)
Falkland Islands (UK)    Faroe Islands (DEN)
Froya (NOR)              Gibraltar (UK)
Gotland (SWE)            Greenland (DEN)
Guernsey (UK)            Hitra (NOR)
Isle of Man (UK)         Isle of Wight (UK)
Jersey (UK)              Menorca (SPA)
Orkney (UK)              Prince Edward Island (CAN)
Rhodes (GRE)             Saaremaa (EST)
Sark (UK)                Shetland Islands (UK)
St. Helena (UK)          Western Isles (UK)
Ynys Mon (UK)

## Appendix 5. ISLAND GAMES FOOTBALL TOURNAMENT

| Year | Host | Winner | Runner-up |
| --- | --- | --- | --- |
| 1985 | Isle of Man | Not held | n/a |
| 1987 | Guernsey | Not held | n/a |
| 1989 | Faroe Islands | Faroe Islands | Yns Mon |
| 1991 | Aland | Faroe Islands | Yns Mon |
| 1993 | Isle of Wight | Jersey | Isle of Man |
| 1995 | Gibraltar | Isle of Wight | Gibraltar |
| 1997 | Jersey | Jersey | Yns Mon |
| 1999 | Gotland | Yns Mon | Isle of Man |
| 2001 | Isle of Man | Guernsey | Yns Mon |
| 2003 | Guernsey | Guernsey | Isle of Man |
| 2005 | Shetlands | Shetlands | Guernsey |

**Source: IGA**

# SOURCES

Most of this book is derived from original research or interviews but information has also been taken from other sources and publications. This is either included in the text or listed below in order of their use in each chapter. Also included here are other sources that have proved vital. All the facts and figures on constitutions, populations and local geography come from the world fact books of either the Central Intelligence Agency or Yahoo.

## Chapter 1

*'Zanzibar revive Tanzania ties'*
by Emmanuel Muga, Dar es Salaam, BBC Sport, 12 November 2005

*'Many are called but few are chosen for Cayman's World Cup campaign'*
by Ian Ross, The Guardian, 1 March 2000

*'Courting in vain'*
by Mark Gleeson, World Soccer, March 2007

*'World Football'*
on BBC World Service, December 2006

*'When is a National Team not a National Team'*
Presentation by Steve Menary, Play the Game conference, 2005

*'When is a National Team not a National Team'*
by Steve Menary, Sport & Society Volume 10, No.2, March 2007

*Letter to the Jersey FA from Geoff Thompson of the English FA*
Presentation by Ian Magic Hughes at Play The Game 2005

## Chapter 2

*'Muratti Vase Centenary celebration'*
by Frank Cusack, Tony Williams Publications

*'The Match of the Century'*
2005 Muratti Vase final centenary programme published by Cherry Godfrey

# OUTCASTS: The Lands That FIFA Forgot

*'Minor Countries'*
by Steve Menary, When Saturday Comes, March 2005

*'Changing Channel'*
by Steve Menary, World Soccer, September 2006

Working Party to review the organisation known as the Jersey Football Association

*'Maderian football should follow the British model'*
Interview with Miguel de Sousa, Journal de Madeira.
Translated by Rafael Maranhoa

*'Morbo - the Story of Spanish Football'*
by Phil Ball, WSC Books

## Chapter 3

*'The New Federation Board World Cup'*
by Steve Menary, When Saturday Comes, July 2005

www.nf-board.com

www.somaliland.org

*'Rebels put viva-voom into cup'*
by Matthew Weiner, The Times, 27 February 2006

*'South Moluccas Clinches 1st UNPO Football Cup Tournament'*
by Daniel Arenas & Maarten Rottschäfer

www.unpo.org

## Chapter 4

*'Give us a game'*
by Steve Menary, World Soccer, January 2006

*'Gronkjaer buys into the master plan'*
by Alex Hayes, The Independent, 8 February 2004

# Sources

*'Football in Greenland'*
www.gif.gl

*'Football From The Heart: How Two Davids Beat a World of Goliaths'*
Presentation at Play The Game 2002 by Jens Brinch & Michael Nybrandt

*'Small Wonder'*
by Steve Menary, Panstadia, Volume 10, No.3, January 2004

Play the Game newsletter, 17 March 2006

Articles from Sermitsiaq newspaper by Irene Jepson,
translated by Soren Andersen

## Chapter 5

Falklands Islands Overseas Games Association - www.horizon.co.fk

*'Press release from the St Helena National Futsal Association'*
www.futsalplanet.com

*'Islander's Boca farewell'*
by John Sinnot, BBC Sport online, 18 July 2002

*'ICC's new recruits swap Goose Green for Gatwick'*
by Matthew Pryor, The Times, 13 July 2007

*'Story of Falklands football traitor inspires new film'*
by Paul Harris, The Observer, 4 August 2002

## Chapter 6

Shetlands in Statistics 2004 published by Shetlands Islands Council

www.islandgames.net

Football Programme
NatWest Island Games XI

NatWest Island Games 2005 programme
www.shetland2005.info

Island Games supplements
Shetland Times, 11 July 2005

www.rhodes2007.info

## Chapter 7

*'The Ball Keeps Rolling - One Hundred Years of the Isle of Man FA 1890-1990'*
by Eric Clague and Colin Moore, Nelson Press

Isle of Man Guide
24 January 2006

*'Isle of Man fall at final hurdle'*
by Mike Appleby, www.thefa.com, 20 April 2007

*'Euro dream lives on'*
by Mike Appleby, www.thefa.com, 20 April 2007

*'Narrow defeat for England'*
by Mike Appleby, www.thefa.com, 18 April 2007

*'Man of the world'*
by Steve Menary, World Soccer, July 2007

## Chapter 8

*'Colonies don't want to break ties with colonial powers'*
www.panorama.gi, 28 May 2001

www.cricinfo.com

www.gfa.gi

*'Rock set to roll?'*
by Steve Menary, World Soccer, November 2006

# Sources

*'For the love of the game'* Gibraltar Football Association UEFA
*Membership Proposal*
News release distributed by PR Newswire on behalf of Gibraltar Badminton
Association, 25 May 2001

*'GFA scores goal and moves nearer joining UEFA'*
www.panorama.gi

*'Letter from… Gibraltar'*
by Tim Stannard, When Saturday Comes, January 2007

*'Diplomacy in the air as Iberia flies to Gibraltar'*
The Guardian, 18 December 2006

*'Gibraltar fears that its UEFA application will not succeed after all'*
by Kirtsen Sparre Play the Game newsletter, 22 December 2006

## Chapter 9

*'Grim up North'*
by Steve Menary, World Soccer, March 2006

Cyprus PIO: Turkish press & other media
www.hri.org, 26 April 2002

*'Football in the twilight zone'*
by Simon Bahcelli, Cyprus Mail 2005

*'Arsenal and FA score own goal over racism with Emirates Flag ban'*
www.embargoed.org, 13 February 2007

## Chapter 10

*'Mind your language'*
by Steve Menary, World Soccer, June 2006

*'Moussu T'*
by Philip Sweeney, Songlines, January/February 2007

'*Discussion with Pèire Costa*'
So Foot, 10 December 2005

## Chapter 11

'*For Chirac read Canute*'
by Keir Radnedge, World Soccer, November 2006


'*Walk in the shadow*' by Nicholas Gettliffe
Onze Mondial, May 2005. Translation by Jennifer M Tennant

'*Kosovo national team has just returned home after their win in Monaco*'
www.albaniasoccer.com

'*Matter of principality*'
by Steve Menary, World Soccer, June 2007

## Chapter 12

'*FIFA offers support to FA of Montenegro*' *FIFA press release September 7 2006*
FIFA press release, 21 February 2006

'*A Different Pitch*'
by Douglas Aubrey, Autonomi Films 2005

'*Kosovo junior football team wins second prize at the Dana Cup International*'
www.unmikonline.org

'*The Big Question*'
by Stephen Castle, The Independent, 26 January 2007
www.streetfootballworld.org/Projects/spiritofsoccer

'*Kosovo prepares for entry*'
by Steve Menary, World Soccer, March 2007

## Chapter 13

'*Going Wild*'
by Steve Menary, World Soccer, August 2006

# Sources

*'Greenland favorites to land Wild Cup'*
Yahoo News, 5 May 2006

*'Also-rans find World of their own'*
New York Daily News, 4 June 2006

www.wild-cup.de

## Chapter 14

*'Zanzibar back to square one'*
by Steve Menary, World Soccer, April 2006

*'Strains within Tanzania's union'*
by Daniel Dickinson, BBC News, 26April 2004

*'Dual role for Suleiman'*
www.fifa.com, 16 March 2006

## Chapter 15

*'Tibet do the business'*
by Steve Menary, World Soccer, April 2007

*'A history of Tibetan football, starting from polo'*
Tibetan Journal, Volume 8, issue 3, May-June 2004

*'International football association apologises to China over Tibet reference'*
by Kate Saunders, Free Tibet Campaign, 10 December 2004

Interview with Rasmus Dinesen & Arnold Kroigard
www.theglobalgame.com

*'The Liberation Game'*
by Gavin Willacy, When Saturday Comes, November 2006

*'Junior football team performs well'*
Official site of the Central Tibetan Administration 25 November 2003

Correspondence between Jonathan Motzfeldt & Chinese embassy in
Denmark, letters dated 17 May 2001 and 31 May 2001

## Chapter 16

*'Deux tournois pour les oublies de la FIFA'* by Jean-Damien Lesay
Liberation, 23 November 2006, Translated by Jennifer M Tennant

*'Worlds apart'*
by Steve Menary, World Soccer, October 2006

*'Normark to lead Sami team'*
by Jonathan Tisdall, www.afternposten.no, 26 October 2006

*'Kick-off for countries that don't exist'*
by Natasha Mann, Scotland on Sunday, 19 November 2006

*'Then there were three..."*
by Steve Menary, World Soccer, February 2007

## Chapter 17

*'OFC - OFC Celebrates 40th anniversary at Congress'*
www.oceaniafootball.com

*'NIMFA host VIPs at Fiesta'*
Saipan Tribune, 10 January 2006

*'Junior soccer players look to enjoy Beijing'*
Saipan Tribune, 19 July 2006

*'NIMFA juniors arrive safely, see action today'*
Saipan Tribune, 21 July 2006

*'Guam strikers draw first blood'*
by Jon Perez, Saipan Tribune, 26 March 2007

*'CNMI preparing for first road game'*
by Brad E Ruszala, Saipan Tribune, 28 March 2007

*'Team CNMI: Mete the midfielder'*
by Brad E Ruszala, Saipan Tribune, 1 April 2007

# Sources

*'Pacific Vim'*
by Steve Menary, World Soccer, May 2007

## Chapter 18

*'North Cyprus in good ELF'*
by Steve Menary, World Soccer, January 2007

www.elfcup.org

## Chapter 19

*'Original sin-bin part of football's counter reformation'*
by Marina Hyde, The Guardian, 1 March 2007

*'Italy holds priestly world cup'*
BBC News, 21 February 2006

*'Matches made in heaven'*
by Stephen Tomkins, BBC News, 22 June 2006

*'Vatican wants to play priests in Serie A'*
by Malcolm Moore, Daily Telegraph, 19 December 2006

*'Cassocks for goalposts: Cardinal plans Vatican FC'*
by Peter Popham, The Independent, 19 December 2006

*'Vatican squashes soccer team idea'*
Italy magazine, 20 December 2006

*'Pray as you play'*
by Paul Saffer, www.uefa.com, 29 December 2006

*'Vatican football tournament ends in an unholy row'*
by Tom Kington, The Guardian, 28 May 2007

## Chapter 20

*'Arctic Magic'*
by Chris Campon, Observer Music Monthly, January 2007

# OUTCASTS: The Lands That FIFA Forgot

*'The Sami - an indigenous people in Sweden'*
published by the Swedish Ministry of Agriculture, Food & Consumer Affairs

*'National team takes on Monaco and Northern Cyprus'*
www.samiradio.org, 31 October 2006

www.tnsa.info

224